D0592586

ENDURING FREEDOM ENDURING VOICES

ENDURING FREEDOM ENDURING VOICES

US OPERATIONS IN AFGHANISTAN

MICHAEL G. WALLING

First published in Great Britain in 2015 by Osprey Publishing,
PO Box 883, Oxford, OX1 9PL, UK
PO Box 3985, New York, NY 10185-3985, USA
E-mail: info@ospreypublishing.com

Osprey Publishing is part of the Osprey Group.

A CIP catalogue record for this book is available from the British Library.

ISBN: 978 1 78200 829 3
E-pub ISBN: 978 1 78200 978 8
PDF ISBN: 978 1 78200 977 1

Index by Zoe Ross
Cartography by Peter Bull Art Studio
Typeset in Bank Gothic, Univers and Sabon
Originated by PDQ Digital Media Solutions, Suffolk
Printed in China through Worldprint Ltd.

15 16 17 18 19 20   10 9 8 7 6 5 4 3 2 1

Osprey Publishing is supporting the Woodland Trust, the UK's leading woodland conservation charity, by funding the dedication of trees.

www.ospreypublishing.com

Front cover: A Marine from RCT 7 provides security at a mortar range in Helmand. (USMC)
Back cover: Images courtesy of the Department of Defense.

CONTENTS

Dedicated to the women and men who have sworn
to protect and defend us from our enemies.
Thanks for all you've done.

ACKNOWLEDGMENTS

First and foremost is my wife Mary for her unwavering faith and support through another all-consuming project. Marcus Cowper, my editor at Osprey, showed remarkable patience and provided terrific input throughout the long process of bringing this project to print.

Obtaining access to and interviews with a remarkable group of women and men was made easier through the efforts of Public Affairs Offices, institutions, and their dedicated staffs. Among these wonder people are Jennifer Elzea, Office of the Secretary of Defense; Ken Gott, Combat Studies Institute; Cheryle Rivas, US Army Special Operations Command; Captain Israel Miller, Pennsylvania Army National Guard; Amy L. Forsythe, US Navy; Lieutenant John Bonds, 3/7th Cavalry, US Army; Senior Airman Mariah C. Tolbert, US Air Force; 2nd Lieutenant Rebecca Ennis, US Air Force; Lieutenant Colonel Sharon K. E. Kibiloski, US Air Force Reserve; Major Christian Hodge, North Dakota Army National Guard; Major Penny Ripperger, North Dakota Army National Guard; Senior Airman Naomi M. Griego, US Air Force; Staff Sergeant Susan Hanson, US Air Force; Lieutenant Colonel Kirk Luedeke, US Army; Colonel Beth Thelen, US Army; and Staff Sergeant Jamal Sutter, US Air Force.

There are many Air Force, Army, Navy, and Marine Corps personnel who shared their memories with me, not all of which made it into this book. For that I apologize. Every one of your memories helped shape this work and will not be forgotten.

Thank you all for helping me keep the faith.

Chapter 1
ATTACK

Tuesday, September 11, 2001

The morning was clear along the eastern seaboard as passengers boarded their flights at Boston Logan International Airport, Newark Liberty International Airport, and Dulles International Airport. No delays were expected as people settled in their seats and aircrews readied for takeoff. American Airlines Flight 11 from Boston departed at 7:59am, 14 minutes late. The next, United Airlines Flight 93 from Newark, pushed back from the gate three minutes later. At Dulles, American Airlines Flight 77 was scheduled to leave at 8:10am. The fourth flight, United Airlines Flight 175, also out of Boston, took off at 8:14am.

The first sign of trouble came at 8:14am, when American Airlines Flight 11 did not respond when the air traffic controller instructed the aircraft to climb to 35,000ft.

Five minutes later, Betty Ong, a flight attendant on Flight 11, alerted American Airlines via an airphone: "The cockpit is not answering, somebody's stabbed in business class – and I think there's Mace – that we can't breathe – I don't know, I think we're getting hijacked." She then told of the stabbing of two flight attendants.[1]

Within a minute Federal Aviation Administration flight controllers in Boston concluded Flight 11 had probably been hijacked. The hesitation was understandable, since no US airliner had been hijacked since December 7, 1987.[2] A decision that it was a hijacking was reached at 8:34am. Boston Center then alerted North American Aerospace Defense Command (NORAD) of the event. Boston flight control called the Massachusetts Air

National Guard Otis Air Base on Cape Cod directly at 8:34am. Major Daniel Nash (call sign "Nasty") and Lieutenant Colonel Timothy Duffy (call sign "Duff") were the two F-15 pilots scrambled to intercept Flight 11.[3]

Duff recalls: "I was just standing up by the ops desk and I was told I had a phone call. I asked who it was and they said the [Boston] tower calling and something about a hijacking. It was Flight American 11, a 767 [sic], out of Boston going to California. At the time we ran in and got suited up." Two unarmed 102nd Fighter Wing F-15s scrambled to intercept the plane.

As soon as the pilots were strapped into their aircraft, the green light directing them to launch went on. Duff radioed his command post for guidance, asking, "Do you have words?" The response was, "Possible hijack, American Flight 11, 737, flight level 290 [29,000ft], over JFK."

But it was already too late. At 8:46am American Airlines Flight 11 crashed into the World Trade Center's North Tower, and 17 minutes later United Airlines Flight 175 impacted the South Tower.

When Flight 175 hit, the F-15s were 71 miles – about eight minutes' flying time – from Manhattan. Both pilots were together, near John F. Kennedy Airport, about 15 miles from the World Trade Center, when the first tower collapsed. Visibility was extremely clear that morning, and Nasty could see the plume of black smoke pouring from the first tower. He was flying about 5,000ft above the second tower when it, too, folded into a torrent of dust and debris. Nasty recalls Duff saying over the radio, "It looks like the building collapsed." He thought to himself, "There were just tens of thousands of people killed. I thought it was the start of World War III."

Even if the F-15s had arrived in time, they did not have the necessary presidential authorization to shoot down civilian aircraft. "If we had shot down four airliners on September 11, we wouldn't have been heroes," Nasty said. "You don't have the choice of outcomes. They're all bad. We didn't have the authority to [shoot it down]. We didn't suspect they would use kamikaze tactics that morning. We weren't ready for that type of an attack, to quickly shoot down one of our own airplanes. We did everything we could do to get there in time. I was the same as everyone else. I was shocked and disbelieving, and frustrated that we were so late."

American Airlines Flight 77 smashed into the western side of the Pentagon at 9:37am. At 10:03am, the hijackers on United Airlines Flight 93 intentionally flew into the ground 80 miles southeast of Pittsburgh, Somerset County, Pennsylvania, to avoid being overpowered by the passengers.

"I remember sitting in my civilian office down in Lancaster [Pennsylvania] when things started happening," recalls Colonel David A. Wood, G Company, 104th Aviation Regiment, Pennsylvania National Guard. "I grabbed my gear, grabbed my flight suit, and jumped into my car. Within an hour I was flying the governor and the commander of the State Police to the crash site in Shanksville. We were there about an hour after the plane hit and saw the devastation and how you can reduce an airplane to very small pieces."[4]

General Tommy Franks, Commander in Chief (CINC), US Central Command (CENTCOM) was in Crete resting after a ten-hour flight from Andrews Air Force Base. A few minutes after 4:00pm local time, his aide-de-camp, Navy captain Carl V. Mauney, informed General Franks of the World Trade Center attacks. "As I watched the flames and roiling black smoke, a colorful graphic appeared on the bottom of the screen: 'America Under Attack.' Osama bin Laden, I said *Son of a bitch!*"[5]

Master Sergeant Mike Elmore was with 5th Special Forces Group at the time of the attacks:

> On September 10 we were on a training exercise with another team from 5th Group using Zodiacs on the Cumberland River. On the morning of the 11th we came back and put the Zodiacs on the trailer getting ready to go back to Fort Campbell.
>
> We turned the radios on and heard the news of the second plane hitting the towers. After finagling for about two hours to get on post we put the

Zodiacs back in the dive locker [and] we went straight to palletizing and packing. We weren't given any formal instruction about leaving at that point, but we knew that sooner or later we would be leaving, so we started getting our stuff ready to go, waiting for the word telling us about leaving.

We received an e-mail from Colonel Mulholland, 5th Group command, to everyone in the Group saying "Make no mistake, we're leaving. Don't know when, but we will be the tip of the spear in this fight. Don't doubt yourself because now is not the time to question yourself whether you know your job or not. Be cognizant at all times and be prepared to fight."[6]

By the time the fourth plane crashed into the ground, General Franks was gathering information on what assets were available for an immediate counterstrike against al Qaeda targets in Afghanistan. The answer was that within 24 hours, 80 Tomahawk Land Attack Missiles (TLAMs) would be within strike range and another 120 a day later. But this time cruise missiles wouldn't be enough. In 1998 the Clinton administration launched cruise missiles to attack known or suspected terrorist training camps in Afghanistan after al Qaeda-led attacks on several US embassies. The missiles had little effect. The attacks showed that only ground troops could effectively locate and kill terrorists.

The world quickly condemned the attacks against the US. On September 11, 2001, the General Assembly of the Organization of American States "condemned in the strongest terms, the terrorist acts visited upon the cities of New York and Washington" and expressed "full solidarity" with the US Government and people.

On September 12 the United Nations Security Council issued Resolution 1386 (2001), part of which unequivocally condemned the "horrifying terrorist attacks which took place on September 11, 2001 in New York, Washington, DC and Pennsylvania and regards such acts, like any act of international terrorism, as a threat to international peace and security."[7] It also called upon all States to work together to bring justice to those responsible for the attacks.

Also on September 12, for the first time in its history, NATO invoked Article 5 of the Washington Treaty, which states that an armed attack against one or more NATO countries is an attack against all NATO countries. However, despite invoking Article 5, NATO did not authorize any specific military action.

On September 18, 2001, the United States Congress passed a joint resolution, later signed into law as Public Law 107-40. The law, which is still on the books, states that:

> The President is authorized to use all necessary and appropriate force against those nations, organizations, or persons he determines planned, authorized, committed, or aided the terrorist attacks that occurred on September 11, 2001, or harbored such organizations or persons, in order to prevent any future acts of international terrorism against the United States by such nations, organizations, or persons.[8]

Discussions between President Bush and his advisors, the State Department, the Defense Department, the Central Intelligence Agency (CIA), and the National Security Agency (NSA) led to a strategy of first ousting the Taliban from Afghanistan and dismantling al Qaeda, although some members considered actions in Iraq, including long-standing plans for toppling President Saddam Ḥussein. Plans for operations against Iraq were tabled until al Qaeda and the Taliban were defeated.

President George W. Bush addressed a joint session of Congress on September 20. His statement to the Afghan Taliban government was straightforward:

> By aiding and abetting murder, the Taliban regime is committing murder. And tonight the United States of America makes the following demands on the Taliban.
>
> Deliver to United States authorities all of the leaders of Al Quaeda [sic] who hide in your land.
>
> Release all foreign nationals, including American citizens you have unjustly imprisoned.
>
> Protect foreign journalists, diplomats and aid workers in your country. Close immediately and permanently every terrorist training camp in Afghanistan.
>
> And hand over every terrorist and every person and their support structure to appropriate authorities.

> Give the United States full access to terrorist training camps, so we can make sure they are no longer operating.
>
> These demands are not open to negotiation or discussion.
>
> The Taliban must act and act immediately.
>
> They will hand over the terrorists or they will share in their fate.[9]

However, talking about striking back against al Qaeda was easy; planning how to do it was more complex. Fighting in Afghanistan presented a challenge different from any the US had ever faced.

Chapter 2
PRELUDE TO WAR

Afghanistan has been a battleground for almost 3,000 years. The first recorded invasion, by Darius I of Persia, occurred in the 6th century BC. It later fell to Alexander the Great in 330 BC. In the 19th century, Great Britain twice invaded Afghanistan (1839–42 and 1878–80). Both invasions were defeated by the fierce resistance of Afghans to outside rule. In 1884, Russian expansionism created a crisis with Great Britain when Russian troops seized the oasis of Merv in what is now Turkmenistan and later fought with Afghan troops over the oasis of Panjdeh.

After a 39-year hiatus, conflict again broke out between Britain and Afghanistan in 1919, when Afghan forces crossed the Khyber Pass into India. The war, lasting three months, was a minor British victory thanks in part to airpower. Afghanistan then remained free of foreign military interference until the Soviet invasion on December 24, 1979. The purpose of the invasion was to prop up the failing communist government and provide the means for quelling uprisings in the majority of primarily Muslim provinces. Within days, 80,000 heavily mechanized Soviet troops were in country, which in turn led to more uprisings. Pakistan's Inter-Services Intelligence Directorate (ISI) began training and equipping groups of these Muslim warriors (mujahedeen – meaning one who fights in a jihad) to fight the Afghan Government and its Soviet ally.

The US, seeing a chance to strike at least indirectly at the Soviet Union, purchased all of the Soviet weapons Israel had captured during its wars with Egypt and Lebanon and in action against Palestinian fighters. Through the CIA-run Operation *Cyclone*, these weapons were then funneled through the ISI to the mujahedeen. Central Intelligence

Agency personnel became involved in clandestine training and operations.

As the war progressed, heavily armed and well-trained groups emerged in the south. Among these were the Pakistan ISI-backed Taliban and Osama bin Laden's al Qaeda. The Taliban, whose name mean "students" in Pashtun, was one of the mujahedeen factions. Its recruits came from seminaries located in Pakistan, where the Taliban imposed a particularly fanatical, anachronistic, and rigid variation of Islam heavily influenced by Wahhabism, a conservative Islamic tradition prevalent in Saudi Arabia. During the 1980s the Taliban emerged as a powerful force in southern Afghanistan, with Pakistan supplying military training, financial support, and weapons.

Osama bin Laden was a Saudi who in 1979 began funneling money, arms, and fighters recruited in Arab countries to mujahedeen forces. Nine years later, wanting a more active military role, he split off from Sheikh Abdullah Azzam's "The Office of Services" mujahedeen faction and formed al Qaeda, its members drawn from across the Arab world rather than the Afghan-centric mujahedeen.

In the north, several strong anti-Soviet, anti-government warlord-led groups emerged. Among these warlords were Abdul Rashid Dostum, Ahmad Shah Massoud, and Ismail Khan. In the east Gulbuddin Hekmatyar emerged as one of the strongest leaders. Because of the difficult terrain and lack of safe havens in bordering countries, the northern forces were often not as well funded or equipped as those in the south. Among the strongest of these groups was that led by Ahmad Shah Massoud. Collectively this loose association of warlords became known as the Northern Alliance.

When the Soviets withdrew in February 1989 over 14,000 of their soldiers were dead, almost 54,000 had been wounded, and roughly 300 were missing. Their Afghan ally's casualties amounted to 18,000 killed. In contrast, mujahedeen losses were estimated at between 75,000 and 90,000 killed and over 75,000 wounded. The communist government ruled by Dr Mohammad Najibullah Ahmadzai lasted into 1992. Following the Soviet withdrawal, the US withdrew its support of the mujahedeen. Having provided the means to defeat the Soviets, the US now failed to provide the means for rebuilding Afghanistan, assist in the reintegrating of the mujahedeen into an already broken society, provide humanitarian aid, or establish a strong diplomatic presence. Afghanistan was in ruins, what little existing infrastructure there was had been destroyed, tribal groups were broken apart in refugee camps, and families were displaced, leaving a generation of men and women who had never lived in peace.

After Ahmadzai's government was overthrown, Afghanistan devolved into civil war for the next four years. Whatever governing there was happened through the shifting alliances between Abdul Rashid Dostum in the northern stronghold surrounding Mazar-i-Sharif, Ahmad Shah Massoud in the Panjshir valley, Ismail Khan in western Herat province, and Gulbuddin Hekmatyar in the east.

The desire for a stable government in Afghanistan increased support for the Taliban. With backing from the Pakistan military and ISI, Taliban forces captured Kandahar and other southern Afghan cities in 1994. After suffering a major defeat at the hands of Ahmad Shah Massoud when attempting to capture Kabul in 1995, the Taliban, again with strong backing from the Pakistan ISI, finally captured the city in September 1996.

However, the Taliban failed in its drive to control all of Afghanistan. In the winter of 1996 Massoud united all opponents of the Taliban under his guidance in the first so-called "Jab-e Nejaat-e Melli bara-ye Aazaadi Afghanistan" (Front of National Rescue for the liberation of Afghanistan) and "Jab-e Motahed-e Melli" (National United Front, which is more frequently known as the Northern Alliance, and will be referred to as such from now on). The alliance was between warlords Ahmad Shah Massoud, Abdul Rashid Dostum, Haji Mohammad Mohaqiq, Abdul Haq, and Haji Abdul Qadir. These warlords and their followers controlled approximately 30 percent of the Afghan population. They managed to keep control from 1996 until US forces arrived in October 2001. Over the next five years Massoud became the spokesman for the Northern Alliance and was its most visible leader. In a speech to the European Parliament on April 6, 2001, he warned that his intelligence network had credible information about an imminent attack on the US. At the time, no US agency took the information seriously.

Ahmad Shah Massoud and the Northern Alliance still threatened the Taliban's control of Afghanistan. The population's resentment was growing against their harsh laws, and upwards of a million people had fled their rule, many to the area controlled by Massoud. Massoud and the threat he posed needed to be eliminated. On September 9, 2001, two al Qaeda assassins posing as Belgian journalists from Morocco set off a bomb hidden in a video camera, killing themselves and fatally wounding Massoud. His assassination was never directly linked to the 9/11 attacks, but the loss of his leadership was a significant blow to the Northern Alliance.

At the end of the Soviet-Afghan war, bin Laden returned to Saudi Arabia and al Qaeda went underground. Bin Laden perceived US involvement in the Gulf War as an attack on Muslim people, and spoke out publicly against the Saudi Government's dependence on the US military, which led to his leaving to live in exile in Khartoum, Sudan, in 1992. While there, he declared jihad in order to force US military and commercial interests out of the Gulf region. Within months al Qaeda began its attacks, beginning with two bombings of hotels in Aden, Yemen, where US service members were believed to be staying. In 1993 al Qaeda provided financial support to Ramzi Yousef, who rented a van, packed it with explosives, and detonated it in the parking garage beneath the World Trade Center, killing six and injuring more than 1,000.

Under pressure from Saudi, Egyptian, and US governments, the Sudanese allowed bin Laden to leave for a country of his choice. He chose Afghanistan, and established his headquarters in Jalalabad in 1996. Al Qaeda stepped up its attacks, including the Luxor massacre of November 17, 1997, which killed 62 civilians and outraged the Egyptian public. In mid-1997 the Northern Alliance threatened to overrun Jalalabad, causing bin Laden to abandon his Najim Jihad compound and move his operations to Tarnak Farms in the south. On August 7, 1998, al Qaeda operatives bombed the US embassies in Kenya and Tanzania, killing 223 and injuring more than 5,000.

In response to the bombings, President Bill Clinton authorized Operation *Infinite Reach* on August 20, 1998. The operation consisted of launching approximately 75 cruise missiles against four al Qaeda training and logistical bases located in Afghanistan, and others directed at the Al-Shifa pharmaceutical factory in Sudan, which the United States claimed was helping Osama bin Laden build chemical weapons. The strikes had no measurable impact psychologically or materially on bin Laden or al Qaeda.

The next direct attack on US forces was on October 12, 2000. Al Qaeda suicide bombers sailed a small boat near the USS *Cole* (DDG-67) anchored in the Yemeni port of Aden and detonated explosive charges. The blast created a hole in the port side of the ship about 40ft (12m) in diameter, killing 17 crewmembers and injuring 39.

Neither the Clinton nor Bush administrations responded to the attack. According to a source in the 9/11 Commission Report, bin Laden complained in February 2001 about the fact that the US had not attacked in response to the *Cole* bombing, and if it did not, that he would launch something bigger.[1]

Chapter 3

RECKONING: OPERATION *ENDURING FREEDOM*, 2001

On September 21 General Franks, Chairman of the Joint Chiefs of Staff (CJCS) General Hugh Shelton, Vice CJCS General Dick Myers, and JSOC commander Major General Dell Dailey briefed President Bush and Vice President Cheney on a four-phase operations plan:

> Phase I: Set conditions and build forces to provide the National Command Authority credible military options: build alliances and prepare the battlefield.
> Phase II: Conduct initial combat operations and continue to set conditions for follow-on operations; begin initial humanitarian operations.
> Phase III: Conduct major combat operations in Afghanistan, continue to build coalition, and conduct operations.
> Phase IV: Establish capability of coalition partners to prevent the re-emergence of terrorism and establish support for humanitarian operation: expected to be a 3–5 year effort.[1]

In addition to complex internal tribal alliances, the geography of Afghanistan presents formidable geographic obstacles to any invader. This land-locked country is roughly the size of Texas. It is a land of towering mountain ranges and remote valleys in the north and east, and near desert-like conditions on the plains to the south and west. Road and rail communication nets are minimal and in disrepair. The rough terrain poses major logistical challenges to any military effort. All supplies and personnel have to be either flown or trucked in. Mountainous routes along the Afghanistan–Pakistan border provide excellent locations for mines and ambushes. Throughout the winter many passes, including the crucial northern routes through the Hindu Kush from Tajikistan to Kabul, are choked off by snow. Mountains in the north are too high for helicopters to operate in, while throughout the country dust-induced "brown outs" flare up unexpectedly, blinding pilots. Mountains and deep valleys block radio transmissions. Extremes of heat and cold stress both equipment and personnel. It is a feudal land populated by Pashtuns (the ethnic majority), Hazaras, Kaffirs, Tajiks, and Uzbeks among others, many members of which are illiterate. It is a place that in many ways has not changed in several millenia. The history, terrain, and fiercely independent people of Afghanistan present major challenges to any invader.

Initially, Pentagon officials labeled the impending campaign Operation *Infinite Justice*. Later, Secretary of Defense Donald Rumsfeld abandoned that code name after Islamic scholars objected on the asserted grounds that only God could impose "infinite justice."

Planning for the strikes would take time to set up. There were (and still are) only two ways of getting the necessary assets in place to conduct operations. The first is from the south through Pakistan. Materiel could either be landed by ship in ports on the Arabian Sea and then trucked north, or flown into Islamabad and then trucked through the passes into Afghanistan. From the north, airbases in either the former Soviet republics of Turkmenistan or Uzbekistan were the only options. Of these two, Uzbekistan was the best choice. There was an old Soviet airbase at Karshi-Khanabad (K2), which provided a starting point. It was also attractive because of its proximity to Afghan Northern Alliance forces.[2] (See Map 1.) Although it was in place, K2 needed significant work to be usable.

The plan was for US and coalition forces to concentrate on destroying al Qaeda's organization and persuading or forcing other nations and non-states to stop supporting terrorists. Concurrently, armed forces were to support humanitarian operations to convince the Afghans and the Islamic world that the war was not directed at them. At this point the US military was not to participate in nation building.[3]

Map 1: Afghanistan, 2001

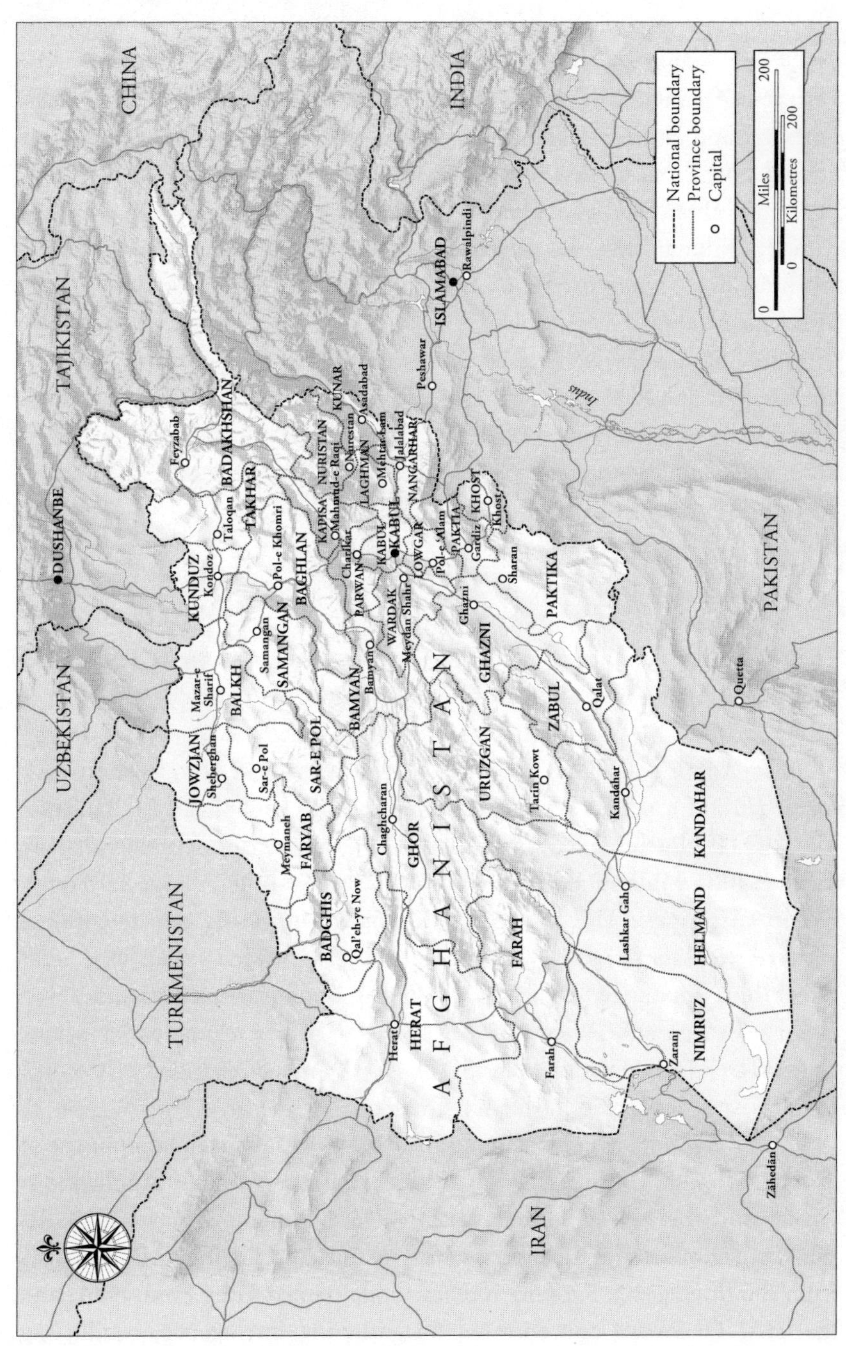

The initial stages of the war in Afghanistan were to be fought by the Northern Alliance with support from integrated Special Forces and US Air Force ground and air elements. The concept of the operation was to insert Special Forces teams first into the northern areas of Mazar-e Sharif and Bagram–Kabul, followed almost simultaneously by insertions into the Kunduz–Taloqan region. These combined forces were to establish a foothold in northern Afghanistan and drive the Taliban and al Qaeda forces into Kabul.

Once these areas were secured, the plan was to move teams south to liberate Kandahar, the center of the Taliban movement. Then the focus would shift to a likely area of enemy concentration in the extensive Tora Bora cave complex situated in the White Mountains of eastern Afghanistan, near the Khyber Pass.

The in-theater commander of Special Forces was the CENTCOM Combined Forces Special Operations Component Command, led by Rear Admiral Albert M. Calland III, who reported directly to General Franks.

Rear Admiral Calland established two joint special operation task forces (JSOTF), which separately covered north and south Afghanistan. The JSOTF North, called Task Force (TF) Dagger, was commanded by Colonel John Mulholland, and was formed around the 5th Special Forces Group (Airborne). This group would engage in classic unconventional warfare, working directly with native forces. It waited at K2 base until Uzbekistan announced that it was offering humanitarian assistance and Combat Search and Rescue (CSAR). Special Forces teams, under Major General Dell Dailey, included in JSOTF North and commanded by Colonel Frank Kisner, were responsible for CSAR.

JSOTF South (TF 11) was built around a two-squadron component of Special Mission Unit (SMU) operators from the Combat Applications Group and the Naval Special Warfare Development Group (DEVGRU [SEALs]), supported by Ranger security teams, and intelligence specialists from the Intelligence Support Agency (code named Grey Fox), NSA, and the CIA. TF Sword concentrated on gathering intelligence, conducting operations against sensitive sites, and eliminating individual terrorist threats.[4, 5]

Task Force K-Bar, a component of TF 11, and consisting mostly of Navy SEALs along with foreign Special Forces, and elements of the 3rd Special Forces Group (Airborne) under the command of Navy Captain Robert Howard, set up operations in Oman.[6] TF K-Bar was tasked with conducting anti-smuggling missions, including interdiction of vessels in the Arabian Gulf suspected of carrying arms that would be offloaded in remote areas of the Pakistani coast, and reconnaissance missions involving the insertion of teams throughout southern Afghanistan. A major part of TF K-Bar's work was Sensitive Site Exploitation – the surveillance and raiding of locations in southern Afghanistan suspected of containing al Qaeda or senior Taliban individuals, arms, and intelligence materials.[7, 8]

Although there were US air assets based around the Persian Gulf enforcing the "No Fly Zone" over southern Iraq as part of Operation *Southern Watch*, none had the legs to reach Afghanistan without mid-air refueling going both ways. Also, the bases themselves had to be upgraded to sustain the increased traffic.

On September 26, two weeks before ground operations began, the first seven-man CIA Northern Afghanistan Liaison Team (NALT) (code named Jawbreaker), led by Gary Schroen, flew into the Panjshir Valley north of Kabul to establish working relationships with Tajik generals Fahim Khan and Bismullah Khan, and the overall Northern Alliance military forces. Millions of dollars in cash was given to Northern Alliance leaders, which was used to purchase weapons and supplies. The team's tasks included ensuring Northern Alliance cooperation with the planned US invasion, collecting intelligence on the location of Taliban and al Qaeda leaders, locating al Qaeda training camps, and mapping frontline positions of the Taliban for later use in air strikes.[9]

At 1:00pm Eastern Time, Sunday, October 7, 2001, President Bush spoke to the nation on live television from the White House: "On my orders, the United States military has begun strikes against al Qaeda terrorist training camps and military installations of the Taliban regime in Afghanistan."

Operation *Crescent City* opened the air war with strikes by F-14 and F/A-18 carrier-based fighters from *Carl Vinson* (CVN 70) and *Enterprise* (CVN 65), Air Force land-based B-1, B-2, and B-52 bombers, and BGM-109

TLAM launched from US and British submarines. The massed attack struck targets such as aircraft on the ground, airfields, antiaircraft and surface-to-air missile batteries and radar sites, command-and-control nodes, and terrorist training camps. Critics questioned the raids on the camps because al Qaeda had largely abandoned the facilities, but the assaults destroyed terrorist infrastructure.[10] Air Force F-15E and F-16 fighters joined the fray, flying missions from bases on the Persian Gulf.

On October 9, Commando Solo, EC-130, from the Pennsylvania Air National Guard 193rd Special Operations Wing headed east to Afghanistan from its base on the Persian Gulf. Commando Solo was equipped with nine radio transmitters and a special 300ft drogue antenna extended from the plane's underbelly. The five-man crew consisted of a commercial pilot, a police officer, a machine-shop owner, an electrical engineer, and a social worker.

Moments later, a transmitter crackled to life and broadcast a message to the enemy combatants below in their native tongue:

> Attention Taliban! You are condemned. Did you know that? The instant the terrorists you supported took over our planes, you sentenced yourselves to death. The armed forces of the United States are here to seek justice for our dead. Highly trained soldiers are coming to shut down once and for all Osama bin Laden's ring of terrorism and the Taliban that supports them and their action. When you decide to surrender, approach United States forces with your hands in the air. Sling your weapon across your back, muzzle towards the ground. Remove your magazine and expel any rounds. Doing this is your only chance of survival.[11]

Although the US established ties with Tajik leaders in the north, these men would not be acceptable leaders to Afghanistan's Pashtun population. This need for Pashtun leadership was filled by two well-known Pashtun opponents of the Taliban regime: the expatriate Hamid Karzai and Gul Agha Sherzai, who had been hiding in Afghanistan. Both men had fought the Soviets and both had experience from their post-Soviet government positions when the Taliban came to power.

Karzai entered Afghanistan from Pakistan on October 8–9. Over the next three weeks he met with local leaders and managed to assemble a small, 50-man force. He used his satellite telephone to call the US consulate and ask for support. Within 48 hours large amounts of weapons and supplies were parachuted to him. In addition to arms, Karzai requested US advisers. These were provided by Operation Detachment Alpha (ODA) 574 on November 14.[12]

For Master Sergeant Dale G. Aaknes, 5th Special Forces Group, working with the logistics needed to launch the war from K2 proved to be a nightmare. In addition to food, water, clothing, and ammunition he had to find items that had not been ordered by anyone in Army for decades:

> We started to get requests for horse and animal feed. I never realized how many different kinds of feed there are. The problem being reported is that the animals were getting sick on the feed we shipped. We found out that the oats we shipped were a better quality than what they were used to, this caused the horses to get sick. To fix the problem we shipped the lowest quality oats I could find. The next little problem was the availability of horse saddles. We knew absolutely nothing about saddles, so we had to get some help. Our group comptroller's wife was a horse person. I called her and asked her to purchase 100 saddles with blankets with my credit card. She bought them at Fort Campbell and from there they were shipped to our position. In less than one week we had the saddles delivered to the ODAs.[13]

The ground war started on October 19 with the insertion of Special Forces based at K2 into Afghanistan. ODA 555 was inserted into the Panjshir Valley and joined the Jawbreaker team to contact Northern Alliance forces dug in on the Shomali Plains, where they controlled an old Soviet airbase at Bagram. Working closely with Northern Alliance troops under General Fahim Khan and General Bismullah Khan, ODA 555 proceeded to call in air strikes on to Taliban positions along the Shomali Plain.[14]

ODA 595 was the second TF Dagger team inserted, flying across the Hindu Kush Mountains by SOAR MH-47s. The team was inserted in the Dari-a-Souf Valley, south of Mazar-e-Sharif, linking up with the CIA and General Dostum, commander of the largest and most powerful Northern Alliance faction. Master Sergeant Mike Elmore, part of ODA 595, remembers the insertion:

> We got on the birds [helicopters] the night of the 19th. We didn't know what to expect. We'd heard all the stories about the Northern Alliance, what type of men they were, the continual fighting in Afghanistan for the past 15, 20 years. We had the understanding we were going to link up with a bunch of seasoned fighters.
>
> It was one, two in the morning when we landed and it was pitch black outside. I got off the bird and people were coming out of caves and adobe huts. The first impression I had was, "Where's Jesus?"
>
> We were carrying 110–115lb rucksacks. The Northern Alliance guys came to help get gear off the helicopter, and watching these guys trying to pick up this stuff was interesting.
>
> Meals were different. For breakfast we had raisins and an assortment of walnuts, peanuts, and cashews. Lunch was an MRE [Meal Ready to Eat] and dinner was usually some kind of goat.

Getting used to the horses and the horses getting use to the ODA team took some adjustments on both of their parts:

> I'd maybe ridden horses along little horse trails once or twice before I got there. Might as well call them little ponies. I weigh 220 pounds and with all our equipment you can probably add another 50 pounds to that. The horses were used to a 150lb guy. At one time the horse like, "Hey, forget about it, I'm done, I'm not moving. You're way too heavy for me, get the heck off."

ODA 595 split into two units, Alpha and Bravo. Alpha accompanied Dostum on horseback as his force pushed towards the city of Mazar-e Sharif, calling in strikes from US warplanes against a series of Taliban positions. Initially Bravo stayed behind to arrange for logistical support before joining Alpha and General Dostum. Master Sergeant Elmore was part of Bravo, but hadn't yet come to a mutually agreeable arrangement with his horse.

> We were moving into position and I was going from one hill top to another. In between the hill tops is called a saddle, fully exposed because it was a pretty steep drop off. I couldn't go below to where I wouldn't skyline myself. The horse just stopped in the saddle. We start taking fire. Bullets are flying all over the place and I'm kicking the horse, hitting, yelling at him.

He's just like: "Hey buddy, I'm not moving." I'm yelling, screaming, and kicking him. No go, so it was exit stage right, do a roll, and go down a little bit so I wasn't skylining myself. He's just standing there, eating grass. No animals were hurt, so I'm sure the animal rights activists will be pleased.

Another Special Forces team, ODA 534, inserted by SOAR helicopters on the night of November 2, was tasked with supporting General Mohammad Atta, a Northern Alliance militia leader. ODA 534, along with CIA officers, eventually linked up with ODA 595 and General Dostum outside Mazar-e Sharif.

This insertion in modified CH-47s was also conducted at night into mountains up to 16,000ft high with clouds, rain, and even sandstorms dramatically limiting visibility.[15] Technical Sergeant William Calvin Markham, USAF, 23rd Special Tactics Squadron, inserted with ODA 555 to coordinate close air support (CAS) for the Northern Alliance:

> We arrived in country around mid-October and were the only team operating behind enemy lines for the first two weeks. I have worked with SFs in the past and knew several of them from previous scuba training, so we came together quickly as a unit. We knew what our mission was – to help the Northern Alliance break through the Taliban lines and liberate the capital.
>
> We went into the area with just the essential gear, traveling as light as possible. Going as light as possible meant "rucking" up mountains with more than 100 pounds of gear. We had all the communications gear and air traffic control equipment needed to do CAS calls, as well as providing the ground-to-air interface with the aircraft.
>
> We had to contend with the mountainous terrain and the weather elements, as well as the fact that we went in with just enough supplies to last a day and would end up staying nearly ten days. I have done a lot of real-world missions and training exercises in this type of scenario, so I was better prepared for the challenge.

The first day of the operation started what is reported to be the longest sustained close air support operation conducted by combat controllers. "We set up an observation post in a mountain ridge overlooking the Taliban," said Markham. "The valley was literally filled with enemy tanks, personnel carriers, and military compounds. Working with the Northern Alliance leadership, the target was selected – a command-and-control building. I called in the first CAS and a US military fighter arrived over the area and dropped his ordnance and hit the building."

That first strike not only made an impression on the Americans, it made an impact on the Northern Alliance forces working with this SOF team.

> I wouldn't say they [the Northern Alliance] mistrusted us initially. But there was a certain sense they weren't sure how we could help them. After that first CAS run, the wall was broken and they seemed to realize we were there to help them.
>
> With no maps that reflected all the caves, the task would fall to the extensive training we had in land navigation and CAS. The first obstacles were the fact that we didn't have a detailed map. When you're talking a pilot on to a target, you have to understand from his perspective that the mountains and desert all looks similar.
>
> The CASs I called in on the site were making an impact, but not sealing the entrances. Many of the caves were lined with concrete and steel. Our team commander told us to figure out how to make the sites inaccessible.

Using a compass, a GPS, notebook, and pen the team set out on the task of creating maps of the caves.

> To get exact coordinates and the layout of the cave, we had to create a sketch for each site. It took hours of pacing off the inside and outside of the caves to get good data so we could give exact data to the pilots. We gave each cave a number, then plotted its height on the mountainside, noted any surrounding obstacles, and began pacing off the inside of the tunnels – the slopes, the direction it was dug in, the turns... We tried a few different bombing runs: bringing the bombs in at different angles to get the best possible attack on the sites. After a few runs, we found the best attack was to crack the entranceway and then use a second bomb to collapse the site. The double-bomb drop worked perfectly. The impact was incredible. We had one run that literally blew the cliff line down over the entrance. We secured and destroyed every cave, and ensured they would be inaccessible to anyone ever again.

As the bombings continued, resistance from the Taliban forces decreased and the Northern Alliance gained ground. Then, one day, the enemy counterattacked: "We were on top of a two-story building when they began attacking," says Markham. "The gunfire was intense. Then, they turned the guns on us. It was like large, flaming footballs flying at our position. The buttons on my uniform were getting in the way of me getting low enough. All I kept thinking was I needed aircraft. I grabbed the radio and called for immediate CAS."

As the SOF team got on the roof for cover, a Northern Alliance officer pushed in front of Markham, shielding him from the attack. Later, through an interpreter, the officer told him why he had done it: "He said if something happened to him, he knew someone else would step in to take his place in the fight. But if something happened to me the planes could not come and destroy the targets."[16]

Navy and Air Force fighters and bombers arrived and blunted the attack, and the offensive continued. A total of 25 days after the first call for ordnance, the Northern Alliance moved into Kabul. After ensuring the city was secure, the SOF team headed to the American embassy, which had been evacuated in 1989. Before fleeing the city, the Taliban had used the building as a staging area. Markham relates: "We gained access and one of the first things I saw was an American flag. It was on top of a pile of straw. Someone had tried to destroy it; the straw was burnt and there were ashes all over the flag. When I picked up the flag, it was untouched – not a burn mark on it. With the help from a teammate I carefully folded the Stars and Stripes. I presented that flag to my unit after I got back to the States."

Air Force 1st Special Operations Wing (SOW) AC-130H Spectre gunships working out of K2 were part of the CAS assets.[17] On one mission Captain Allison Black, USAF, the squadron's first female navigator on an AC-130H Spectre, earned the nickname "Angel of Death."

> We were in Greece for a while until they sent us to K2. We fly into K2, hit our tents for 12 hours because they figure if we go more than 12 hours we'll turn into pumpkins. After 12 hours they pull us out of our tents and said "Hey, you've got a mission."

It was a call sign, radio frequency, and a [map] grid or latitude longitude. That was it. We got on the plane, pulled out the chart and figured out how we were going to get there. Our squadron was staying in the northern part of Afghanistan – Mazar-a-Sharif, Kunduz, and north of the [Hindu] Kush.

It was unique from my perspective. Unique but not scary, I was nervous about being one of the only girls out there. I think maybe there was more concern on the guys' side than there was for me. Don't care; I wanted to be part of this great mission set.

The customers at the time were primarily ODA teams with our JTACs imbedded, some of which had had worked with me, some who had not.

This first combat mission set we made contact with our ODA team on the ground collocated with the Northern Alliance under General Dostum. He heard me talking on the radio and couldn't believe it. He said to the ODA leader:

"Americans bring their women here. They must be so determined."

"Yeah, of course we bring our women to kill Taliban." was the ODA leader's reply.

This was my first combat mission and I have to be very professional, bring my A-game. We identified this meeting house and there were multiple vehicles and lots of people which led down the path that we were clear to engage and we unloaded all our ammunition on the target.

At the time the gunship pilots had high power laser pointers, something like you'd use in a classroom. With your NVG [Night Vision Goggles] you can see this. The general saw it and believed it was a Death Ray that we could put on something and it would explode or turn to flames. He turned to the ODA leader and said: "Is that your Death Ray?" believing America had created such a thing. The ODA guys looked at each other and said: "As a matter of fact it is. Yes we have one."

So General Dostum got on his walkie-talkie and called the enemy we were engaging and said, "You're pathetic. American women are killing you. It's the angel of death raining fire upon you."

As I was communicating to the team what we were doing and what we were seeing he was keying the mike so the enemy could hear the conversation.

Our first mission was very successful. We shot 400 rounds of 40mm and 100 rounds of 105mm. The effects on the battlefield were so impressive that most of the al-Qaeda and Taliban forces surrendered to General Dostum the next day.

So this all goes down and I know nothing about it. We land and about a week later the team comes back to K2 from down range. They come to our hooch with an AK 47 from General Dostum telling us the whole story about how this unfolded and that "You are the Angel of Death, raining death and destruction on our enemies."[18]

While TF Dagger was being organized at K2, TF Sword had been embarked on the carrier USS *Kitty Hawk* (CV(A)-63)[19] from Masirah Island off Oman in the Persian Gulf. TF Sword was comprised of an Army SOF command including approximately 600 soldiers and 20 MH-60 Blackhawk and MH-47E Chinook helicopters. For operational security a 5-mile bubble was established around the carrier and her escorts. *Kitty Hawk* then moved to her station in the northern Arabian Sea to form TG-50.3.

On the night of October 19/20, operating primarily from *Kitty Hawk*, TF Sword raided the compound of Mullah Omar, a key Taliban leader, near Kandahar, and an airstrip near Bibi Tera, approximately 80 miles southwest of Kandahar. That same night 3rd Battalion, 75th Ranger Regiment, and SOF personnel parachuted on to a landing strip southwest of Kandahar designated Objective Rhino, and Objective Gecko, demonstrating the US's capability to attack Taliban strongholds.

The plan called for pre-assault fires and then a Ranger airborne insertion on Objective Rhino and a helicopter insertion/assault on Objective Gecko. Objective Rhino, a desert landing strip roughly 100 miles southwest of Kandahar, was divided into four objectives: Tin, Iron, Copper, and Cobalt (a walled compound). Before the Rangers parachuted in, B-2 Stealth bombers dropped 2,000lb bombs on Objective Tin. Then, AC-130 gunships fired on buildings and guard towers within Objective Cobalt, and identified no targets in Objective Iron. The gunships placed heavy fire on Objective Tin, reporting 11 enemy KIAs and nine "squirters" (enemy forces who escaped the initial attack).

After the pre-assault fires, four MC-130s dropped 199 Army Rangers, from 800ft and under zero illumination, onto Objective Rhino. A Company, 3rd Battalion, 75th Rangers, with an attached sniper team, assaulted Objective Tin. They next cleared Objective Iron and established blocking positions to repel counterattacks. C Company assaulted Objective Cobalt, with psychological operations (PSYOPS) loudspeaker teams broadcasting messages encouraging the enemy to surrender. The compound was unoccupied.

An Air Force MC-130 Combat Talon landed 14 minutes after clearing operations began, and six minutes later a flight of 160th SOAR helicopters landed at the Rhino forward arming and refueling point (FARP). Air Force Special Tactics Squadron (STS) personnel also surveyed the desert landing strip, and overhead AC-130s fired upon enemy reinforcements. After more than five hours on the ground, the Rangers boarded MC-130s and departed, leaving behind PSYOP leaflets.

While the Rangers took Objective Rhino, a helicopter-borne assault of Delta Force and Rangers were hitting Objective Gecko. This was a large walled compound belonging to the one-eyed Taliban leader, Mullah Mohammed Omar, situated near the city of Kandahar.

Four MH-47s infiltrated 91 SOF troops into the compound. Security positions were established, and the buildings on the objective were cleared. While the ground forces were clearing the buildings, MH-60s provided CAS, while the MH-47s loitered waiting to pick up the force. It has been reported that as the assault force were preparing for extraction, they were ambushed by a large number of Taliban who were armed with a large supply of rocket-propelled grenades (RPGs). They were extracted from the area under heavy fire. An MH-47 Chinook helicopter was hit, and lost a piece from its landing gear as it took off. At least one soldier was injured during the firefight, reportedly having a foot blown off by an RPG. The ground force spent a total of one hour on the objective.[20]

While Objectives Rhino and Gecko were being assaulted, four MH-60K Special Operations helicopters inserted 26 Rangers and two Air Force STSs at a desert air strip, to establish a support site for contingency operations. One MH-60K crashed while landing in "brown-out" conditions, killing two Rangers and injuring others.

To the east, Air Force bombings had so severely weakened Taliban defenses around Bagram that they crumbled when General Khan's forces attacked on November 13. The next day, Northern Alliance forces occupied Kabul without a fight.[21]

On November 25, 750 Marines of the 15th Marine Expeditionary Unit Special Operations Command (MEU SOC) occupied Objective Rhino, which was henceforth known as Camp Rhino. Marines along with an Australian Special Air Service Regiment (SAS) unit began operations against the Taliban to secure Sherzai's flank as he moved toward Kandahar.[22]

Major Lou Albano, a Marine CH 53 Chinook pilot, talked about Camp Rhino and the often horrendous flying conditions.

> It was desert. They called it a hunting lodge. There were a couple of buildings off to one side and a very austere dirt runway that we weren't even using to land on, since the dirt was like silt. Every time you'd land you'd kick up so much dust that you couldn't see anything and you'd just brown out. That was actually the big danger the entire time we were there. On the other side of the runway opposite from where the small set of buildings were we created landing pads.
>
> They were just sandbags that were spray painted and had been set out in a crow's foot configuration. We'd just land on the sand pads. That's what it was; it was very austere. We had all our equipment there but there was just one warehouse, three small buildings, a small mosque, and that was it.
>
> We actually ran the gamut [of weather]. It was December when we actually got there and we were there all of December, January, and February. Our detachment was only in Afghanistan for three months. There was freezing rain and that was pretty treacherous and there was a lot of blowing dust which would bring the visibility down, especially at night, to your minimums which was 3 miles visibility. With night vision goggles on that's treacherous in itself, especially with a low cloud layer. The clouds would come in at night so you'd have maybe 1,000 feet of clearance before you were in the clouds and it snowed a couple of times. It was pretty interesting flying around in the snow. The base altitude even at Camp Rhino was 4,500 feet and at Kandahar it went up to close to 5,000 feet. The service limit of the helicopters is 10,000 feet, so already you're halfway to the service limit just taking off from the deck. The higher up in altitude you go, the less lift capability you had. It was always a concern. With some of the peaks you had to fly at or a bit above 10,000 feet just to get over them. We didn't have good maps either. We had these very wide angle maps; the kind of ocean navigation maps. You'd know there was a mountain range but you'd see

> these gigantic mountains in front of you. You had no idea where you really were on the map and we relied heavily on the GPS. I could pinpoint where I was on the map but what I was seeing in front of me had no relation to where I was on the map. You'd go up and down and over the tops of mountains. It was odd. It was the most unique kind of navigation and the terrain was pretty treacherous.[23]

Operational tempo for aircraft flying CAS was intense. Captain Black, 1st Special Operations Wing, recounts what it was like.

> We were flying almost every day. Occasionally fly three days and get a day off. We flew always at night. We're fat, heavy, and predictable. We flew low enough to get good fidelity on our sensors which doesn't work in the daylight particularly when you're shooting at people and they want to shoot back. We very concerned about the moonlight, flying only after EENT [end evening nautical twilight, i.e. nautical dusk] and before BMNT [begin morning nautical twilight, i.e. nautical dawn]. We lost airplanes and crew members because they were exposed in the daylight.
>
> We were at Mazar-e Sharif, Kunduz, working with different ADO teams. It was fairly easy because all the lights were out and the towns were dark. If the lights were on it got your attention. If people were out during the times we were flying 95 precent of the time they were up to no good. All the folks who didn't want to get into trouble were home tucked away quietly so it was easy to spot activity. When we engaged the enemy it was apparent they didn't know what we were. How they were trying to be deceptive wasn't working. They expected ground artillery fire, but it was coming from the air. It took a few weeks and then we saw their body language change. They would stay still when we engaged. They would hide more effectively.

The US efforts in the fighting up north suffered a setback on December 5. While the Special Forces were calling in CAS, a 2,000lb joint direct attack munitions (JDAM) bomb landed in the middle of their position. The soldiers were literally blown off their feet. Three Americans were killed and dozens wounded, along with many of their Afghan allies.[24] Major Richard Obert, USAF, remembers this well.

> We were launched to go land in a flat spot in the desert and do a CASVAC because an ODA team had dropped a JDAM on themselves. There was a bunch of dead Afghanis, a couple of dead Americans and a bunch of really hurt guys that needed treatment immediately. They were pulled out on helicopters and again this was early on where Bagram and Kandahar weren't secured.
>
> We landed in a flat spot in the desert, transloaded off the helos to us and then flew them to Oman where there was a better level of care; I guess that is how I should say it. Me and the loadmasters were cutting up everything we had in the back of the airplane to make bandages ... there were some guys that were bad off. There were also guys that had been living there on the compound, or the hangar, with us, for a week or two before we went in and computer emergency response team (CERT'd) them; we knew some of them. I don't want to say that that made me feel good because I didn't like seeing it; I didn't like having the guy that didn't have an eye anymore ask me for my magazine and give me a thumbs up when I gave him my magazine because he's the least hurt guy in the back of the airplane.
>
> I wasn't that young, like 24, but that's a different feeling when you see a guy like that when you were throwing a football around with him the week before...
>
> The doctor actually gave us the feedback that in his opinion getting them to that care that quickly – it was about a three hour flight to Oman from where we were – saved a couple of the guys' lives.
>
> The treatment from the flight doctor that we had with us, the loadmasters, and I had provided in the back significantly reduced some of the trauma in terms of blood loss. We had water and other stuff like that to help with the shock because some of the guys had shrapnel wounds and that water had really helped them a lot in terms of treating them once they got there. That's a feeling of knowing that those guys were really having a bad day and we were able to help them out."[25]

Following the loss of Kabul and Kandahar, Taliban and al Qaeda forces retreated south to two refuges. One was in the Shah-i-Kot Valley in Paktia province and the other was the Tora Bora Valley located in the Spin Ghar (White Mountain) region of Nangarhar province. The valley is six miles wide, 6¼ miles long, and surrounded by 12,000–15,000ft mountains that form a concave bowl facing northeast. The primary avenue of approach into the area is from the town of Pachir Agam south through the Milawa Valleys that joins the Tora Bora Valley at its eastern end. The valley is only 12 miles from the Pakistan border. Most of the al Qaeda positions were spread along the northern wall of the valley.

The CIA-led Jawbreaker Team Juliet, supervised by Gary Bernsten, arrived on a ridge overlooking the Milawa Valley north of Tora Bora in late November and saw hundreds of al Qaeda combatants, command posts, vehicles, and other facilities spread out in the valley below.[26] There were strong intelligence indications that bin Laden and other senior al Qaeda leaders were in the complex when the fighting began on December 5.

Assault forces included ODA 572, under the command of Master Sergeant Jefferson Davis, and coalition ground and air forces aircraft, in addition to a collection of local militias totaling approximately 2,500 fighters grouped under the label "Eastern Alliance" (EA). The alliance was comprised of four anti-Taliban groups led by commanders Hajji Qadir, Hajji Zahi, Mohammed Zaman Ghun Shareef, and Hazrat Ali. Unlike the Northern Alliance forces, these militias were mutually hostile groups – so hostile in fact that at times they fired at each other.

Special Forces teams set up observation posts along the east and west ridgelines of the complexes and began calling in air strikes. The battles took place during the Muslim holiday of Ramadan, during which no food or water is to be consumed from dawn to dusk. Each day, fighting began at first light and continued into the night, when the EA forces would withdraw from the valley to their camps while the enemy remained in the valley. When enemy forces lit campfires at night, SF teams used thermal-imaging scopes to call in attacks by bomb-equipped aircraft and gunfire missions by AC-130 Spectre gunships.

Captain Black was on one the gunships flying CAS at Tora Bora.

> At Tora Bora we were looking for the cave complexes. At the time we didn't have the fidelity to show the elaborate caves they ended up having. We looked for anything man-made – trails, any 90-degree angles, anything that stood and shouldn't be up on 14,000ft mountains. We found and engaged

> entryways and could see the effects from the top of the ridgeline. If we were shooting from the side of the ridgeline we could see smoke from the top. We didn't know what it was at first. It was coming from the air ducts. Probably the most dangerous part of our mission set was when we flew close to the mountains. They could get up close and personal. If they had the weaponry they could get a good shot at us.

The EA forces' withdrawal each night meant that much of the same ground would have to be taken again the next day. Air strikes coordinated by Jawbreaker and SF teams continued almost continuously for 72 hours. On December 9, TF 11 arrived and took control of the operation. Task Force 11 consisted of 50 US Army Delta Force troops from A Squadron, Navy DEVGRU, Air Force STS, along with 12 British Special Boat Service (SBS) commandos, and one British Royal Signals Specialist from 63 Signals Squadron. German KSK Kommando Spezialkräfte (Special Forces Command, KSK) forces moved in to help protect the flanks and run reconnaissance missions.

The battle went on and included 17 more hours of continuous air strikes between December 10 and 11. Finally, on December 17, most of the remaining al Qaeda and Taliban fighters slipped away, their retreat covered by al Qaeda's most fanatical fighters lodged in caves. At the time, CENTCOM did not have forces trained or equipped to operate in the severe Spin Ghar winter conditions or the air assets needed to block the routes into Pakistan.

In the aftermath of the battle the cave complex was carefully examined. Instead of a massive fortress complex, only a natural cave system to which minor improvements had been made was found. No evidence was discovered that any major leaders of al Qaeda or the Taliban had been killed, although there was proof that bin Laden had been there when the fight began.

Kandahar, the last Taliban-controlled city, fell without significant fighting on December 7. The Taliban movement had started in Kandahar, and the city was considered the true capital of Afghanistan by the largely Pashtun population. No one expected an easy fight. While Sherzai positioned his forces to attack the airport, Karzai was negotiating for the Taliban to surrender. On December 7, Sherzai began his assault on the airfield. His forces moved carefully to the entrance, but unexpectedly found no resistance. In the midst of the operation he received a phone call informing him that the Taliban had completely evacuated Kandahar as a result of Karzai's negotiations.

Two days earlier, members of the UN Afghanistan Committee had met in Bonn, Germany, to sign the "Agreement on Provisional Arrangements in Afghanistan Pending the Re-establishment of Permanent Government Institutions." The agreement contained the terms to transfer power to an interim Afghan administration effective from December 22, 2001. Hamid Karzai was selected as chairman of the administration.

The agreement also established the International Security Assistance Force (ISAF), a NATO-led security mission whose main purpose was to train the Afghan National Security Forces (ANSF) and assist Afghanistan in rebuilding key government institutions, in addition to fighting insurgent groups.[27] ISAF, led by a two-star general (COMISAF), was headquartered in Kabul. ISAF's area of responsibility at this time only covered Kabul and the immediate surrounding area. The British Major General John McColl was ISAF's first commander.

As the fighting rapidly progressed across Afghanistan, General Franks and Secretary Rumsfeld discussed post-combat troop strength. Not wanting to repeat the Soviet mistake of flooding the country with tens of thousands of foreign soldiers, General Franks recommended that the total be kept to approximately 10,000 Army, Air Force, Marine, and Special Forces personnel, with enough assets for air assault operations as needed. The 10,000 included three brigades of the 10th Mountain and the 101st Airborne (Air Assault) Divisions and the 15th Marine Expeditionary Unit (and attached units). These forces were placed under the newly formed Combined Forces Land Component Command (CFLCC) Forward. CFLCC was responsible for controlling conventional operations, coordinating with Special Operations Forces, and providing logistical support in the Afghan theater. Major General Franklin Hagenbeck, 10th Mountain Division commanding general, was placed in charge of CFLCC.

On December 12, Major General Hagenbeck and his division headquarters staff arrived at K2 to set up shop. The staff of the headquarters totaled slightly more than 150 soldiers to handle forces more than six times its size.

In Afghanistan, the Army 1st Battalion, 87th Infantry, 10th Mountain Division, and Air Force units established a primary operating base at the old Bagram Soviet air base, while the Marines moved from Camp Rhino to Kandahar Airport. They were replaced there by the 3rd Brigade of the 101st Airborne Division.

By the end of 2001, organized al Qaeda and Taliban resistance ended and a new government was in power. Since Afghanistan no longer had an army tracking down and eliminating remaining Taliban and al Qaeda fighters, this was left to coalition forces. The 10th Mountain and 101st Airborne units swept the countryside looking for weapons caches and any remaining enemy fighters.[28]

At this time there were two distinct military commands operating in Afghanistan, with different focuses. The first was Operation *Enduring Freedom*, the American-led coalition operating throughout the country and focused on eliminating the Taliban and al Qaeda threat. The second, mentioned above, was the UN-sanctioned ISAF based in Kabul. ISAF was tasked with the security and stability of Kabul, not the broader national threats and regional instability. Thus, combat operations, nation building, stability operations, and humanitarian efforts were directed by the US and (primarily NATO) coalition forces in the majority of the country.

In previous wars Afghanistan combat operations had been curtailed during the winter months due to the severity of the weather. Snow closed mountain passes to traffic and made flying a nightmare when pilots were caught in whiteouts. Extreme cold affected not only men, but also made metal brittle and froze oil in motors. Most enemy fighters went to ground, fading into villages or crossing into sanctuaries in Pakistan. But there would be no break this winter. As the new year dawned, coalition forces were to pursue al Qaeda and Taliban fighters through some of the bitterest weather and on some of the highest peaks in the world.

Chapter 4

RECKONING PART II: OPERATION *ENDURING FREEDOM*, 2002

By January, all major Afghan cities were under the control of coalition and anti-Taliban forces. Although there was an increasing number of regular Army and Marine units in country, most of the war fighting was still conducted by small Special Forces units in collaboration with militias supported by close air support. Following the failure to defend fixed positions with out-of-date weapons, and lacking armored vehicles, artillery, and surface-to-air-missiles to counter the coalition's modern arsenal, the Taliban and al Qaeda changed tactics, reverting to unconventional (guerilla) warfare. Bin Laden's al Qaeda and Mullah Omar's remaining Taliban forces retreated to sanctuaries in the mountains in eastern and southern Afghanistan and Federally Administered Tribal Areas in Pakistan. There they began to regroup, rearm, and prepare to strike back. However, before they disappeared into the mountain vastness, the most hardened enemy veterans assembled in the Zhawar Kili cave complex.

During the Tora Bora operation in December, CENTCOM approved a plan to move against the Zhawar Kili cave complex and what is known as the Gardiz–Khost–Orgun triangle close to the Pakistani border in Paktia province. This was one of the four al Qaeda bases hit by cruise missiles in August 1998. Al Qaeda still used the base as a command-and-control center, training ground, and logistics base. (See Map 2.)

The mission began on January 2, with a TF K-Bar SEAL Team being inserted to carry out area reconnaissance. The team was supported by troops of 1st Battalion, 187th Infantry (1-187) (TF Rakkasan based out of Kandahar) and a small Afghan security force, on what was planned to be a nine-day mission. They expected to find the old Soviet compound established by mujahedeen fighters. Instead of this relatively small complex, Zhawar Kili now consisted of one above-ground area containing more than 60 buildings and two separate cave areas covering roughly nine square miles containing over 70 caves. The facilities included a hotel, a mosque, arms depots, repair shops, a garage, a small hospital, a communications center, and a kitchen. Within the complex were towed artillery, tanks, military vehicles, and more than a million pounds of explosives.[1]

Using this information, air controllers on the ground directed B-52 and B-1 bombers, F-18 fighters, and AC-130 gunships to neutralize and destroy the compounds. They did not encounter any enemy forces. Clearing operations lasted until April 7, whereupon the TF Rakkasan deployed back to Kandahar.

While Army, Marine, and Special Forces units sought out and engaged enemy forces, the hard work of building bases, ensuring the smooth flow of materials, and providing the personnel to back up combat operations went on. Army National Guard (ARNG) and Air National Guard (ANG) units augmented regular forces in combat and support roles. ANG C-5 and C-17 transports did the majority of the heavy lifting needed to sustain operations. Air-to-air refueling tankers helped ensure F-15 and F-16 fighters had the fuel for long flights to and from Persian Gulf bases, as well as having the sustainability to be on scene when calls for close air support came in for troops in contact (TIC) with enemy forces in Afghanistan.

ARNG forces with diverse skills, including special operations, teamed up with their reserve and regular Army counterparts. ANG members with Arabic language skills carried out missions in dangerous places. Among these was Sergeant 1st Class Mahmood Qadri who, in early 2002, deployed with SF operators to the rugged mountains of Afghanistan.

Map 2: Major US Special Forces Operations, October 2001–March 2002

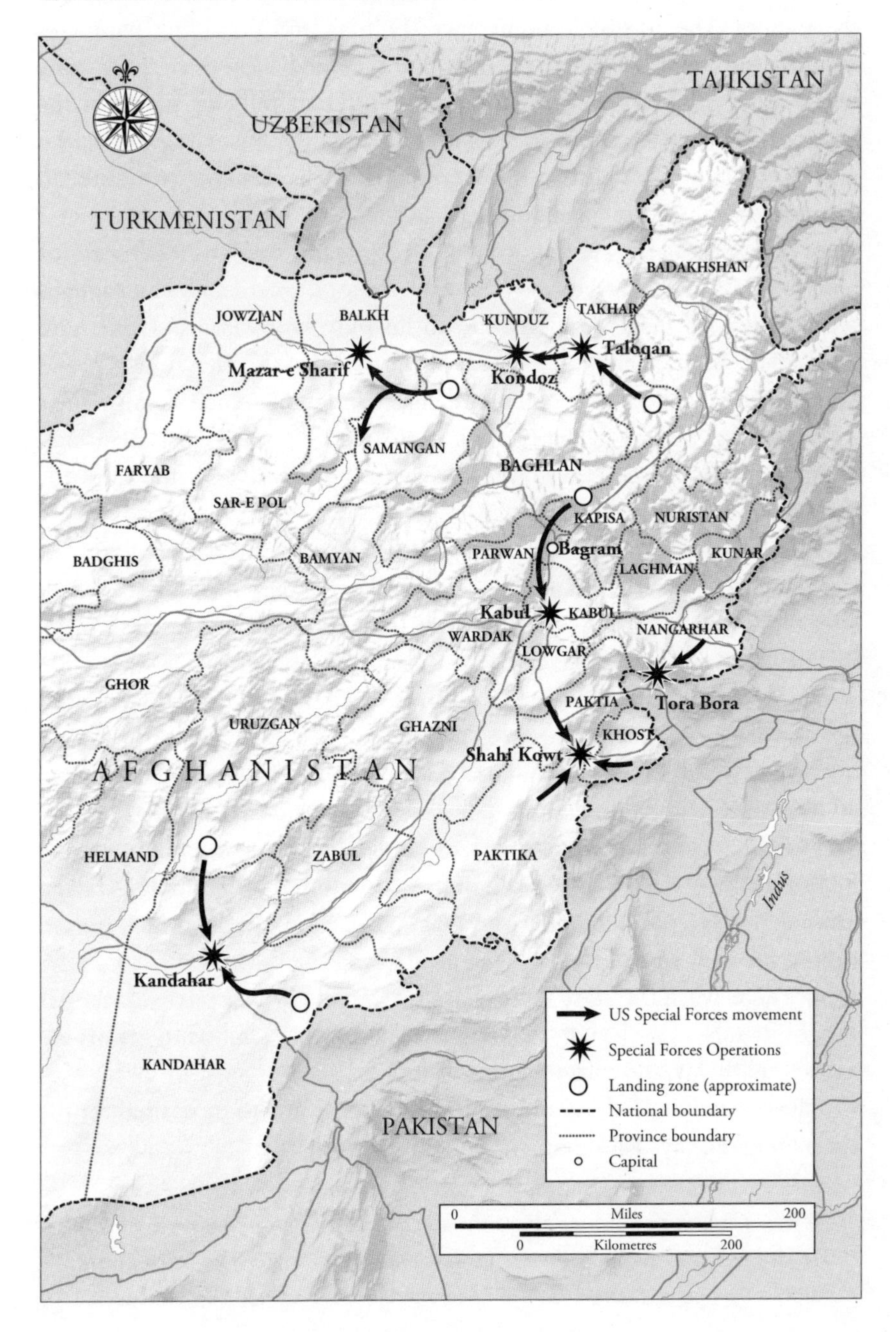

"They were fighting over me in Afghanistan," he said. Qadri and three other linguists quickly joined the Special Operations troops, who traveled throughout Afghanistan training local militias and providing perimeter security for coalition forces. "It was like the Wild West over there, only worse," he says. "There are all of these different military gangs in the country. They're like the mafia. Then, you have the business people who want protection and different governors. But the government can't do anything because they have nothing."

With a beard and wearing local clothing, Qadri trained Afghan troops and was an interpreter between the Afghans and Americans. The Afghans responded with meals. "There was no hostility between us," Qadri said later. "The Afghan people are very hard working and they are a proud people. Their concerns were about basic things like their family, their safety, eating, getting water, getting their children educated. They don't want the Americans to leave because they feel there will be better hope for the future if we stay."[2]

North Dakota ANG 119th Wing firefighters deployed to Bagram. At the time at Bagram and Kandahar, leftover Soviet equipment lay strewn all over the landscape, and the ground was thick with mines. The bases were in bad shape and living accommodations almost nonexistent.

Staff Sergeant Scott Kaufman and Master Sergeant Ernest Svenkerud relate what Bagram was like.

"We flew out of Qatar on a C-17 packed with 101st Airborne troops in all the seats with Humvees and trailers chained down in the middle," Svenkerud recalls. "At that time Bagram only had about 5,000ft of a 9,000ft runway open and about half its width, too, from old bombs laying around. It was a rough landing and a chain came off a trailer, which started rolling around. I got off the plane and it was the darkest night I'd ever seen. There wasn't a star; there wasn't a moon. It was pitch black. Air Force guy met us and said: 'Follow me.' They didn't want us to get off the marked pathway and into the mines."

Their accommodations and scenery left something to be desired for the six-man team, says Kaufman:

> It was a tent with a heater about the size of a soda can. It was cold, maybe 28 degrees, and all we had were jackets and gloves to keep us warm in the tent. We woke up the next morning, opened up the tent door, and it was like

> waking up in the middle of a Russian junk yard. Everything was covered with a couple of inches of snow with mountains in the background. We saw buildings that were bombed. "Alright, I guess we're here, but not quite sure what to do yet."
>
> The base was a big open area with a single chain-linked fence for security. One day we're walking around base and run into a ten or 12 year old Afghan kid carrying an AK-47. We were armed with pistols, which wouldn't have done us much good if the kid wasn't on our side.

The rest of the amenities matched the cold tent in austerity. For the entire six-month deployment their meals consisted of MREs. Latrines were large pipes driven halfway into the ground. Svenkerud remembers the showers: "The only shower was a small inflatable tent one that the Special Forces guys had, but it didn't work if the pump wasn't hooked up to a pickup part of the portable pump. It didn't help much. By the time you got back to your tent you were covered in fine dust again."[3]

Army Major David King, an intelligence officer (S2) for 3rd Battalion, 160th Special Operations Aviation Regiment (SOAR), described what Kandahar was like when he arrived in January.

> My impression of it all was just a complete Wild West town. I mean, every place you're going it was not the normal, sterilized military environment, where everything had its place and its purpose, where everything was nice and orderly and here are the sidewalks you're supposed to walk on. It wasn't that way at all. It was signs that said, "Stay out of this area because of land mines."
>
> You had SF guys walking around in beards and leg holsters. We were walking around in khaki; they were not desert camouflage. We were wearing leg holsters and boonie caps. The 101st guys, on the other hand, were walking around in pro' [protective] masks, flak vests and all this other stuff. You'd be looking at them like they were from another planet and they were looking at you the same way. It was obviously two very different standards. The SOF guys had beards. They looked like they'd been living in the mountains for the last two or three months – and they had been. But it

> was just very surreal. It felt very adventuresome. It wasn't a normal military deployment.
>
> There was one shower point in the whole place. You have to go in planning on using a piss tube and you're going to be crapping in a barrel and burning it with diesel fuel. It was like going back to the Vietnam War. For me, that was a big impression. This is the same stuff, listening to my dad talking about Vietnam. There wasn't any honey wagon or portapotties or that stuff, at least at that point. It was very primitive.[4]

There were few reliable Intelligence, Surveillance, and Reconnaissance (ISR) assets available. King describes his part in analyzing intelligence input: "I didn't go out into the hinterland. I didn't deal with people. I will tell you that during the early phases of that operation, specifically from a special-operations standpoint, it was pretty much search and destroy. It was find targets, eliminate targets; find more targets, eliminate more targets. That was *our* mission."

Providing intelligence to forces conducting special reconnaissance and resupply missions, as well as infiltrations and exfiltrations, were among his responsibilities during a four-month period when Afghanistan was basically a "shooting gallery." "The time I was there," he says, "the missions amounted to little more than man hunting." King also worked closely with international forces operating in theater, dubbing the scene the "Olympics of SOF" because of all the coalition partners present.[5]

Although there was a hiatus in major combat operations there was no hiatus for CSAR squadrons. On February 16, Sergeant Andrew Russell, serving with Australian Special Air Service Regiment, was wounded when the long-range patrol vehicle he was in struck an antitank mine southwest of Kandahar. He was one of five Australian personnel travelling in the vehicle, but was the only one wounded in the explosion. A three-member US military rescue team parachuted into the scene to stabilize him in preparation for evacuation by helicopter.

US Air Force major, Jeremey Turner – a member of the 66th Rescue Squadron stationed at Kandahar, piloted that helicopter accompanied by a second one.

We were alerted that a coalition soldier had been injured and that we were needed to go get him and bring him back. It was about a two-and-a-half to three-hour flight to the location. Because of the time it was going to take for the helicopters to arrive on station, it was determined that the parajumper (PJ) team on the HC-130 would be able to get to this soldier more rapidly, so we had the HC-130 overfly the area – since there was not a significant threat to it – and a PJ team parachuted into the area. The uninjured SAS team members cleared an area in the minefield into which the PJs jumped.

My aircraft had blood on it, meaning our PJs were able to get actual blood products for trying to help this soldier out. As a result, the survivor went back on my aircraft. Since it was a relatively short time and there wasn't any issue of exhaustion, the PJ team on the ground maintained primary care and I recovered the survivor, one team member from the ground and my two PJ team members. The other aircraft in the formation recovered the rest of the team from the team that jumped.

Our PJs worked exhaustively to try and keep him alive, but he had effectively lost all his blood. With about 45 minutes left in flight, the lead PJ told me the soldier had expired and they were going to continue doing CPR throughout the rest of the recovery. So for about 45 minutes in the back of the helicopter, they tried to keep him alive

Once we turned him over, it did not take long for the doctors to say he was beyond being saved. The fact that we were able to get him close to home and obviously get his body back to his family was a small victory, but we would have rather had a happier ending.[6]

Sergeant Andrew Russell was the first Australian casualty of Operation *Enduring Freedom*.

After the Zhawar Kili operation the fighting wound down, with no major operations taking place in February. During a meeting, Major General Hagenbeck, 10th Mountain Division commander, and his staff in Kuwait reached the conclusion that the war was essentially over. Even as they reached this conclusion, signals intelligence (SIGINT) and human intelligence (HUMINT) sources on the ground in Afghanistan indicated that al Qaeda and Taliban forces who escaped from Tora Bora were gathering in the Shah-i-Kot Valley and Arma Mountains near the towns Gardez, Khost, and Ghazni close to the Pakistan border. Intelligence analysis placed the number of fighters in the area anywhere between 150 and 300 and the number of civilians at 800–1,000.

The Shah-i-Kot Valley is a 60-square-mile bowl-shaped area about 15 miles due south of Gardez. It's bound on the east by a range of tall, steep mountains known as the Eastern Ridge, and a smaller, lower hill mass named Tergul Ghar on the west. The valley runs northeast to southwest and has two primary entrances/exits. The first is at the north end of the valley and enters from the northwest. The other, larger entrance enters the valley from the southwest past the village of Surki. The Eastern Ridge was dominated by a 10,500ft-high mountain known as Takur Ghar located across the valley adjacent to the southern entrance. (See Map 3.)

Acting on the intelligence analysis, plans were made for a multi-pronged assault, which included inserting blocking units positioned to the east and sweep units moving in from the west. The operation was codenamed *Anaconda*. The Concept of Operations (CONOPS) called for "nonlinear simultaneous operations in noncontiguous areas of operations" oriented on the following priority objectives:

1. Capture/kill al Qaeda key leaders;
2. Destroy al Qaeda foreign fighters;
3. Prevent the escape of al Qaeda foreign fighters; and
4. Defeat Taliban forces that continue to resist.[7]

Because of the valley's shape, US planners decided the assault would employ the "hammer and anvil" technique. The day before the battle, several SOF teams would set up observation posts on high ground at the northern and southern ends of the valley, enabling them to track the arrival of US and friendly Afghan troops and help provide spotting for air strikes. US air strikes were to be conducted against 13 targets, principally machine-gun positions on the Tergul Ghar Mountain (nicknamed "the Whale" by US forces) and other ridgelines shortly before ground troops arrived on D-Day.

Major David King Intelligence Officer (S2), 3rd Battalion, 160th Special Operations Aviation Regiment, talks about one crucial part of the planning:

> One of the real hard parts about this stuff was finding HLZs [Helicopter Landing Zones]. The reason that was significant: if people were caught off

> guard up on the ridgelines, it may have been that they didn't have nice, flat, level HLZs where they could just zoom into, kick people out of the back and go. It was just extremely, extremely hard to find helicopter landing zones up in these areas.
>
> This may be an oversimplification, but the bottom line is, "Mountains get pointy on top, and the higher you go, the pointier they get." These mountains were very rugged mountains, very steep. They're not like the rolling Appalachians where you can just go find a round hilltop and land on there, no problem. These are very steep, jagged areas and, plus, you're already putting a significant demand on the helicopter working at those elevations.[8]

Command and control of US forces was hampered by the newly established command relationships Operations Order (OPORD) published on February 20, which drastically changed how military forces operated in Afghanistan. Operations changed from a geographically dispersed SOF-centric force with decentralized planning of most ground operations at the JSOTF level, to a geographically concentrated large conventional ground force with operations requiring detailed functional component planning. There wasn't time between when the OPORD was published and Operation *Anaconda* began to effectively implement the new structure.

Although close air support was a critical part of the plan, the Combined Forces Air Component Commander (CFACC), Lieutenant General T. Michael Moseley, wasn't informed of the operation until February 23, only five days before the target start date of February 28. Operation *Anaconda* was the first time US Army battalions were involved in ground maneuvers against hostile forces that required significant CAS. Heretofore, US ground forces were primarily small Special Forces units working with a limited number of Afghan militias. At this point in the war, the joint military infrastructure needed for interoperability was not fully in place. This further compounded the already complex Command, Control, Communications, Intelligence, Surveillance, and Reconnaissance (C3ISR) situation.

Assault forces consisted of 1,200 US Army conventional units, Army and Navy Special Operations Forces, and CIA forces; 2,000 Afghan Military Forces; and 200 Australian, Canadian, Danish, German, and Norwegian Special Forces teams. The combined ground forces were designated Combined Joint Task Force Mountain.

US Navy, Marine, Army, Army National Guard, and Air Force units were tasked to provide CAS and CSAR. Close air support operated in vertical layers, starting with AH-64 Apache and AH-1 Super Cobra attack helicopters on the bottom ascending to AC-130 gunships, A-10 Warthog and AV-8 Harrier jets, then Unmanned Aerial Vehicles (UAVs, Predator drones) overflown by F-14, F-15, F-16, and F-18 fighters, which in turn were under B-1B and B-52 bombers, and all capped by an AWACS. Tanker aircraft circled outside the area. CSAR and other helicopters wove between layers on their way in and out of the confluence of other aircraft.

Since helicopters have short operational ranges another critical task involved setting up the forward ammunition and refueling points (FARP) with extra fuel, rockets, and missiles at a point near the objective to allow the Chinook, MEDEVAC, and Apache gunships more on-station time.

Major Mark Quander, commander of Charlie Company, 326th Engineer Battalion, part of 3rd Brigade, 101st Airborne Division (Task Force Rakkasan) was given the assignment to set up the FARP called Texaco.

> Since we were just right outside the objective area, we could be there very quickly and be very responsive. To do this I had some air traffic controllers from 7th Battalion, 101st Aviation Regiment. I had some Air Force parajumpers for medical evacuation [MEDEVAC]. I had a three-person tactical PSYOPs team and a two-person counterintelligence [CI] team. I had a 3/5 Platoon from 7-101 and my engineer platoon – 3rd Platoon – from Charlie Company, 326th Engineer Battalion.
>
> I had several Javelins [missiles] which had been fielded no more than nine months prior to provide a great nighttime surveillance capability. The big thing we had to do was to safeguard the aircraft that were on the ground. We had an HH60, a MEDEVAC helicopter, a CH47 and there was a lot of munitions on the ground. At one point we had close to 30 aircraft on the ground at the FARP and most of them were for the rescue operation.[9]

The specific Special Forces units involved were part of a combined and joint organization, consisting of 3rd Battalion, 3rd Special Forces Group (3-3 SFG), US Navy SEAL teams, and SOF teams from various coalition nations including Denmark, France, Germany, and Norway. The 3-3 SFG also allocated five ODAs (372, 381, 392, 394, and 395) to the operation, of which three were assigned to help prepare the participating Afghan militia units. An Australian SASR unit was also included.

Afghan militia forces consisted of three Pashtun units. The first force, led by Commander Zia Lodin (TF Hammer), consisted of approximately 600 men. ODAs 594 and 372 advised and trained Zia's force. The other two Afghan units were led by Zakim Khan and Kamal Khan, and each consisted of about 400 to 500 fighters. ODAs 542 and 381 partnered with Zakim's force and ODAs 571 and 392 worked with Kamal's unit.[10]

Task Force Rakkasan, consisting of 1-187 IN and 2-187 IN from the 101st Airborne Division and 1st Battalion, 87 Infantry (1-87) of the 10th Mountain Division, as well as helicopters and the 3rd Princess Patricia's Canadian Light Infantry, were to secure the blocking positions. Special Operations teams from the Advanced Force Operations (AFO) detachment were to provide on-location reconnaissance in the Shah-i-Kot Valley.

Based on previous operations and battles, planners believed the opposition would be armed with AK-47s, RPG-7s, 82mm mortars, and Soviet DShK 12.7mm machine guns. And, once the fighting began, that the rank-and-file fighters would resist long enough for their leaders to escape before they, too, would withdraw along trails into Pakistan or mix with the local population.

D-Day for Operation *Anaconda* was set for February 28 but a blizzard lasting two days forced the assault to be pushed back until March 2.

The ground assault was to be conducted at dawn by TF Hammer and TF Rakkasan. Task Force Hammer, as the "hammer," would advance across the valley floor from the north by vehicle and engage, destroy or capture enemy forces. Task Force Rakkasan was to insert using CH-47 Chinook helicopters and act as the "anvil," establishing seven blocking positions (referred to as Battle Points [BP], named from south to north as Heather, Ginger, Eve, Diane, Cindy, Betty, and Amy) at the passes leading through the mountains on the valley's eastern side.[11]

Shortly after midnight a 39-vehicle assault convoy of military Humvees (HMMWVs) and civilian vehicles under Zia, accompanied by ODAs 372 and 594, quickly became bogged down. The recent snow had turned the dirt roads into thick mud and morasses, which trapped some trucks and caused a bus to overturn. The convoy was scheduled to arrive in their target area around 6:30am.

One hour before Zia was scheduled to hit the jump-off point, a B-1 bomber, a B-2 bomber, and two F-15E fighters were scheduled to bomb the 13 enemy targets in the Shah-i-Kot Valley. Soon after arriving and commencing their bombing, they received a radio message, possibly from an SOF unit on the ground, to cease bombing because friendly troops were endangered. The aircraft halted their operation with only about one half of their targets bombed.

Before reaching one of its two objectives, an HMMWV was hit by what was first believed to be enemy mortar fire, killing Chief Warrant Officer 2 Stanley L. Harriman of ODA 372 and two Afghans, as well as wounding two other ODA team members and 13 Afghans. Enemy mortar fire was not responsible; the attack came from an AC-130 Spectre gunship, which had, due to poor communication, identified the convoy as enemy vehicles and opened fire.

After reaching their objective, Zia's forces ran into minefields and accurate fire at the northern entrance to the valley, causing several casualties. Unwilling to sustain any more losses, he retreated to Gardez. With his withdrawal, what was to be the anvil was left without its hammer.

At about 5:00am, six CH-47 Chinook helicopters carrying half of TF Rakkasan's 400 troops took off from Bagram Airfield, linked up with two UH-60 Blackhawk command-and-control (C2) helicopters, and several AH-64 Apaches. Lieutenant Colonel Ronald Corkran and his security team were on one of the Blackhawks. The helicopters immediately ran into a thick fog, making an already difficult flight worse. The pilots, Corkran stated, "flew that cloud layer through the mountains right up to the objective."

For security, the C2 Blackhawks' door gunners kept doors open all the way to the objective area so they could return fire if necessary. Corkran recalled, "I was so cold I couldn't move my fingers, which had only been clad in a pair of raggedy nomex gloves so that I could write and track the air assault execution matrix in our alternate C2 aircraft."

On approach to the HLZ, the high ridge west of BP Heather, Wiercinski's Blackhawk was struck by small-arms fire and possibly RPG fire. Corkran, Wiercinski, the brigade TAC, and the security team were joined by a two-man SOF Special Reconnaissance (SR) team called Mako-31. The 11 men were on a high, steep ridge that would soon become known as Rak TAC Ridge.

Wiercinski surveyed the valley below: "Very early on I could tell there were no civilians in those three towns. There were no colors, no smoke, no animals, no hanging clothes, nothing to identify it as a populated area with people living there. I looked down and asked, 'What's wrong with this picture? There were no civilians in there. They had moved them out.'"

Wiercinski continued studying the villages to the north of his position. "There was nothing but bad guys there. The place did not have the look of anything else in Afghanistan; it had the look of a battlefield." He then thought, "This is going to be a fight."[12]

The troops started take heavy fire as they unloaded from the Chinooks. The 10th Mountain troops took the heaviest amount of fire, which drove them into a defensive position called "Hell's Halfpipe." They fought from there for the rest of the day and were finally evacuated that night, along with the first day's wounded. Bad weather and enemy fire forced the postponement of the insertion of the remaining 200 troops.[13]

Heavy enemy fire also took a toll on the five Apaches of 3rd Battalion, 101st Aviation "Killer Spades" Regiment flying CAS. As soon as they began their sweeps, the enemy opened fire with rifles, machine guns, RPGs, 57mm antiaircraft guns, and MANPADs (man-portable air-defense systems). Because of the terrain, they were forced to make moving gun runs along a canyon-like route, firing into the side of the mountain as they went. To use their rockets they would have to stop, hover, and take aim to have any hope of hitting the enemy. These tactics exposed the Apaches to close-range direct fire, but they accepted the risk in order to cover the ground troops.

Technical Sergeant John McCabe, the battalion's enlisted terminal attack controller (ETAC), stated, "I do recall seeing 2.75 [inch] rockets coming off of the Killer Spades. They shot their 30mm at them... Again, they would fire their weapon systems, continue flying, and they received heavy ground fire from the guys. I believe they made probably four attacks, at best."[14]

In less than 90 minutes, two of the five helicopters were so badly damaged they had to leave. The remaining three, reinforced by two more, provided fire support to troops trapped on the ridges, making runs as close as 200m away from the enemy.

Throughout the day the Apaches rearmed and refueled at nearby FARP Texaco and headed back into the fight. When they returned to base that night every one of them had been hit multiple times by small-arms fire. Five of the seven were so badly damaged they couldn't fly the next day.

By the end of the first day's fighting, many of TF Rakkasan's troops had been wounded, mostly by mortar fire. The second batch of 200 TF Rakkasan troops were inserted on March 3, bringing with them a mortar unit. Reinforced, the men continued to clear the ridges.

Unlike Army CSAR helicopters, the Air Force mounts either two 7.62mm GAU-2Bs, 4,000rpm Gatling guns, or .50-cal machine guns, one on each gunner's window in each of the aircraft. The Air Force helicopters fly in pairs on missions so one can provide overhead protection while the second makes the rescue.

Although he didn't fly a mission that night, Major Jeremy Turner was one of the pilots assigned to go in on the night of March 3: "If it's considered to be too hot of a landing zone and beyond usual medical evacuation capability, we're usually the ones they call. Our mission is to fight our way in to isolated personnel and fight our way back out. Personnel recovery is what we focus on and what we train for."

Turner and Lieutenant Tom Cahill (piloting the second helicopter) and their crews spent March 3 at FARP Texaco. That evening they got their mission and launched just after dark.

> As we flew in, we started getting more information. We had a litter-critical patient and there were also two injured who were not litter critical but needed to be evacuated. It was very dark, so we spent most of the time trying not to hit the ground or each other. As we flew into the area, we had antiaircraft artillery fired at us... The northern side of the mountains that we were working around was a higher threat, so even though we were north of the position we had to go to, we had to fly around the south side. As we flew to the west of the mountains, we were fired at by something maybe the size of 23mm.
>
> Once we got around the south side of the mountain and started flying north, the AC-130 came back and started some fires on targets they were able to identify on our route of flight as we went in.
>
> The team we were going to recover either did not have a radio to talk to us or was not in a position that allowed them to talk to us, and the team

we had radio communication with was not located with the team we were trying recover. We didn't know where they were, we couldn't identify where the radio guy was we were talking to, and the radio guy was the one who knew where the other team was. It became challenging.

My gunner, then Staff Sergeant Kevin Stewart, [finally] saw the communications signal we were looking for. He then talked my eyes onto it. While we were approaching we were being fired at with small arms, rocket-propelled grenades, and mortars. I was very much focused on the things I needed to focus on.

We made our approach and were enveloped in a brownout dust cloud at about 20 to 30ft off the ground. We got to the ground and, interestingly enough, were about 5ft from a fairly significant hill. We were very lucky. Because of the very low illumination conditions, we just couldn't see it until we were right there.

We recovered the litter-critical patient as well as three others, not two. Three of them were actual saves and then the fourth was just a recovery because he wasn't hurt that bad.

Once we dropped them off, we turned and flew all the way back to Kandahar. From notice to shutdown was almost 24 hours.[15]

During the first days of the operation, pilots flying night CAS missions when most aircraft flew blacked out had problems avoiding other aircraft in the chaotically crowded airspace above the ground where the fighting was occurring. Air Force Lieutenant Colonel Scott "Soup" Campbell, an A-10 flight commander and the chief of weapons and tactics in the 74th Expeditionary Fighter Squadron, found this out the hard way.

The first mission, we got briefed up in the morning. Our maps were no help because they have all these friendly positions plotted out, these enemy positions plotted out and it all looks to me like a big collage of blue and red mess. It doesn't look like when you looked at the *Anaconda* briefing on the map. It's a mess. I said, "Wow, this is not going to be pretty. There aren't any friendlies on this side – good guys, bad guys, here's the line. It's just a mess."

We had a sheet that probably had 100 freqs [frequencies] on it. It didn't have who was assigned to any of them; it just had all these tactical air direction (TAD) numbers. Well I have to make that decision. It's who's screaming the loudest. That's the best I can do. I have to use, at this point, my experience of going, who really sounds like they're in deep shit? Who is the guy who has that tone of voice that tells you it's a little closer than the other guy. Because everybody is screaming, "Danger Close! Troops In Contact!" So we get pushed to this call sign, "White Lightning Bravo."

I talk to White Lightning Bravo and they're in contact in the north end of the valley. I have no reference points. I don't know where any HLZs are. I don't know any of the blocking positions. I can't tell you Betty from Diane from Ginger at this point. I haven't been given any of that. I have no ground scheme of maneuver. I just know there are dudes all over the place. So, we're kind of going from scratch. He's screaming, "We're getting mortared, DShK fire, we're getting hammered!" These guys are about a klick [kilometer] south.

He tells me, "Move about 300 meters towards me, that's the target." So K9 [Campbell's wingman] at this point is in position to roll in and we've pretty much sectored the target because we're blacked out. I tell him to roll in and rip two airbursts down.

He put two airbursts down and the ETAC reports contact is completely ceased, that they're taking absolutely no fire. He reports a direct hit on where these guys were. They were out in the open and we're putting two 500-pounders down.

I'll find out that on one of my passes on that first attack a good buddy of mine, Mike Martin, who's a combat controller, is riding onboard the gunship to try to help out with the coordination and cleaning up the mess that's over on Ginger. I end up pulling off what his and the pilot's estimation say was about 300 yards off the nose of the gunship. It's the dead of night, I'm blacked out and they could see the entire silhouette of my A-10 playing for them as I pull up, and I don't know they're there. That's how close we passed in the night.

As we're continuing to work with some ETACs an F-18 split right between me and my wingman. I have a Predator that almost bounces off the top of my canopy. Nobody is really in charge of deconfliction [establishing safe and exit air corridors]. Then I'm talking to an ETAC, trying to get a talk on, maybe looking into an area of possible bad guys, and all of a sudden a 2,000-pounder blows up as I'm sitting there looking down at the ground. That means it probably just dropped right through my formation off a bomber at 39,000 feet.

It quickly dawned on us that this is a mess and the threat is not from the ground really, from guys shooting at us, it's from each other.[16]

At the close of day on March 6, US forces had control of all blocking points, but the enemy still controlled the abandoned villages in the valley and had forces on the Whale.

As TF Rakkasan fought to clear the ridges on March 2, plans were made to deploy two SEAL teams with Air Force Combat Controllers (Mako 21 and Mako 30) as observers to help oversee enemy movements and coordinate air strikes. Two 160th SOAR Chinook MH-47 helicopters (call signs Razor 03 and Razor 04) would provide transportation for the teams. Razor 04 was to deploy Mako 21 on the north end of the valley and Razor 03 would deploy Mako 30 on Takur Ghar on the valley's east side. Insertions were timed to arrive on scene before dawn to minimize the risk of enemy fire as the teams deployed.[17]

At 3:00am, Razor 03, carrying Mako 30, approached its HLZ in a small saddle atop Takur Ghar. As Razor 03 approached, both the pilots and the men in the back observed fresh tracks in the snow, goatskins, and other signs of recent human activity. As the pilots and team discussed a mission abort, an RPG struck the side of the aircraft, wounding a crewman, and machine-gun bullets ripped through the fuselage, cutting hydraulic and oil lines. Fluid spewed about the ramp area of the helicopter. The pilot struggled to get the Chinook off the landing zone and away from the enemy fire. SEAL Aviation Boatswain's Mate (Handling 1st Class) Neil Roberts stood closest to the ramp, poised to exit onto the landing zone. He and an aircrew member were knocked off-balance by the explosions and the sudden burst of power applied by the pilot. As Neil and the crewman reached to steady each other, both slipped on the oil-soaked ramp and fell out of the helicopter. As the pilots fought to regain control of the helicopter, other crewmembers pulled the tethered crewmember back into the aircraft. Untethered, Roberts fell approximately 5–10ft onto the snowy mountaintop below. He was now alone and in the midst of an enemy force. Roberts survived the fall from the helicopter and engaged the enemy with his squad automatic weapon (SAW) and grenades. An AC-130 gunship moved to Takur Ghar and reported seeing what they believed to be Roberts, surrounded by four to six other individuals. After expending all his ammunition the enemy closed in and executed Roberts.

As Roberts fought alone, Razor 03 executed a controlled crash landing about 3 miles away. Combat Controller Technical Sergeant John Chapman, a member of the team, began coordinating CAS and a rescue effort to retrieve Roberts.

A short time later, Razor 04, after inserting Mako 21, arrived on the scene and picked up the downed crewmen and SEALs, taking them to Gardez. The SEALs and pilots of Razor 04 quickly formulated a plan to go back in and rescue Roberts, despite the fact that they knew a force of heavily armed al Qaeda manned positions on Takur Ghar.

Razor 04 approached the HLZ atop of Takur Ghar at around 5:00am, as dawn was breaking. Despite enemy fire cutting through the MH-47E, the remaining six members of Mako 30 safely inserted, and the helicopter, although damaged, returned to base. Once on the ground near Roberts' last known location, the team assessed the situation and moved quickly to the high ground. The most prominent features on the hilltop were a large rock and tree. As they approached, Chapman saw two enemy personnel in a fortified position under the tree. He and a nearby SEAL opened fire, killing both enemy personnel. They immediately began taking fire from another bunker position some 20m away. A burst of gunfire hit Chapman, mortally wounding him. The SEALs returned fire and threw hand grenades into the enemy bunker position to their immediate front. As the firefight continued, two of the SEALs were wounded by enemy gunfire and grenade fragmentation.

Finding themselves in a deadly crossfire with two of their teammates seriously wounded and one killed, and clearly outnumbered, the SEALs decided to disengage. They shot two more al Qaeda as they moved off the mountain peak to the northeast, with one of the wounded SEALs taking point. As they moved partly down the side of the mountain for protection, a SEAL contacted the overhead AC-130, "GRIM 32," and requested fire support. GRIM 32 responded with covering fire as the SEALs withdrew.

About an hour later, Razor 01 and Razor 02 arrived, carrying a 23-man Ranger Quick Reaction Force (QRF) team and four Air Force personnel: Staff Sergeant Kevin Vance, Staff Sergeant Gabe Brown, Technical Sergeant Keary Miller (123rd Special Tactics Squadron, Kentucky ANG), and Combat Controller Senior Airman Jason Cunningham. Because of communications failures, the QRF landed in the same spot as Razor 03. Razor 01 was hit with multiple RPG warheads and riddled with machine-gun fire that killed or wounded several of those onboard. Miller managed to drag a wounded helicopter pilot to safety. He said later: "We continued to treat the patients, continued moving ammunition and grenades to where they were needed. I grabbed a radio and set up satellite communication and then returned to the rear."

Cunningham dragged injured helicopter crewmen and Rangers out of the burning helicopter. Miller and Cunningham worked hard to keep the patients from succumbing to hypothermia. They put them in the helicopter and removed its insulation and wrapped it around the wounded Rangers.

Approximately 10 minutes after the Rangers took control of the hill, they began to receive more frequent enemy mortar and automatic weapons fire. The Rangers, Army crewmembers, and Air Force personnel began moving the wounded up the steep slope; it took four to six men to move one casualty. As the soldiers moved the wounded, additional al Qaeda began firing from a small ridgeline some 400m to the rear of the downed helicopter's position. The casualty collection point was completely exposed to the enemy fire, which wounded an Army medic and fatally wounded Cunningham. In a few hours, Cunningham would bleed out before rescue came.

With Cunningham out of action, Staff Sergeant Gabe Brown took over coordinating CAS with call sign Snake 01.

Colonel Christopher M. Short, F-15E Strike Eagle Flight Lead, 335th Fighter Squadron, and his wingman had been over the area for two hours tasked to go the Whale when he received a call to contact Mako 30.

> We pass the location to our wingman and he looks down and sees a helicopter on the ground with the rotors spinning. It's probably 15–20 minutes and can't contact MAKO 30, no one knows who MAKO 30 is. Finally we get a call to contact Snake 01.
>
> He's yelling: "I'm on a mountain top with a downed helicopter and I need CAS now. I need guns only. I got wounded [men] and enemy 75 meters way. Danger Close so I need guns and need you to come in from the north."
>
> In my two ships no one had ever fired the gun [a M61A1 20 mm Gatling gun] in the Strike Eagle. I'd done it once on kind of a fan ride on an A-10 range, two trigger pulls. We hadn't practiced CAS using guns.
>
> Snake 01 comes back up: "The helicopter's is at 12-6 and the enemy is at two o'clock 75 meters towards the 4 o'clock position of the helicopter."

> We do three hot passes on that target and get good feedback. I'm using 100–120 round bursts. My wingman makes a great pass. He does with good ranging and 100 round bursts which is perfect. I can see the sparkles from the ricochets as they come off range so I get him to come in steeper to prevent ricochets going too near our guys.
>
> Snake 01 comes on says: "So you know I've got friendlies 75 feet forward of my location."
>
> It was the first we time found out the Rangers had moved forward. 150 meters is Danger Close. I thought we were 75 meters away. In essence we were 75 feet away which was very high risk.
>
> We hung over him and suppressed the enemy. We started yo-yoing [one plane remaining on station while the other refuels] to the tanker so one of us remained over the friendlies.
>
> We're out of bullets and it's fairly quiet now, they're not taking fire like before. So we're ordered home. We didn't want to go. I start beating on the canopy saying we can't go home. I found out later that Snake 01 [was the] son of the man who had taught me how to strafe when I was flying A-10s earlier in my career.[18]

Though hit with mortar rounds, RPGs, and small-arms fire, the team on the ground continued to battle the enemy for hours. With the essential support of air power, they slowly silenced the enemy.

At about 8:15pm, four helicopters from the 160th SOAR extracted both the Rangers on Takur Ghar and the SEALs down the mountainside. The QRF and SEALs had suffered 11 wounded and seven dead.[19]

From March 6–18, three operations were mounted to clear out the remaining enemy forces and secure the area. The first, Operation *Glock*, was carried out by an all-Afghan force composed of Pashtuns commanded by Zia, and Tajiks from the north under General Gul Haidar, along with ODA teams. The operational objective was to take control of the Whale.

The Afghans were not completely successful, which led to Operation *Harpoon* from March 13–17. The task force for *Harpoon* comprised the Canadian 3rd Battalion, Princess Patricia's Canadian Light Infantry Regiment, supported by US Marine HMM-165 Helicopter Battalion composed of three CH-53 "Sea Stallion" heavy-lift helicopters, six CH-47 Chinooks, and five AH-l Cobra attack helicopters. The operation eventually cleared the Whale of enemy troops and supplies.

The third operation was Operation *Polar Harpoon*, carried out on March 18–19. Company C, 4th Battalion, 31st Infantry Regiment inserted from Chinooks 800m from the peak to clear the summit and provide security for A Company, which cleared the valley below.

On March 19, Operation *Anaconda* was over. US and coalition casualties were 15 killed, including eight Americans and 82 wounded. Estimates of enemy losses ranged between 500 and 800 wounded or dead.[20]

Operation *Anaconda* was considered a success even though the initial battle plan didn't survive first contact with the enemy. Ground operations supported by air power won the battle. There were several lessons learned from this operation. Among them was that air power's effectiveness could have been enhanced if circumstances had permitted systematic airstrikes against enemy forces and positions in the Shah-i-Kot Valley in the days and hours before US Army forces were deployed.

Lack of coordination between US, coalition, and Afghan forces hampered smooth operations and, in one instance, resulted in deaths due to friendly fire. Even within the US forces, there was no single overall commander. Special Operations Forces had its own separate chain of command, and had differing priorities, as well as authority to request and receive support from a variety of the same assets that also supported Combined Joint Task Force (CJTF) Mountain operations, such as the AC-130s. These competing command structures utilizing the same assets in the same operating area led to confusion and frustration during the execution phase of the operation. CJTF Mountain did not have tactical control (TACON) or any control at all of these organizations, which reported directly to the CENTCOM Commander.

Despite the operation's flaws, ultimately the enemy did what the US forces wanted them to, which was stand and fight rather than withdraw. This decision cost the enemy heavy casualties, as it had at Tora Bora.

Operation *Anaconda* did not completely eliminate the Taliban and al Qaeda from Afghanistan, or bring stability to that country. A report by

UN Secretary General Kofi Annan cited the continued presence of Taliban and al Qaeda militants as one cause of the general sense of insecurity, but added that conflicts between political and military groups vying for power and criminal organizations were the primary reason for the instability.[21] Complicating the problem was the fact that international law and the rules of engagement didn't allow US, NATO, and ISAF forces to cross into Pakistan. There was concern that violations would trigger the collapse of President Pervez Musharraf's Pakistan government. The situation was exacerbated in May when terrorist attacks in India that the Indian Government believed had been sponsored by the Pakistani Government pushed the two countries to the brink of war.

In Afghanistan, Major General Hagenbeck, now CJTF Mountain commander, and his staff began formulating a new approach that would establish the direction of future military operations, the first such change since the original Operation *Enduring Freedom* plan in November 2001. According to the new approach, coalition efforts would revolve around full spectrum operations, which involved the simultaneous execution of offensive, defensive, and stability operations (such as reconstruction projects).[22]

As this approach was being developed, Hagenbeck and his staff saw an opportunity to fatally cripple the remaining al Qaeda and Taliban in Paktia, Paktika, and Uruzgan provinces along the Pakistani border. To accomplish this, Operation *Mountain Lion* was set into motion.

This was the first major US operation following *Anaconda* in the Gardez and Khost regions, and it began on April 15 led by 1-187 Infantry, 101st Airborne (Air Assault) Division. Task Force Rakkasan planned a 90-day campaign consisting of week-long missions launched by battalion-size or smaller elements. The target was a large training and supply base near the village of Zhawar Kili.

The objectives included intelligence gathering, cordon and search, raids, and humanitarian assistance, all focused on capturing or killing Taliban and al Qaeda groups.

"Well, we think we had a successful mission" said Lieutenant Colonel Ron Corkran, 101st Airborne, who commanded the operation.

We did three basic things. We did exploitation of a cave system in the Zawar Kili area. We did operations with Afghan forces in the area. They helped us do that mission. And then, we also were able to coordinate and work some humanitarian assistance for the village of the Afghan forces that were working with us.

Since we don't normally work in caves and that kind of environment, we took some of the tactics, techniques, and procedures we use in the city fighting and applied them to the caves.

So there are ways of clearing rooms and hallways and buildings, we applied to the caves. And the guys were able to do that. They provide themselves with over watch security and then, checking for booby traps using grappling hooks and that type of thing to look for tripped wires and all and then, moving through the caves very methodically with security all around.

There's really two different kinds of caves. One are natural caves by erosion and whatever else that have occurred and some are actually underground facilities that were developed 15 or 20 years ago, hardened, rebar, supported roofs, arches that support a lot of stress as we tried to destroy some of the caves. Some of them were very difficult to do that with.

Wiring that had been running inside where they were running power and all. So they were very sophisticated complexes and I guess complex is right word, multi-room, interconnected, multiple entrances or escapes out of them. So it was a complex place.[23]

After six months of war there was still not a unified US Command in Afghanistan. Major General Hagenbeck as commander of CJTF Mountain did not have either the rank or the authority to coordinate assets from other branches. A CJTF commanded by a three-star general was needed to coordinate Navy, Air Force, Army, Marine Corps, and coalition forces operations, which would rectify the situation. In mid-March, CJTF 180 formed at Bagram Airfield under the command of Lieutenant General Dan K. McNeill, who commanded XVIII Airborne Corps. The CJTF 180 staff was formed from XVIII's own headquarters corps augmented by coalition staff and liaison officers. With a multinational staff, the CJTF could synchronize the operations of US and coalition forces. CJTF 180 efforts were directed toward tactical combat operations; establishment and training of the Afghan National Army; and support to ISAF, civilian military operations (CMO), and information operations. CJTF 180 officially assumed control of coalition operations in Afghanistan on May 31, 2002.

Lieutenant General McNeill also reorganized the US forces' command structure, including 10th Mountain Division, Special Operations Forces, and the Combined Joint Civil-Military Operations Task Force, comprised of mostly civil-affairs units. CJTF 180's structure allowed McNeill to focus on theater strategic- and operational-level concerns, which included relations with Afghan military and political officials. McNeill placed the burden for tactical-level operations on Combined Task Force (CTF) 82, which had been constructed from the US Army's 82nd Airborne Division headquarters and was commanded by Major General John Vines.[24]

In planning future operations, the CJTF 180 staff had to consider how many and what types of troops would be available. The coalition set a cap on the total number of military personnel to ensure its military organizations created only a light footprint in Afghanistan. Thus, the US was limited to 7,000 servicemen and women. About 400 people were in the task force headquarters, including staff officers from coalition partners. Some 20 nations had contributed forces to the coalition effort in the region. About 7,000 Americans, including US forces training the new Afghan National Army, were among the roughly 14,000 troops under McNeill's command. He did not command ISAF, which was under Turkish command.

Brigadier General Robert L. Caslen, Jr. served as chief of staff for CJTF 180 in Afghanistan from May through September 2002. Upon arriving in Afghanistan, he immediately realized that their biggest challenge would be finding and fixing the enemy in an enormous area using limited resources coordinated across the different service components. Another difficulty CJTF 180 faced was getting subordinate units to adopt more than a purely kinetic approach to the fight, with the ultimate goal of providing a secure environment in which the Afghan Government could prosper. ISAF played an invaluable role by providing legitimacy to the government in Kabul. Caslen relates:

> We had Tora Bora then we had *Anaconda*. They [Taliban and al Qaeda] had no more safe havens, so they had scattered in Afghanistan and went across the border to Pakistan. Then we had remnants of them coming back and forth across the border.

We didn't call it a counterinsurgency. We just saw it as a typical search-and-attack type mission. You go find the enemy, fix them and then kill them. At the same time, you're working with populations of people.

We all learned the importance of working with populations, which are the grassroots of counterinsurgency fighting. You go in there with kinetic attitude, you have to realize you're working with populations of people who respond to different approaches, and they certainly don't respond to getting their doors kicked in all the time.

You've got to work with the people and understand them, so therefore that was my approach as chief of staff when we did our operations and the targeting piece during that particular time. So we really had to work on the strategic effects. Every time we did a combat operation, we now had them work on the immediate aftermath, to bring blankets, food and water and talk to the village people and have meetings. We started trying it that way.[25]

One other problem Brigadier General Caslen encountered was the lack of accurate information about coalition forces' actions and what was heard by government officials:

We conducted a raid against Osmani, who was a Taliban corps commander. We had done the raid on Thursday. We were all high-fiving that we had killed the guy. We had pictures and everything. It looked just like him. On Sunday, General McNeill, who was going to be the JTF 180 commander, came in and did a pre-deployment site survey. So General Hagenbeck [10th Mountain Division commander] brought him into Kabul to meet Karzai.

We walk into Karzai's office. There's Hagenbeck, McNeill, me, and Karzai. Hagenbeck has a relationship with Karzai and we had just killed this guy on Thursday down by the Kandahar area. Karzai just launches into Hagenbeck and says, "Why did you go down there and kill that old man for? Why did you throw the girl down the well and drown her? Why did your men put all the women in that compound into a room and start fondling them? What are you doing?"

Here's the president of the country just lambasting us. This just shows the ineffectiveness of our strategic communications, not only to the leadership of Afghanistan but to the people in the area.

It was nothing like that. It was a special ops raid. They went in there and they had a couple of bad guys, so they shot them. They took this one guy who resisted and he was shot and brought back. It turned out he was not Osmani. He was somebody else but he was still a bad guy. But all the accusations that Karzai got wind of were not true.

On the Osmani raid, they had obviously drummed up their own story and it worked its way up to Karzai, totally independent of what we did – and we thought we were doing pretty good.

We thought Karzai would be pretty happy that this Taliban corps commander was killed, but it was a totally different story. So we immediately realized that you cannot fight a kinetic fight against this type of an enemy and this type of a people, because we're going to have to connect with the people. So we started making modifications to how we conducted warfighting. If we're going to do a raid, then we brought in a unit in the aftermath with public affairs that would not only communicate to the people, they would talk to the press and things like that as well.

While much of the US and coalition focus was on Operation *Anaconda*, low-intensity operations took place throughout Afghanistan. Among these was the relief of Special Forces ODA teams who had been in country since November.

ODA 922, B Company, 1st Battalion, 19th SFG(A) deployed to K2, Uzbekistan on March 2, 2002 to conduct a relief in place (RIP) for the 5th SFG(A). Master Sergeant Carl A. Richards was Company Training NCO and Operations SGT for ODA 922 at that time.[26]

"When we arrived, Operation *Anaconda* was being conducted. We attended daily briefings and waited for a mission," Richards recalls.

After a couple of days of helping the ISOFAC [Isolation Facility] construct resupply bundles, my Team was placed in Isolation and began planning for a RIP of an ODA that had linked up with Ismail Khan and taken control of Herat and essentially western Afghanistan. This was a true UW [Unconventional Warfare] mission. After five days of detailed planning we INFILed [infiltrated] with a CA [Civil Affairs] team and a PSYOP team. Half of the ODA we RIPed EXFILed and we spent a week with the remaining ODA elements in order to conduct hand off operations. This was 12 March, 2002. We were a ten man ODA, six man CA and three man PSYOP element.

Our Commander's intent was to provide ground truth. This was a marathon that lasted almost seven months. Initially gaining situational awareness was the priority. Working with our Afghan counterparts was true unconventional warfare. Learning the Area of Operations, developing emergency plans and SOP's was the priority. We conducted Low Level Source Operations, CA and PSYOP operations, Concept of Operations [CONOPS] in western Afghanistan, and numerous Dignitary Personal Protection operations. During the CONOP operations the team, by doctrine, split into two elements.

One to maintain contact with host nation forces in Herat and the other conducted the sometime 10 day operations in remote locations along the Iranian border, North Western and central Afghanistan.

This was not a high intensity combat operation. Long in duration and tedious in nature.

Throughout the spring and early summer other units were transitioning in, replacing, or relieving units finishing their six-month deployments. Three battalions of the 82nd Airborne, 505th Parachute Infantry Regiment (PIR) arrived to take over from the 101st. Command Sergeant Major Richard Lopez was one of the new arrivals:

The 10th Mountain and 101st were already on the ground. It was hot during the day – 110–130 degrees. Lots of dust everywhere. We came in with three battalions. Command was structured around brigade task forces. We had responsibility for the majority of the east side of Afghanistan. It wasn't really a big threat.

We pushed out to Bagram and then to what is now FOB [Forward Operating Base] Salerno. We started venturing out. A lot of our information was fed to us by the locals. "Here's where rockets are being stored. We know where a cache of weapons is."

We were always prepared for the worst. You get a few pop shots now and then. The Taliban worked in four- or five-man fire teams. They'd set rockets on a timer, lean it against a rock and leave. It was literally hit or miss.[27]

The Air Force brought in the 75th "Tiger Sharks" Fighter Squadron, 23rd Fighter Group, which had A-10s, to augment the F-15s, F-16s, and AC-130s in close air support missions. Staff Sergeant Antuan Ray, a weapons loader, recalls his arrival in country and working the night shift:

> We were supposed to land at Kandahar, but the plane was getting shot at so the pilot basically did a touch-and-go and went to Bagram. On top of our ten-to-12-hour shifts we had to help clear up the base. We're clearing debris and there are all kinds of snakes and vipers, unexploded ordinance in the port-a-potties, rats in the MREs.
>
> We'd load the aircraft at night. It was black with only the stars out and we didn't have flashlights, but we did have glow sticks. So I'd put my glow stick around my head so I could see. They would yell, "Ray, take the thing off your head. There could be a sniper out there." I always disobeyed that order.[28]

There was one mission the squadron took part in he wishes he could forget being a part of. On July 1, US and coalition forces near the town of Tarin Kowt in Uruzgan province conducted sweeps looking for suspected Taliban personnel and weapons caches. They had already found several large caches, including one containing 29 shoulder-fired antiaircraft missiles. During the operation, SF units called in CAS when unknown enemy forces fired on them. B-52 bombers and AC-130s struck several ground targets, including antiaircraft artillery sites that were firing at the gunships. A-10s from the 75th Fighter Squadron were among those responding to the call.

"Every once in a while there'd be a scramble," said Ray. "One day we found a whole village full of bad guys. We armed the jets up and they went on the mission. They came back a couple of hours later with empty racks. The pilots were quiet. Turned out the target they hit was a wedding."

The small-arms fire was from a wedding party whose members were firing off their weapons in celebration. The air strikes killed more than 40 civilians and injured more than 100.

"I know mistakes happen, but I felt particularly bad because the jet that came back completely empty of ammo was the one I'd loaded," Ray said. "The rest of the deployment was a downer."

On August 19 soldiers of the 82nd Airborne, 1st Battalion, 505th Parachute Infantry Regiment (1-505 PIR) and 3rd Battalion, 505th Parachute Infantry Regiment (3-505 PIR) boarded helicopters at Kandahar and Bagram airfields and flew south toward Paktia province. The 82nd was joined by Army Rangers, a CMO team, and two Special Forces ODAs. These units formed the main maneuver force of Operation *Mountain Sweep*, the largest security mission in Afghanistan since Operation *Anaconda* in March.

Over the course of the six-day operation, units moved from village to village across the district. In most cases they used helicopters, landing near their objectives and then quickly moving into position near the village, but not always. In one instance the battalion conducted a 13km foot march to approach one site.

Despite the massive operation, the 3-505 PIR did not find the Taliban official thought to be in the district. Colonel Huggins, the TF Panther commander, suspected that intelligence leaks had led to the loss of the element of surprise. On August 25, the last day of *Mountain Sweep*, Huggins stated, "I have no doubt that [the enemy] had advance warning that we were coming."[29]

The 3-505 PIR followed up Operation *Mountain Sweep* with Operation *Village Sweep* in early October. The operation focused on four villages near the Pakistani border that intelligence reports indicated contained Taliban fighters and weapons caches. Keying off comments from Special Forces teams who had worked in the area for months, the unit took a less aggressive approach this time.

Instead of conducting unilateral searches, unit leaders explained their intentions to village elders, asked permission to search homes, and had female soldiers search the women. In addition, while searches were in progress, CA teams politely inquired about medical conditions and the general needs of the villages to identify potential reconstruction projects.

Company Sergeant Major Lopez was part of the operation. "Every one of our missions was 72–96 hours," he says. "Go through two to three villages, spend the night in one, get resupplied, spent the night there, and move on. One of our main objectives was winning hearts and minds – bring in services, food, blankets, school supplies for the kids, stuff to prepare them for the winter time. Sit with them, break bread, meet with the local warlord."

The searches located significant stockpiles of weapons and ammunition, including one cache of 250 RPGs and thousands of rounds of heavy machine-gun ammunition, and a second large cache was discovered in a village less than a mile from the Pakistan border.[30]

A significant change in US operations took place in TF Panther's area with the construction of forward operating bases (FOBs) just north of the city of Khost and near the towns of Asadabad, Shkin, and Orgun-e. The FOBs enabled US forces stationed at Bagram and Kandahar airfields to establish a permanent presence closer to where Taliban and al Qaeda groups were finding refuge in Pakistan. FOB Salerno was the largest, manned by the entire 3-505 PIR, part of an aviation battalion, an SF ODA, and other units.

A key part of the overall military operations included US military-led humanitarian efforts on the ground, which started soon after combat operations. These efforts were spearheaded by US Civilian Military Operations (CMO) battalions. The 96th Civil Affairs Battalion (Airborne) was one of the first units on the ground as part of US Special Forces. This was part of initial counterinsurgency (COIN) efforts. However, the US and other force commanders remained focused on insurgency guerilla operations rather than the broader counterinsurgency aspect of the war.

Counter-guerilla operations focus on detecting and defeating the armed insurgent or guerilla, without solving the society's underlying problems. Military efforts alone, however, cannot defeat an insurgency. Thus, the need for COIN. This involves all political, economic, military, paramilitary, psychological, and civic actions that can be taken by a government to defeat an insurgency. Operations include supporting a Host Nation's military, paramilitary, political, economic, psychological, and civic actions taken to defeat an insurgency. Avoiding the creation of new insurgents and forcing existing insurgents to end their participation is vital to defeating an insurgency. COIN operations often include security-assistance programs such as foreign military sales programs, foreign military financing programs, and international military training and education programs.[31]

Working as attached four-to-six-man teams called Coalition Humanitarian Civilian Liaison Cells (CHCLCs, pronounced "Chicklets," later designated Provincial Reconstruction Teams [PRTs]) they carried out missions involving population resource control, helping dislocated civilians, and paying reparations for civilian property losses incurred during a fight. It also covered any other area that involved civilians on the battlefield.

The Army Reserve 489th Civil Affairs Battalion arrived at Bagram in February 2002 to relieve the 96th CA Battalion. Eight 489th teams co-located with Special Forces and PSYOP teams in locations spread out in Herat, Bamyan, Bagram, Khost, Gardez, Kandahar (two teams), and Jalalabad. Many of the teams served in isolated areas, with no more than 20 other US soldiers within hundreds of miles. In one case, a team member provided medical care under fire to an Afghan district governor who was shot accidentally by his own men during a confrontation with village residents.

The battalion also provided civil affairs support in combat operations along the Pakistani border. Teams accompanied units from the 82nd Airborne, 101st Air Assault, and 10th Mountain Divisions, as well as the British Royal Marines and other special-operations forces. They also assisted US combat troops in raids seeking "high-value targets" (HVTs). "Our job is to help find people to point out the HVTs, calm the local citizens, and reassure the village elders," said Lieutenant Colonel Don Amburn, the unit's commanding officer.[32]

Company Master Sergeant James W. King eloquently recalled his impressions and experiences of Afghanistan as part of the 489th Civil Affairs Battalion:

> The C-130 touched down in Bagram under cover of darkness. As the rear ramp slowly came down the reality of total darkness set in. We waited, not really knowing what was to happen next. In the distance the glimmer of a green nightstick could be seen slowly approaching. "Grab your gear and let's go," shouted a voice in the dark. We filed out in a column and quickly set off into the night. After a short half-mile walk we were told to bed down in one of the blown-out buildings from the Russian days, and we would figure everything else out in the morning. Welcome to Bagram.
>
> The perimeter was triple-strand concertina wire and you had to chase the kids out of the area every morning as they tried to sell you everything from watches and coats to old Russian bayonets and pistols.
>
> I was the detachment 1st Sergeant assigned to the CMOC [Civilian-Military Operations Center] in a house in downtown Kabul. Sand bags and film taping the windows gave us a certain degree of comfort and protection. We were just a few blocks down from the headquarters of the controlling Northern Alliance Commander. Our guards were provided by him and we were his guests and under his protection. It was an amazing feeling when Mamadeen, an Afghan guard, said to me, "Don't worry. I will give my life for you."

As I traveled throughout the central Afghanistan countryside I was astonished to see Afghan villages that hadn't changed in 300 years. No electricity except for an occasional gas-powered generator; crops sustained by irrigation canals that were hundreds of years old; farmers plowing fields using an ox team and a tree trunk. And yet the villagers themselves were some of the happiest, most thoughtful people I have met. Always ready to share what they have with you. The children still laughed and played and it seemed like a very good life. Perhaps similar to the American West in the early 1800s.

I was reminded of the level of poverty on several occasions during my year-long stay in the country. The first came to me as a story from one of my team sergeants. His team had been assigned to return the remains of a small boy who had died. The boy had been brought to the medical facility at Bagram and had been treated for several days before he passed away. The Bagram CA team was asked to return the boy's body to his village and his family. After arranging the helicopter transportation to return the boy, the team stayed for the brief funeral service. After the service the boy's body was taken out of the wooden coffin it had been in and placed in the ground. My team sergeant asked the family why the boy had been taken out of the coffin and the sad reply came back, "The boy is dead. He doesn't need any wood. We do."

The second reminder came when I was asked by a few Afghan men I had hired if they could have some rice. We had received a wooden pallet of 50lb bags of rice on wood pallets from the World Food Organization (WHO). The wooden pallet was out back in our compound and after a few weeks and a host of birds a few bags had opened and some rice had spilled onto the ground. After the last bags were gone we gave the pallet away to an Afghan who wanted the wood. He asked if he could also have the rice. I told him the rice was all gone. He touched my arm and pointed to the ground where the rice had fallen out of the bags.

I didn't quite understand so I got my interpreter Rayhaun. "Sir, he wants the rice on the ground." There couldn't have been more than a few pounds of rice on the ground but to this man it was everything. I stood and watched as first he swept all the dirt and rice into a pile and then as he sifted the rice from the dirt. I gave him a black garbage bag to put the rice in and stood there humbled as he thanked me several times for a bag of rice that would feed his family the next day. I realized then that I would never again feel sorry for the way my life had progressed.[33]

During the remainder of 2002, US forces continued running security missions throughout eastern and southern Afghanistan. The northern and western parts of the country were relatively secure, with no major actions reported. CJTF 180 faced the challenge of maintaining the momentum, focused on eliminating opposition forces through the next year.

CJTF 180 also placed increasing emphasis on stabilizing Afghanistan. To accomplish the mission, two new organizations were set up. One was PRTs consisting of 60–90 soldiers and civilians that included security enforcement, force protection, and reconstruction capabilities. The first PRT deployed to Gardez on December 31, 2002. The second was Combined Joint Task Force (CJTF) Phoenix to assist with training a new Afghan National Army (ANA).

In 2002 there was a shift from SF-centered operations to ones employing regular forces for major operations. Special Forces still played a major operational role, but the numbers employed in these operations were smaller than they had been. Also, the role of the Northern and Eastern Alliance forces was diminished as the major fighting ended. Their leaders were still powerful figures, but the internecine fighting had ended.

However, as at the end 2001, the fight against Taliban and al Qaeda forces didn't slack off as the new year started.

Chapter 5

RESURGENCE, 2003

In the beginning of 2003 there were approximately 10,000 US troops in Afghanistan. The reason for this low number was to avoid giving the Afghan people the impression that they were an occupying army, a mistake the Soviets made by investing the country with large concentrations of forces. The US forces were augmented by the 5,000-strong multinational ISAF force based in Kabul. However, ISAF operations were still limited to the area around Kabul only.

The ANA, which had been trained by the British and by US Special Forces, numbered less than 6,000 soldiers, and was not in a position to actively intervene. To offset the paucity of US, coalition, and ANA troops, roughly 100,000 anti-Taliban forces commanded by warlords provided security at the local and, in some areas, regional level. Not all of the warlords were benign, with some engaging in oppression, narcotics operations, and power struggles amongst themselves.

This mixed bag of security enforcement led to an increase in criminal operations fueled by increasing opium production and heroin trafficking. This increase in criminal activity had a corollary effect of corrupting Afghan officials, which in turn led to a worsening of the situation. Initially these activities were not addressed by the US forces, which instead focused on the anti-terrorist mission. The overall lack of a cohesive security blanket and enough US and NATO forces to provide adequate national security on their own gave the Taliban and al Qaeda time to reconstitute their forces.

On a tactical level, TF Devil (1st Brigade, 82nd Airborne) relieved TF Panther on December 5, 2002. Task Force Devil was based in Kandahar and deployed units to FOBs in areas where Taliban and al Qaeda were seeking refuge. Along with conducting routine security patrols, CA and PSYOPS teams worked with the population in surrounding villages.

Major Del Monroy, Intelligence Officer (S2) for the 3-504th PIR, explains the mission at that point: "In early 2003 it was a very new fight. We were going into a combat-intensive situation and al Qaeda and the Taliban were still around. We weren't going in to build bridges and build schools. We were going in to seek, find, and destroy the enemy while also creating relationships with the mayors and city councils. We had to understand the tribal culture of it all; I couldn't recite any Pashtu for you right now but I could probably speak a couple of sentences for you in Iraqi [sic]. It was just different then. We were going into the fight."[1]

Task Force Devil launched Operation *Mongoose*, the year's first major combat operation, on January 23. The objective was to search for enemy groups and weapons caches in the Adi Ghar Mountains near Spin Boldak southeast of Kandahar. Intelligence suggested hundreds of Taliban soldiers were hiding throughout the cave complexes in the area. A force consisting of 300 US, SOF, and coalition forces supported by B-1 bombers, US and Norwegian F-16s, Apache helicopters, and an AC-130 gunship spent two days clearing caves. Taliban soldiers fought back, losing at least 18 men in exchange for no friendly fatalities.

Operation *Eagle Fury* from January 9–28 kept up the pressure in the Bahgran Valley, located in Helmand province. The 82nd, 7th SFG(A), and SEALs, along with Afghan troops, spent the two weeks searching villages for weapons caches and suspected Taliban members.

No troops were safe, even when not conducting combat operations, because the enemy could be anywhere around them. Major Monroy tells of the situation: "In our first two weeks we saw probably one of the first bicycle improvised explosive devices [IEDs] ever used. A kid rode up with an IED in his bike and was traveling along with the convoy. He rode up beyond them and stopped. The kid walked away and it went off. There were at least two Purple Hearts from that. The enemy was there but it was difficult to find them because they were in the population."[2]

Staff Sergeant Dean McMurry, 3rd Battalion, 2-505 PIR, 82nd Airborne, TF Sabre, staged into Kandahar in January and spent two weeks there before moving to Bagram. From there his unit was sent out to FOBs.

> We got chopped up and sent to Fire Base Osamabad. Our FOB was in that area. Two main Ops – Bull Run, the highest elevation that overlooked the FOB, and Shiloh a little lower. The FOB and the two Ops had been Russian positions. They put artillery piece on both Ops. At one time the Taliban overran the positions and turned the guns on the Russians in the valley below. The Russian officers air evacuated and left the troops. The Taliban captured and executed them all.
>
> The problem was that the only coverage we could provide was with .50-caliber machine guns and 81mm mortars at the FOB. At the FOB were SF, Rangers, and some federal guys there; you didn't really know because they're running around with beards. We were FOB bitches pulling gate guard, tower guard, and LZ patrols. They'd kick out with their own mortar to Route Orange and Route Blue, which were traditionally hot areas.

McMurry also talks about the difficulties he encountered when searching locals for IED materials, and how relations could sometimes be tense.

> One day I was told to take my guys up and do a traffic-control patrol. We got reports of IED trafficking in the area. The IEDs look like light ballast. So we roll up and search the village. We get little pieces of det cord and we're detaining people. You knew what was going on, but you couldn't just nail them down.
>
> There was a village elder. I asked him through my interpreter: "Why are they not showing us who are carrying these IEDs?"
>
> The elder said to come with him. So we walk back down a little ways the way we came. He explained to me that years ago a battalion of Russian tanks came through this pass and got to this point. Then he turned around and walked away. I didn't get it at first. Then I realized he was saying that if they didn't want us here we wouldn't be here. Basically he was saying: "So just shut up and do your deal. We're allowing you to do your deal."
>
> Some of the other platoons would rough up people if they found some det cord or batteries. We knew we couldn't detain them if they didn't have certain materials on them, and they'd get roughed up pretty bad. The Afghans would retaliate by ambushing SF teams.[3]

The tempo of Special Operations missions was still high, with forces going out to find and eliminate the opposition, often with AC-130 gunships feeding them information and providing CAS. Master Sergeant Todd Millhouse, AFSOC AC-130H gunship airborne operations sensor operator, was there.

When we got in country we were living in tents and when you hear the siren go off warning the mortars are coming in it's kind of scary. Then at the end of the 60-day trip you don't even hear the siren anymore because you're kind of used to it. If it hits, it hits and if it doesn't I'm still going to the chow hall. I got to eat and I got to go. It's hard to fathom. You get numb to it after a while because it's so inaccurate, unorganized. You have a better chance of hitting me with a rock than one of these things.

The first time we got shot at – antiaircraft, triple-A, artillery coming up over the aircraft – at the moment you don't think because you're doing what you're supposed to be doing, and then you land. I was with my buddy Brad and I kissed the pavement. I walked around the airplane, sure that something had hit it – there was nothing. I said "alright" and hit the chow hall, ready to do it again tomorrow. I remember seeing a guy the first time he had to engage the enemy in combat. He basically shut down afterwards. He sat in the corner with his head in his hands and didn't say anything.

You go out to do missions and then the helicopters bring the Navy guys and the Army guys back. Then you have a debrief and they say, "Thanks for saving my ass." They came back because of what you and your crew did.

There were several nights I was flying and my roommate, a JTAC, was on the ground. It's gratifying that the guys on the ground make it home safely. Somebody is not going to leave the valley that evening. Preferably it's the guys on the other side.

I've been on missions where we lost people on the ground. The plane was so quiet you could hear a pin drop because you probably knew Jim or Bob or whatever his name was. It's always hard because we're so close and our paths had crossed at some time at a permission planning or post-mission, planning or cycles. You met that person, it's not some face in the newspaper. It makes it that much more a tougher pill to swallow knowing you weren't there fast enough or something like that.

What I did is what I did. To me it's not a big deal. I know a lot of the ground guys. Those guys to me are more important than what I do because I know them on a personal level. That's what drives me to continue to do this.[4]

The only major security operation during February was launched by TF Devil on February 19 and lasted until March 2. Paratroopers of the 2-504 PIR air assaulted into the Baghran Valley, a known Taliban stronghold, to conduct cordon-and-searches for weapons and opposition fighters.

Captain Andrew Zieseniss, one of the battalion's company commanders, emphasized the deliberate and painstaking character of the operation: "It's not a war where we're fighting a conventional army, like World War II. There are bad guys in civilian clothes. It's old-fashioned detective work, digging through hay stacks, literally."[5]

Sixteen days after completing Operation *Viper*, the 2-504 PIR and the 3-504 PIR, accompanied by US female soldiers and civil affairs specialists along with Romania's 151st Infantry Battalion ("Black Wolves") and ANA units, were inserted by Chinooks into the Sami Ghar Mountains for the four-day Operation *Valiant Strike*. Before boarding the helicopters, Lieutenant Colonel Charlie Flynn, commander, 2nd Battalion, 504th PIR, told his troops: "Don't let them bring it to you; you bring it to them."

In the village of Laday, 1st Sergeant Brian Severino, Company B, 3-504 PIR, found weapons hidden in manure piles. Akter Mohammed, a 40-year-old shepherd, told Severino: "We need the guns to protect our sheep from the wolves, or they will eat my sheep."

For the most part the Afghans were friendly. In Narai they brought tea to the troops. Shahghsy, one of the village elders, explained why: "The Americans come to make peace in Afghanistan. When the Russians were here the Americans helped push the Russians out." The Afghans don't forget either their friends or their enemies.

1st Sergeant Craig Pinkley, B Company, 2-504 PIR, said later that the one of the goals of operations like *Valiant Strike* is finding large weapons caches and taking them out of circulation, but there are still some difficulties. "The difficult part is not knowing who's who," he said. "Sometimes they say they're Afghan militia force and they're not; they say they work for the government but they don't, so it gets confusing."

When the operation ended, more than 50 rifles, two heavy machine guns, 170 107mm rockets, and 400 82mm mortar rounds had been collected. Pinkley summed up how the troops felt after walking long distances carrying heavy packs, living on MREs, and not getting a lot of sleep at night. "It's a hard job; the guys feel as if they've accomplished something."[6]

As Operation *Valiant Strike* kicked off on March 20, US and NATO forces launched Operation *Iraqi Freedom*. It began with a massive air campaign quickly followed by a ground assault from Kuwait. By May 1 organized resistance had ended, and at that time there were 466,985 US personnel deployed as part of the operation.[7] Since military commanders held the opinion that the Taliban and al Qaeda were no longer major threats, the military and political focus switched from Afghanistan to Iraq.

Planning for the Iraq invasion began on November 27, 2001. Secretary of Defense Donald Rumsfeld requested General Tommy Franks to prepare a "Commander's Concept" that might form the basis for action. The initial concept was approved by Rumsfeld on December 11, 2001 and the plans for the invasion evolved from there.[8] Through 2002 and into 2003 it appeared as though Afghanistan was stable and anti-government forces were no longer a significant threat to the regime.

Task Force Devil operations continued through March and into April 2003. During Operation *Desert Lion* on March 27–30, troops from 2nd Battalion, 505th PIR, backed by two Norwegian F-16 fighter bombers flying on a routine patrol over the area, air assaulted into the Kohe Safi Mountains near Bagram Airfield. CJTF 180 spokeswoman Captain Alayne Cramer said: "Intelligence sources and tips from local Afghans suggested we revisit the area." The operation netted two caches of weapons that included 107mm rockets, mortar rounds, recoilless-rifle rounds, and cases of machine-gun ammunition, just 5km from the air base.[9]

For a change, the 812th Romanian Infantry Battalion, Major Dorin Blaiu commanding, led operations *Carpathian Lightning* and *Carpathian Thunder*. Operation *Carpathian Lightning* took place on April 14, with *Carpathian Thunder* kicking off on April 22. As usual, elements of the 82nd Airborne were part of the operation along with soldiers from the 450th Civil Affairs Battalion (Airborne), and the 731st Explosive Ordnance Disposal Company.

"CA is always the first vehicle to enter the villages," said Specialist Abram Miear, 450th. "We sit down with the village leader to smooth everything over. While we are doing that, soldiers can focus on their job. They can't perform without CA," he added.

Throughout the mission, the team distributed a total of 1,000 daily rations, shoes, clothes, and other necessities to five different villages, including Hazar Khili. "The people shouldn't be scared. We are here to help. We are very grateful for everyone being cooperative in telling us where the weapons were," said Captain Kevin K. Parker, 450th.

Approximately 43,000lb of rockets, mortars, and small-arms ammunition plus 1,440lb of explosives from both the Romanian and US was blown up. "That was the largest explosion that our unit has done," said Staff Sergeant Baylin Oswalt, 731st.[10]

Not all operations yielded such explosive results for TF Devil. Operation *Vigilant Guardian* began with 2nd Battalion, 504th PIR, travelling through the night over dusty roads on April 23 back to Spin Boldak along with Afghan Military Forces (AMF).

"No one ever knows what you're going to find," said the platoon sergeant, Sergeant 1st Class Joseph Johnson, B Company, 2/504th. For three days they searched the area finding only two hand grenades, multiple rocket-propelled grenades, six 107mm rockets, approximately 40 mortars, and a few AK-47s.[11, 12]

As part of the searches all the women and children were asked to go to one room while the area was being searched, because of past incidents where women hid weapons under their burqas. Usually the US females are military police (MPs), but this time Private Terri Rorke from the 11th Public Affairs Detachment came along. She reveals what it's like to see behind the burqa:

> When I was tasked to go on a mission recently, as a journalist, I thought my primary job would be to take pictures and set up interviews, like I was trained to do. But I realize I am a soldier and I must do what I am needed to do. The last couple of operations I went on I was needed to help out with searching females.
>
> "Peace. I am a woman. I have to search you," I said in Pashto as I entered the dark rooms, taking off my helmet and sunglasses to show the scared and innocent I was a female. Some looked directly in my eyes as I searched them, while others tried to hide underneath their robes. Some were shy and giggled as I patted down on their shoulders. They would pull out metal containers with beads from their dresses sequined with colors of blue, red, purple, pink, and neon variations. Although I didn't totally understand what they were saying, I knew they were trying to tell me, "See, I wasn't hiding anything," after I was finished.

> They were beautiful, yet so hidden. It is something I don't understand as an American and as someone who doesn't follow the Muslim lifestyle in the Middle East and central Asia.
>
> I wished I was a fly on the wall that could just [photograph] away and I would then be able to show the world their beauty. But all I could do was say thanks for cooperating and I would leave them in their dark huts where their beauty remains to be seen strictly by their families, military police females, and maybe a female military journalist from time to time.[13]

Fire Base Shkin was located in Paktika province about four miles from the Pakistan border, at an elevation of 7,800ft. Shkin is a brown adobe mud fort surrounded by concertina wire, and is said to resemble the Alamo. Because of its proximity to the border, Shkin was often hit by mortar and rocket fire. It had earned a reputation as "the most evil place in Afghanistan."

Colonel Roger King, the spokesman for US forces, said the US-led anti-terrorism coalition forces have "made no secret of the fact" that the border region between Afghanistan and Pakistan is where there is the "highest probability of contact," adding that the "more active you are, the more possibility you have of running into enemy elements."[14]

Two US soldiers were killed and an Afghan and two US soldiers were wounded on April 25, 2003, in a daytime clash with suspected Taliban fighters in Shkin. Specialist Stephanie Pavliska and Private Anna Wear stationed at FB Shkin were part of the base QRF during this attack "They started firing on us," said Pavliska. "You could see all the flashes and frag [grenades] blowing up." She talked more about the actions of her fellow soldiers than she did herself. "I can't explain what it's like," she said. "Everything goes through your mind but at the same time you ... you just do it."[15]

On May 1, Donald Rumsfeld visited Kabul for meetings with President Karzai and Afghan military commander Marshal Fahim, in addition to US commanders. At a press conference with President Karzai, Secretary Rumsfeld said:

> The President of the United States and General Franks and I have been looking at the progress that's being made in this country and in cooperation with President Karzai have concluded that we are at a point where we clearly have moved from major combat activity to a period of stability and stabilization and reconstruction activities.

> The situation, first of all, what will be done differently? I think that it's a matter of a shift emphasis. The United States began a process from the very outset of including humanitarian assistance and reconstruction activity and technically non-military activity almost from the first day that we set foot here and brought in forces to work with the local forces to deal with the Taliban and the al Qaeda. What's different however is that we are now at a point where we can actually shift our weight and a considerably larger portion of the effort in the country can be in that direction because of the success in providing a more stable environment here.[16]

He went on to emphasize the constructive role the PRTs were having in bringing about stability and security throughout Afghanistan. This transition is what Lieutenant General McNeill and his XVIII Airborne staff that formed the core of CJTF 180 had been working toward since Operation *Enduring Freedom*'s inception. The transition would have to be carried out by another general and his staff. The change of leadership began in May, when 10th Mountain Division headquarters and combat units arrived to replace the 82nd Airborne. Major General John R. Vines was McNeill's relief. The 10th Mountain headquarters then became the staff for CJTF 180 under Vines.

The core of the revised CJTF 180 was Task Force Warrior, built around the 1st Brigade, 10th Mountain Division, which began arriving in the summer of 2003. Task Force Warrior units included 1st Battalion, 87th Infantry (1-87 IN), which conducted operations from fire bases at Orgun-e, Shkin, and several other locations along the Pakistani border. Also operating out of the Gardez FOB was a troop from the 3rd Squadron, 17th Cavalry Regiment.

The 2nd Battalion, 22nd Infantry (2-22 IN) moved into Kandahar Airfield and provided the QRF for southern Afghanistan. 2-87 IN secured Bagram Airfield as well as a small base near Asadabad and provided the QRF for northern Afghanistan, while 1st Battalion, 501st Parachute Infantry Regiment (1-501 PIR) deployed to FOB Salerno near Khost. The batteries of 3rd Battalion, 6th Field Artillery (3-6 FA) were deployed at various FOBs to provide indirect fire support to these units as they conducted missions near the bases.

Task Force Warrior also contained coalition forces. Some 400 soldiers from Romania's 151st Infantry Battalion, based at Kandahar Airfield, provided airfield security as well as convoy security for civil affairs operations. The 250 soldiers of French Task Group Ares operated in the border region southeast of Kandahar with a primary mission to interdict Taliban and al Qaeda infiltrators. Task Force Nibbio II, the 800-soldier Italian airborne battalion, was based at FOB Salerno, north of Khost, until September 2003.[17]

In order to expand training, the ANA Combined Joint Task Force Phoenix was created. The 1st Battalion, Afghan National Guard was trained by the British Army working as part of ISAF. Then, in order to enlarge training capability, 1st Battalion, 3rd Special Forces Group under the command of Lieutenant Colonel McDonnell trained the follow-on battalions. The 3rd Special Forces Group built the training facilities and ranges for early use, using a Soviet-built facility on the eastern side of Kabul, near ISAF headquarters. The 10th Mountain Division units were the first conventional forces involved with TF Phoenix. When Division rotated home, Army National Guard and other members of the coalition took over.

In addition to major ground-force command and unit changes, there were an increasing number of Reserve and National Guard units integrated into every part of the operations. In February, G Company, 104th "Nomads" Aviation Regiment (Chinook Heavy CAB), 28th Combat Aviation Brigade, Pennsylvania Nation Guard, was the first Guard aviation unit activated. One section came out of Connecticut. Colonel David E. Wood, commanding officer, recalls it was an interesting mix of people from essentially different cultures:

> My POL [Petroleum, Oil, Lubricants] team came out of Hartford. Almost to a "T" all black, urban black men, just with different stories to tell. The Pennsylvania part of the platoon was country farmers, kids that were deer hunters, woodsmen, really rural people. You bring this platoon together and they can't even understand each other. I love them all.
>
> Walking into the POL shack at two o'clock in the morning preparing to do a night op, these guys were playing cards together, working together, they were brothers, and it was truly a band of brothers. Honestly it left such an impression on me no matter how diverse Americans are, when you put them together in this kind of situation they work together. There were no problems. To watch my soldiers live together, work together, and build relationships together was a piece that's always stuck with me. I'm so damned proud of them.[18]

The Nomads were initially slated to be part of Operation *Iraqi Freedom*, but their assignment changed to Afghanistan by the time the personnel and helicopters got to Kuwait in March.

Chief Warrant Officer 4 Larry J. Murphy, who had been in the Army since 1975, mentions what made the Nomads different from the 101st Airborne (Air Assault) aviation unit they replaced. "Their average age was about 28 and average flight time roughly 600–800 hours. Our average age was 41 and average flight hours were 3,300."[19]

Lieutenant Colonel John Kubitz adds: "We had one pilot that had as much flight time as an entire active duty company. Chief Warrant Officer 4 Kevin Dillingham had been doing it since Vietnam. The confidence the ground troops had in our unit was phenomenal. Special ops requested us because they knew we could get the mission done properly and safely. This is a testament to the experience the National Guard pilots have. The other thing interesting about the Guard is we have full-time jobs. When we got into a base camp we had guys who drive bulldozers, we had electricians, we had HVAC mechanics who could make life a lot nicer for us. We choose not to live in misery; we choose to improve it."[20]

They flew all over the country on missions to the Iranian border, south of Kandahar, the edges of Pakistan, and Herat, province supporting French, Australian, and Canadian forces.

"Our biggest threat was the environment, because of the different types of sand," says Chief Warrant Officer 4 Murphy. "Some was like talc and others like beach sand. One thing about landing in brown outs is that in Pennsylvania we do snow landings where the techniques are similar, so it wasn't completely foreign to us. You're blind for a few seconds."

"There are a couple of things that stick out in my mind about the countryside," mentions Kubitz about the flying. "You went from desert to lush green valleys. You would fly over parts of the country where you'd swear Christ and the Apostles could have walked out of any one of the villages. You never see many cities. The majority of the places we flew over you'd think, 'What do these people care about what's going on?' They're tending their fields, herding the sheep, the nomads are going with their camels. They really don't care about what the government's going to do for them and the Taliban."

Wood said: "Soon we were pushed into the south central area where there were a lot of bad guys. There were fairly heavy operations going on

[*United Resolve*, *Warrior Sweep*, *Haven Denial*, *Heavy Debt*, *Devil Fury*, *Mountain Yankee*, and *Viper 1* and *Viper 2*]."

Kubitz recalls one mission he flew with Dillingham. "We were doing an infil and as we were on short final approach I'm listening to the radio. They're telling me there are troops in contact and they threw out the grid. I'm looking at the map and I said 'Kevin that's only 200m from where we're landing.' He replied 'I got off slicks [unarmed helicopters] so I wouldn't have to do this anymore.'"

Other Chinook pilots had demonstrated the same type of finesse flying with troop insertions on narrow ridges and in tight quarters, but the Nomads brought the most experience of anyone to date in the war.

Secretary Rumsfeld's statement in May about moving from major combat activity to a period of stability and stabilization proved hollow. Working from safe havens in Pakistan and the Afghan mountains, the Taliban and al Qaeda struck back. Enemy attacks increased in number and frequency throughout the spring, summer, and fall. The attacks seemed to be focused primarily on Afghan civilians and security forces, ISAF personnel, and people working for nongovernment and international organizations (NGOs and IOs).

When the Taliban retreated in the fall of 2001 they took millions of dollars from the national treasury and established networks in the southeast, where they and al Qaeda had always been strong. The now-dispersed enemy became increasingly difficult to find, and the heretofore successful tactics used by US-led coalition forces were no longer effective.

The inability to effectively fight such a dispersed force was compounded by the fact that after *Anaconda* the coalition was unable to reach the Taliban because of their location in the lawless Federally Administered Tribal Areas (FATA) of Pakistan. There, insurgents could plan and launch actions, train, supply, refit, and regroup all relatively free from Afghan and coalition interference. These areas were also comprised of sympathetic refugees displaced from Afghanistan, which were a ready source of new recruits.[21]

After Operation *Anaconda*, the Taliban used the FATA as a place to reconstitute its forces. Most of its operations were launched into the adjacent Paktika, Khost, and Paktia provinces. In addition, the US invasion of Iraq drew attention away from Afghanistan, which the leaders were quick to take advantage of.

Surviving Taliban fighters and leaders adopted tactics to better counter those US and coalition forces. These included simple things such as knowing the weak points in body armor, to understanding where MEDEVAC helicopters might land during a firefight and mining that area. In July, 1st Battalion, 87th Infantry Regiment, replaced an 82nd Airborne battalion operating mostly in Paktika province. Initially the battalion operated out of three firebases: Orgun-E, Shkin, and Gardez, with operations mostly limited to 15km circles around the firebases. At that time the Shkin area was considered one of the five most dangerous places on earth. Lieutenant Colonel Dennis Sullivan, 1st Battalion's executive officer, describes the situation and the unit's mission at this point in the war.

> One mission was to secure the firebases and provide security to the other elements on the bases so they could perform their missions as well. It eventually evolved into conducting our own combat operations in those areas of operation. We were supposed to focus on the enemy and identify, kill, or capture any enemy forces that we found in those areas. We had so much force committed to securing firebases that we really didn't have a lot of firepower to go out and conduct operations. For the first few months, the most we could get was about a company's worth of infantry to go out and conduct operations. It limited our flexibility because so much was tied down with securing these three firebases.

Another sign of the Taliban and al Qaeda's resurgence was their employment of more sophisticated ambush tactics using larger forces, instead of shooting at the first available targets. This was a classic tactic used throughout history, and one that the Taliban and mujahedeen used with devastating effect against the Soviets. Lieutenant Colonel Sullivan experienced this change first hand.

> A special ops force had been ambushed in a specific area a couple of times. We'd flown some Apaches over the area to do some investigation of the AO to find out what was going on there and they identified a few suspicious locations that we were going to check out.

> So I mounted up and did the mission in Mangretay. On the second day, we headed out of the AO in platoon-sized elements and went along a channelized road with high ground on each side. Two elements passed through there and the third one was ambushed by enemy forces up on a hill."[22]

With CAS suppressing enemy fire, the forward two elements reinforced the one under attack. Fortunately, no friendly forces were killed.

Enemy forces did not challenge operations *Haven Denial* and *Warrior Sweep*, which were run in July. Operation *Haven Denial* involving 800 US forces and 500 Italian paratroopers supported by 25 aircraft; it netted one small arms cache.

The larger Operation *Warrior Sweep* against militants in Paktia and Paktika provinces started on July 20 and continued into September. The operation utilized combined forces from the 82nd Airborne, 2-505th PIR, one company from 3-504th PIR, the Italian Folgare Brigade, the 812th Romanian "Red Scorpion" Infantry Battalion, the ANA, and Afghan militia forces.

As part of counterinsurgency efforts during the operation a CMA team with healthcare providers, medics, traditional birth attendants, veterinarians, veterinarian techs, military police, preventive medicine personnel, Afghan medical students, Afghan physicians, and supporting elements went with the combat troops. In the following ten days the medical teams provided care for 2,300 men, women, and children. Medical educators provided instruction on dental care, malaria, mine awareness, and food preparation to all patients treated at Zurmat, and providers integrated preventative health messages into their treatment of patients at the remaining locations. The veterinary team treated 21,000 animals including camels, burros, horses, goats, cows, and sheep.[23]

At the end of six weeks, caches had been found containing grenades, C4 plastic explosives, a crate of dynamite, more than 20 RPG rounds, a box of antiaircraft rounds, and hundreds of 7.62mm and handgun rounds. One unsubstantiated report indicated that more than 20,000 pieces of ordnance had been destroyed, but no enemy fighters were killed or detained.[24]

Not all the action took place during named operations. Taliban and other anti-coalition/government militia staged attacks across the country. Troops living in or running patrols out of fire bases and FOBs near the Pakistan border skirmished almost daily with the enemy or were hit with mortar and rocket fire. Mounted patrols usually consisted of a rifle platoon in Humvees equipped with a .50-cal machine gun or an MK-19 40mm grenade launcher. Lieutenant Colonel Sullivan describes the mounted patrol vehicles thus: "It was a mixture of gun trucks, and when I say gun trucks I mean turtle-backed Humvees. Some of them were up-armored. It was about 50/50 at the time. Initially we just had cargo Humvees and we had to put sandbags in them for protection. Then we got Kevlar blankets to put in all the Humvees. After that we got the modification kit where we put some Kevlar sheeting down the sides of the cargo Humvees to give them some more protection from enemy fire."[25]

On September 29, 2nd Platoon from A Company, 1-87 IN, was on routine patrol out of Shkin Fire Base. After reaching the designated patrol area they parked their vehicles on the ridges and infantrymen began sweeping through the wadis. Suddenly AK-47s, machine guns, mortars, and RPGs opened up, some firing from within Pakistan. The first barrage wounded Sergeant David Gilstrap in the face and Specialist Robert Heiber in the arm.

Captain Ryan L. Worthan, the company commander, moved out of the fire base with another platoon and together the two platoons advanced toward the sites where they suspected the enemy mortars were located. Assessing the battlefield, Worthan directed the evacuation of casualties, marked enemy positions, and directed fire toward them. He led one platoon through a 150m-deep, 500m-wide wadi as he continued coordinating attacks on the enemy forces.

Following along the wadi, Sergeant Christopher McGurk and his men found wires leading in the direction of the landing zone and where the Humvees were parked. Sergeant Allen Grenz began following the wire. Cresting the hill he spotted three enemy fighters. One of them was holding a detonator, another poised to hurl a grenade, and a third was leveling his weapon at Grenz. Grenz fired three shots, hitting the first man in the forehead, the second in the right eye, and the third in the stomach.

From the other side of the wadi, Worthan's men fought from ridge to ridge as enemy fire continued to come from different directions. Worthan continued marking enemies and calling in their positions to air elements.

A sniper hit Private 1st Class Evan O'Neill twice below his flak jacket, shearing a main artery. A third shot hit O'Neill as he was dragged behind a tree for protection. Braving machine-gun and rocket fire, medic Christopher Couchot administered first aid and then helped carry O'Neill up the hillside to the Humvees. Despite these efforts, O'Neill died.

Elements of A Company quickly moved onto open ground that provided a clear field of fire and a large enough area to accommodate a MEDEVAC helicopter, which was on its way to pick up Gilstrap. As the helicopter flared to land, enemy fighters fired from positions on the ridgelines surrounding the site, forcing it to shear off.

Captain Ryan L. Worthan on the ground and Major Paul Walle, the XO, coordinated CAS to suppress the enemy on the high ground. Soon, several Apache helicopters and two A-10s arrived, hitting the enemy on the ridgelines. "The whole ridge was ripped up," Worthan later recalled. "It was like time stopped." As evening fell, Worthan finished clearing his areas before coordinating the return to Shkin Fire Base.

The firefight lasted 12 hours, and an estimated 20 al Qaeda and Taliban fighters were killed. "The enemy did a good job anticipating what we'd do," Walle said. "They wanted us to take casualties and bring in a helicopter so they could shoot it down."[26]

September also included fatal attacks on Afghan police and other targets in the mountains north of Deh Chopan in Zabul province, which resulted in Operation *Mountain Viper* being launched on August 30. This two-week operation resulted in an estimated 84–95 anti-coalition militia (ACM) killed at a cost of 15 coalition casualties, including one 5th SFG killed in an accidental fall. A disquieting piece of intelligence came to light in that during the operation Taliban forces were supported by troops loyal to Gulbuddin Hekmatyar, a former Afghan prime minister who now led a guerilla-style insurgency against the current government.

In October, Combined Forces Command Afghanistan (CFC-A), now theater strategic headquarters for Operation *Enduring Freedom*, was formed under the command of Lieutenant General David W. Barno. CFC-A focused on building relationships with Karzai's government, the American Embassy, and ISAF.

Analysis of the current military situation showed two separate but overlapping conflicts. One was that of the coalition and Afghan Government forces against al Qaeda and closely related terrorist organizations composed primarily of non-Afghans that operated in the southern and southeastern provinces along the Afghan–Pakistan border. The second conflict featured the insurgent networks of the Taliban and the Hezb-e Islami Gulbuddin faction.

After two years of war, pockets of remaining Taliban and Haqqani network allies tended to be near Kandahar in the south and the adjoining provinces of Zabul, Uruzgan, Ghazni, Paktika, Paktia, and Khost along the Pakistani frontier.

In the northeastern provinces of Nuristan, Kunar, Laghman, and Nangarhar, Gulbuddin Hekmatyar and his insurgent group Hezb-e Islami Gulbuddin (HIG) mounted operations against coalition forces and Afghan security units. Although the HIG, Taliban, Haqqani, and al Qaeda organizations were distinctive, there were indications by the fall of 2003 that leaders were increasingly interested in collaboration.

In Barno's assessment, coalition security operations before mid-2003 had focused too heavily on destroying the enemy and less on winning and retaining the support of the population. From this early assessment, the CFC-A built a COIN campaign strategy based on five lines of operations that Barno called pillars:

1. Defeat Terrorism and Deny Sanctuary;
2. Enable Afghan Security Structure;
3. Sustain Area Ownership;
4. Enable Reconstruction and Good Governance; and
5. Engage Regional States.

CJTF 180 would support the security operations and reconstruction efforts that supported pillars 1, 3, and 4. The Office of Military Cooperation Afghanistan (OMC-A) would focus on pillar 2. Barno, working closely with his staff and US Embassy officials, pursued the initiatives at the center of pillar 5.

To accomplish these objectives there were approximately 10,600 US Army personnel in Afghanistan along with Marine and Air Force units providing additional forces, as did coalition partners and a small number of operational Afghan Army units. ISAF units in Kabul had approximately

5,000 more troops. The total coalition, ISAF, and Afghan Government military strength did not exceed 30,000.[27] At the time, conventional wisdom held that a ten-to-one ratio of troops to insurgents was needed for success. Concurrently the US military taught to plan for a three-to-one numerical superiority when operating in most environments, and a five-to-one ratio in urban-warfare scenarios.[28] Since no one knew the actual strength of insurgent forces, commanders stayed with the ten-to-one ratio. The primary reason for limiting the size of US forces was Secretary of Defense Rumsfeld's concern that too many US troops would create an anti-American backlash, which, in turn, would lead to a wider-spread insurgency.[29]

Using cell-phone intercepts and other ISR resources, Combined Joint Special Operations Task Forces (CJSOTFs) developed information about enemy activity, which included the Hezb-e Islami Gulbuddin militia, operating in Nuristan province in the Hindu Kush region near the Pakistan border. Operation *Mountain Resolve* was to disrupt any ACM operations and deny them sanctuary. No outside force had penetrated the area since Operation *Enduring Freedom* began. The operation was designed around the "hammer and anvil" tactic employed during Operation *Anaconda*.

The "hammer" consisted of the 10th Mountain Division's Warrior Brigade, which air assaulted from Chinooks into farm fields on the outskirts of Namgalam village in the eastern Afghan province of Nuristan shortly after nightfall on November 6.

The "anvil" was formed by CJSOTF elements operating in three northern sectors. The 10th Mountain forces would push up the Waygal River Valley to drive enemy forces north into the net established by CJSOTF.

Infantry units were augmented by field artillery, civil affairs units, military police, PSYOPS teams, combat cameras, and a forward treatment team. Apache helicopters and A-10s provided 24-hour CAS. Chinooks provided logistics support. "Normally when we deploy we have very limited attachments, but this time what we had was pretty impressive," said 1st Sergeant Carl Ashmead, B Company, 2nd Battalion, 22nd Infantry Regiment, 10th Mountain Division.

During the first days of the mission, A Company destroyed weapons, ammunition, and explosives it found while searching through Namgalam village.

"We traveled straight-line distance of 20km, but we ended up walking probably close to 52km total," Moore said. "This terrain is very rigorous and unforgiving," he added. "These [soldiers] were tired, it was cold and raining, and they marched over 50km and didn't complain."

Carrying combat loads often weighing more than 100lb slowed down the operation. Four mules and their Afghan owners were hired to take the heaviest equipment, a solution that had been used before by troops manning observation posts (OPs) farther north.

Keeping the large amount of troops supplied was another challenge. Chief Warrant Officer 4 Larry Murphy's experience came in handy on a couple of the logistics missions.

> In mid-November we had done the infil but they hadn't been extracted yet so we were on resupply on all-day missions. It was toward the end of the day when we got a radio call that there were PUCs [Persons Under Control, i.e. detainees] that needed to be picked up. They gave us a grid that was up on a mountainside.
>
> The elevation was 1,000ft above the ground and the mission was run at dusk. What was different about this was it's the top of a house that's all solid logs. The rest of it was adobe. It was not going to support an aircraft. It was a very crew-intensive operation. The flight engineer looking over the end of the ramp is giving you verbal commands – "aft one, left three, down two," – to get the aircraft in position.

Murphy gingerly set the rear landing gear on the roof, picked up the PUCs, and flew off into the night.

By the fourth day, Warrior Brigade soldiers traveled more than 20km over rocky mountainsides and even moved through a river at one point. Although during the trek they didn't come into contact with ACM forces, they did finally come within view of the mountain where the objective was located without any enemy contact. When they got there they found evidence that ACM fighters had left one to two days before. The next day the force extracted.

Two weeks later, A, B, and C companies reinserted in the Waygal River Valley looking for Mullah Wazir, a low-ranking local Taliban organizer.

Again they found evidence of ACM activity, but no personnel. Although the unit did not find Wazir, information surfaced that he was in the village of Aranas. An air strike was called in. Seven boys and two girls playing nearby and a 20-year-old man were killed in the attack. At a press briefing on December 9, US spokesman Lieutenant Colonel Bryan Hilferty said villagers later told US investigators that Wazir had left the village ten days before the strike.[30]

The US suffered its only casualties of Operation *Mountain Resolve* in its last stages. The night of November 23, Major Steve Plumhoff, Air Force 58th Special Operations Wing, was piloting an MH-53 Pave Low long-range CSAR helicopter conducting combat operations for Operation *Mountain Resolve*. A compressor problem caused one of the two engines on the Pave Low to stall, leaving it with one engine operating and too much weight to carry in the thin mountain air. Plumhoff attempted to jettison the auxiliary tanks without success, and then the other engine stalled while an emergency landing was being attempted.

With all power lost, the helicopter fell from an altitude of about 200ft onto an uneven river bank, rolled over, and burst into flames nine miles east of Bagram Airfield. Major Plumhoff was killed in the accident along with three men of the Air Force 20th Special Operations Squadron – Technical Sergeant William J. Kerwood, Staff Sergeant Thomas A. Walkup Jr., Technical Sergeant Howard A. Walters – and Army Sergeant Major Philip R. Albert.[31]

In a major public relations play the Taliban claimed to have killed 120 coalition soldiers, captured 40 others, and shot down an MH-53 helicopter with 38 people on board.

Operation *Avalanche* was the last major push of the year, and the largest mounted in Afghanistan that year. "The terrorists are going into their winter campaigning season where they don't campaign as much," said Lieutenant Colonel Bryan Hilferty at a press briefing. "We're going to make sure that we get them before they get a chance to hunker down." The four-day operation using 2,000 US forces supported by Afghan troops would cover the eastern and southern provinces to suppress attacks undermining stability efforts. More than 600 men from the 10th Mountain

Division's 2nd Battalion, 87th Infantry "Catamount" Regiment, took part in the operation, which launched on December 26. For the first time since arriving in country the entire battalion was involved in a single mission. "We were able to cover a lot more ground quickly with the whole force out," said Staff Sergeant Charles Haskins, 1st Platoon, C Company.

Having learned from their own and other units' experiences, searches were low in intensity, with no more kicking in doors and herding people out of their homes. The Catamounts' final objective was the village of Surobi. "I've been to a couple other villages but this is huge, just huge," Haskins said. "This village has alleyways, side streets, different tiers, apartment buildings; it's just crazy."[32] Using the low-intensity approach paid off. Villagers led the soldiers to cache sites, and two more were pointed out by children. The take was more than 50 RPGs, over a dozen mortar rounds, a canister of gunpowder, IED-making materials, and dozens of grenades and small arms.

Once again enemy forces chose not to fight, and not much in the way of weapons or explosives were found for the effort expended.

The shift in US operations from counterterrorism to counterinsurgency and stability operations was significant. By the end of 2003, US civil and military forces had completed more than 150 projects, and nearly 300 more had been started. These included improving drinking water, medical care, transportation, communications, irrigation, and agriculture methods. PRTs were operating in Bamiyan, Kunduz, Gardez, and Mazar-i-Sharif, with more planned for 2004. Politically, a Loya Jirga (grand assembly) began meeting on December 13 to draft a new constitution, with national elections scheduled for the summer of 2004. Through the efforts of the US-led Office of Military Cooperation Afghanistan (OMC-A), with assistance from five coalition partners, Combined Joint Task Force Phoenix was established to train and advise new ANA units on a larger scale than was possible using SF personnel. ANA strength at the end of the year was 6,000 men, with another 9,000 projected to be trained by the end of 2004.[33]

Concurrent with rebuilding the ANA was reestablishing an Afghan National Police (ANP) force. Beginning in 2002, the Department of State's Bureau for International Narcotics and Law Enforcement Affairs (INL) concentrated on training noncommissioned police officers and patrolmen at several facilities throughout Afghanistan and at the Kabul Central Training Center. DynCorp International built, equipped, and staffed the various ANP training centers, and provided embedded advisors to the Afghan Ministry of Interior (MOI). The ANP was divided into four branches: Afghan Uniformed Police, Afghan Highway Police, Afghan Border Police, and the Criminal Investigation Department. As of October, approximately 20,000 ANP were operational.[34]

Operations in 2003 focused on defeating the remaining insurgent forces, stabilizing the country, and establishing Afghan Security Forces (ASFs). Secretary Rumsfeld's statement in May that major combat in Afghanistan was over proved hollow. Insurgent forces were gathering strength in their Pakistan sanctuaries and in remote areas of Afghanistan. Although there were major accomplishments, these didn't herald the end of the fighting, and US operations continued unabated through the winter.

Chapter 6
TRANSITION, 2004–05

Continuing the winter operations begun with Operation *Avalanche* the previous December, CFC-A launched a series of cordon-and-searches and other operations to disrupt the opposition's lines of communications (LOCs) along the Pakistan border.

Operation *Mountain Blizzard* kicked off on January 4, 2004, and wrapped up in mid-March. In the 1,731 patrols and 143 raids conducted, 22 enemy combatants were killed and caches with 3,648 rockets, 3,202 mortar rounds, 2,944 rocket-propelled grenades, 3,000 rifle rounds, 2,232 mines, and tens of thousands of rounds of small-arms ammunition were found.[1]

Task Force Linebacker – consisting of the newly arrived 2,000-man 22nd Marine Expeditionary Unit (Special Operations Capable) (MEU [SOC]) and units of the Army 25th Infantry Division – was among the US forces in Operation *Mountain Storm* along with two ANA battalions.

The operation covered 3,300km along the border provinces of Kandahar, Zabul, Paktika, Paktia, Khost, Nangarhar, and Kunar. The operation also moved against Taliban and al Qaeda fighters in the interior provinces of Uruzgan, Ghazni, and Laghman.

Lieutenant Colonel Bryan Hilferty, the chief US military spokesman in Afghanistan, had the following to say at a press briefing: "Operation *Mountain Storm* is a continuation of the operations throughout the east, southeast, and south of the country. Of course, we will continue patrols, vehicle checkpoints, and coordinated searches. We have small-scale air assaults. We have air support – close fire support from the air – 24 hours a day circling overhead, ready to assist coalition forces."

The operation, starting on March 13 and running through July, was primarily aimed at disrupting the Taliban's spring offensive and establishing conditions for voter registration needed for the scheduled October national elections.

Marines concentrated their operations in the Uruzgan province, which was a Taliban stronghold. For their part of the operation the 25th Infantry Division's 2nd Battalion, 27th Infantry Regiment ("Wolfhounds"), accompanied by B Battery, 3rd Battalion, 7th Field Artillery Regiment, operated in Paktika. CJSOTF teams working with ANA troops moved through the Takhar Ghar mountains, at times linking up with local militia fighters to root out weapons caches. The not-always-friendly militia cooperated this time by providing information about suspected Taliban fighters and leading the team to a cache of weapons and ammunition near the village of Petaw. The cache included a large supply of tank shells, antipersonnel mines, Soviet-era rockets, mortar shells, rocket propelled grenades, and C4 plastic explosives.[2]

Along with major operations, there were small-unit actions daily, but not at the same place all the time. As in any war, there are often long periods without any action and then it becomes almost nonstop. Chief Warrant Officer 5 Garrett Hopkins, an Apache Longbow pilot attached to an Arizona Army National Guard aviation company, recalls these times during his second deployment. Most of his time was spent escorting Chinooks, Blackhawks, and Marine Sea Stallions on resupply missions, or waiting for a call to provide CAS. He'd been in country for two months before the ops tempo picked up.

> A State Department Huey helicopter with some special people on it that I really can't go into too much detail about. But it went down, so they called us out and we go over to that area. It takes us thirty, forty minutes, but we're going as fast as we can through the mountains.
>
> We get there, the Huey's on fire and we are trying to sort things out. I always wear my NVGs [Night Vision Goggles], always, along with my FLIR,[3] and I noticed that something is trying to get my attention with an IR [inferred] pointer. It's coming from an unmanned aerial vehicle. But I can't talk to it, I don't know its freq, nobody told me a thing. Well, we find out that this unmanned aerial vehicle has spotted the bad guys that are chasing the State Department guys. So we end up receiving clearance to engage those guys and that unmanned aerial vehicle finds the friendlies, but

the ground forces can't get to them; the ground forces come underneath attack while they're trying to get to the Huey.

We go back to try to help them, but the bad guys quit shooting at them. So we go back and the unmanned aerial vehicle finds the good guys. Nobody's going to be able to pick them up. So I made a decision at that time that I'm going to land and get my wingman to land.

So there's an HC-130 overhead and all the assets that they have, they're helping us out. So we take off our vests, give them to the guys, there's five of them. I put three on the outside of my aircraft. They strap on with carabineers and my wingman picks up two. So we're in the middle of the mountains, not a heavily mountained area where we land at; it's more of a farming field, but it's full of dust. We pick those guys up and we fly them over, back to the ground convoy, the rescue convoy and we head back home.

After four days later the unit received a report that Taliban forces had overrun an ANA outpost.

It was actually, they said, "hey, let us in, take over, or we're going to kill you." So they let them in. They called in the MEDEVAC. They thought MEDEVACs coming in, there's Apache's coming in first, they don't know it, they're shooting all around us, trying to hit us. They don't realize that we're armed. They tell us there's friendlies in there. As we're coming in we see all the tracer fire, we can't get a hold of anybody on the ground. We see a green star cluster go up and we said, huh, that must be where the friendlies are; maybe their radios are out. The tracer fire's still pretty heavy.

But we proceed inbound. My wingman, he's saying there's a lot of tracer fire. My front seater, he's saying, "Do you mind if we don't turn left because I think we might get shot down." I said, "No, there's ground forces down there. We've got to figure out what's going on because we need to help them." Well, it turned out that there weren't any friendlies. We still hadn't fired – we didn't know there weren't friendlies – so we picked an open field where we're not going to get in trouble, because we couldn't figure out who's friendly, who's bad, so we just picked an open field, did our collateral damage estimation and shot that field. Nothing really stopped, but we said, hello, we're armed, basically.

We kept trying to sort it out and finally, my wingman says, "You're just about ready to get shot down and you need to probably return fire." I said,

> "No, we're not going to return fire anywhere close to the compound." We came back in for another pass, same thing happened again. He says, "Can I put a burst close to the compound or we're going to get hurt?" I said, "Okay, go ahead." The moment we did put it down close to the compound where nobody's going to get hit, all the fire stopped, all the tracer fire stopped. We climbed up to altitude, called back and they said, "I guess there's no friendlies there. Come back home."
>
> So we found out the next day they were trying to get MEDEVAC to come in because they said they had somebody who's got wounded with a sucking chest wound, but really, I guess there was or wasn't. I don't know if somebody was really hurt or not. It was an ambush. They didn't get the Blackhawks, and we addressed them.
>
> Then there were just events that started happening every other day. Then it became every day. Then it became two times a night. There were a few times where we'd go out three times a night to shoot. That went on for like six months.[4]

In mid-April 2004 the 25th Infantry Division (Light), command by Major General Eric T. Olson, relieved the 10th Mountain Division-led CJTF 180 and changed the task-force designation to CJTF-76. General Olson organized CJTF-76 into six primary task forces, each operating in newly designated Regional Commands (RCs). The reorganization and assigned units are worth noting because of their role in future operations.

Combined Task Force (CTF) Bronco, commanded by Colonel Richard Pedersen and based on the 3rd Brigade of the 25th ID, assumed responsibility for RC-South. This large area included the provinces of Kandahar, Lashkar Gah, Zabul, Zaranj, and a part of Uruzgan. CTF Bronco's forces included four US Army light infantry battalions, one field artillery battalion, the French Task Group Ares, and a Romanian infantry regiment. The 25th ID's Artillery reorganized as a maneuver force called CTF Thunder under the command of Colonel Gary H. Cheek. The new CTF Thunder included 2nd Battalion, 27th Infantry Regiment of the 25th Infantry Division (Light); 3rd Battalion, 6th Marine Regiment, 2nd Marine Division; 3rd Battalion, 116th Infantry Regiment of the Virginia Army National Guard; and 1st Battalion, 505th Parachute Infantry Regiment of the 82nd Airborne Division, along with many smaller attachments and coalition and Afghan Army units.

In July 2004 CTF Thunder took the reins of RC-East, which comprised 16 provinces including the restive provinces of Paktika, Paktia, Khost, Ghazni, Nangarhar, and Laghman. In area, RC-East was roughly the size of the state of Iowa.

JTF Wings, led by Colonel B. Shannon Davis, provided aviation assets for all coalition operations in Afghanistan. All of the US aviation assets in Afghanistan except those belonging to the US Air Force were controlled by JTF Wings, which included US Army Blackhawk, Chinook, and Apache helicopters, plus Super Stallions and Cobras from the Marine Corps. JTF Wings was staffed by more than 2,500 pilots, crew, and support personnel, and included soldiers from the Alabama, Florida, Georgia, Hawaii, and Utah Army National Guard. The aviation JTF was the backbone of the coalition supply chain and provided aeromedical evacuation and air traffic control services throughout the theater.

The 3rd Squadron, 4th Cavalry Regiment (3-4 CAV) and Company B, 193rd Aviation Regiment made up CTF Saber and operated in the vast provinces of western Afghanistan. In September 2004 CJTF-76 designated this area as RC-West and created a new organization called CTF Longhorn based on 3-4 CAV.

CTF Coyote oversaw engineering operations for CJTF-76 and was commanded by Colonel Nancy J. Wetherill, South Dakota Army National Guard. US Army Reserve and Army National Guard units from Alabama, Iowa, Louisiana, Minnesota, New York, and Wisconsin plus coalition detachments from Australia, Korea, Poland, and Slovakia conducted a wide range of engineering missions as part of CTF Coyote.

The 3rd Special Forces Group (SFG) formed the core of CJSOTF-A. Around 4,000 soldiers from seven different countries made up the Special Operations task force, which was headquartered at Bagram Airfield. Finally, on arriving in Afghanistan, the 25th ID Support Command became the Joint Logistical Command and served all CJTFs from its headquarters at Bagram.

In addition to the six primary TFs organized under CJTF-76, several other US and coalition units operated under Olson's authority during the spring of 2004. For example, the 22nd Marine Expeditionary Unit, located at Bagram Airfield, was designated CTF Stonewall and conducted independent operations in northern Uruzgan province in RC-South. A Military Police TF (TF Enforcer) provided general support services to the regional commands and operated detainee-holding facilities at Bagram and Kandahar.

The 45th Infantry Brigade of the Oklahoma Army National Guard, along with Army National Guard detachments from 20 additional states and contingents from seven coalition countries, continued the CJTF Phoenix mission of training the ANA. In August, the 76th Infantry Brigade from the Indiana Army National Guard would take over from the Oklahoma Guard.

The OMC-A, based in Kabul, was the parent organization for CJTF Phoenix, and planned for six ANA battalions to be trained and ready by the summer of 2004 to assist in voter registration and presidential-election security operations. Approximately 20,000 additional Afghans, graduates of coalition-run Regional Law Enforcement Training Centers, were also expected to assist in election security as members of the Afghan National Police. ISAF, under NATO authority since August 2003, provided security for the Kabul area and commanded the PRT in Kunduz in northeast Afghanistan.[5]

Throughout the spring and summer, ACM forces openly operated in several provinces. Both Paktika and Zabul provinces were headquarters for key Taliban commanders and al Qaeda leadership. Paktika was the AO for a Taliban commander, known to the coalition as "Rocket Man," who had become infamous for his attacks against the FOBs at Shkin and Orgun-e using 107mm rockets. The Daychopan area in Zabul province had become both a training site and a staging area for Taliban operations elsewhere.

In Helmand and Uruzgan and the southern half of Kandahar province the Taliban moved freely through the entire region, using vehicles to position troops and supplies. Coalition intelligence indicated that the Taliban had established command centers north of Deh Rawod in Uruzgan and in the Baghran Valley in Helmand.[6]

Summarizing the situation, Colonel Walter Herd, the commander of CJSOTF-A in 2003 and 2004, quoted an oft-heard aphorism: "[The Taliban's] strength was their ability to endure and [the coalition's] weakness was our willingness to endure... The Americans have all the watches, but the Afghans have all the time."[7]

During the first week of July two ODAs conducted Operation *Independence*, a follow-on sweep of the Baghran Valley. After finding that the Taliban had retreated from the valley, a local villager led the teams to a substantial weapons cache that included T-62 tanks, 105mm howitzers, ZSU-23 antiaircraft guns, 107mm rockets, and tens of thousands of rounds of assorted ammunition.[8]

As part of CJSOTF-A, ODA 364 conducted large-scale operations in the Kunar Valley. One of the most productive operations was a direct-action mission at Hadji Mir Alam Khan's house and a cordon-and-search in the Korengal Valley. Sergeant Major Dwight C. Utley, Operations Sergeant, C Company, 2nd Battalion, 3rd Special Forces Group (Airborne), recalled the mission.

> One day one of our ASF soldiers came to us and informed [us] that he knew of a house where bin Laden had spent the night a few years earlier. The homeowner's name was Hadji Mir Alam Khan, and it was a commonly known fact that he had al Qaeda ties.
>
> Our recce team said that they saw armed men with radios guarding the house, which was indicative of a large cache and perhaps some high-level al Qaeda leadership.
>
> We decided to cordon and search the house and the mosque at first light, hoping to catch all of the males at the mosque for morning prayer. The good news was that the objective was only a four-minute flight from our fire base. Our task organization had ODA 364, three ASF platoons, two AH-64s, and four CH-47s supporting us. When we hit the ground the assault force that was securing the mosque (only ASF entered the mosque) captured about seven bad guys and nothing else.
>
> The assault force found an empty house. The house was huge, and the teams kept clearing empty room after empty room. I was getting worried that the place was going to be a dry hole [i.e. nothing of value was found] after weeks of planning and rehearsing. Before entering one of the rooms an ASF soldier threw a flashbang stun grenade in the room and a fire started. The fire was too big to put out and we had not finished clearing, so we ignored the fire and continued on. By the time that we had cleared the entire house the fire was raging.
>
> I walked over and told the commander how pissed I was that this was a dry hole, and as the house was on fire we were going to have a hard time doing any type of exploitation of papers/pictures/documents.
>
> While we were discussing our next move I began hearing random gunfire. I almost jumped out of my skin. The objective was secure, security

> teams were in place, and we absolutely owned the objective, "how could we be taking fire?" I asked myself. It turned out that the house was constructed of mud bricks and ammo cans. The entire house was a cache, and the ammo was cooking off because of the fire.
>
> The mission was only a partial success; we had destroyed the cache and grabbed some bad guys but we had not gotten the leader. After a couple of days we had the PSYOPS guys start broadcasting that we knew where the IED cell leader's other houses were and that we were going to burn them down as well if he did not come [and] turn himself in to us. It worked: after about three days of spreading the rumor he contacted the provincial governor and made arrangements to turn himself in. The mission turned into a double success when he provided information about other al Qaeda terrorists."[9]

The only effective way to defeat the Taliban, al Qaeda, and other ACM forces was by enlarging counterinsurgency operations, which had begun in 2002. Central to COIN was the expanding role of the PRTs. According to Lieutenant General Barno the teams:

> brought hope with them, they brought money with them, they brought the flag with them, and they brought recognition that this was not just the Americans. This was the [Afghan] Government because there was always a Ministry of Interior representative with the PRTs... They were widely viewed as kind of outposts of hope in the future, and optimism and a positive outlook for people who had not seen any sign of the Government or the coalition except for guys running around in HMMWVs with guns.[10]

A political advisor to TF 180 said in an interview that the focus of the counterinsurgency was against three groups:

> The first group was al Qaeda and Osama bin Laden, and they are regarded as a strategic foe, because al Qaeda operating in the eastern, south-eastern border between Afghanistan and Pakistan, was a foe who was not only attacking Afghanistan, but attacking Pakistan and attacking Saudi Arabia, and they had a strategic aim to hurt the United States. So they were the strategic foe, and they were the best equipped, and they had the most tenacious fighters.

> The second foe of the three groups that we were fighting in the counterinsurgency was the Taliban. Again, we were dealing with remnants of the Taliban because the main forces had been thoroughly defeated earlier in '01 and '02. Nevertheless, they still persisted, they were still out there and in some provinces, particularly in places like Helmand and Uruzgan, and Kandahar and Kalak, in southern and southeastern Afghanistan, they were still a serious security problem. Many of their leaders had sought refuge in these very difficult border areas with Pakistan.
>
> The third foe we were fighting was the militia contingent of Gulbuddin Hekmatyar, who had been a former prime minister of Afghanistan in the civil war that followed the Soviet departure. He was bitter foe of the United States, and he was based out of a refugee camp near Peshawar, in northern Pakistan. He operated north of Kabul, in Nangarhar and Kunar, north and east, Nangarhar and Kunar provinces, and also in Kabul proper.[11]

PRT efforts focused on both large- and small-scale projects such as digging wells, building or rebuilding schools, or improving a town's road or communications. Many of the smaller projects were organized at the battalion level and below. The funds for these projects came from the Commander's Emergency Response Program (CERP), and ranged from $25,000 to $200,000 in Afghan currency. These funds paid for materials and paid for the hiring of locals to do the work. Two problems that were not fully addressed were drugs and the role of women in Afghanistan. These were major cultural and economic issues, and the PRTs did have the resources or time to work on them.[12]

According to the PRT commander in Ghazni province from September 2004 through June 2005:

> The primary focus was to try to help rebuild the infrastructure and also establish security by training the police and doing certain things like that. While we were doing this, we were also on the lookout for illegal weapons. If the police had them and we felt like, "hey, these can easily fall into the hands of the bad guys," we'd take them from some police. There was also mujahedin in villages that had stuff stuck away.
>
> I would use different techniques to go in, like just go in and say, "Hey, we're here," and if we spot something we'll take it away from them. We'd come in and say, "Look, we're trying to get these weapons out of their

hands. We don't want people being killed accidentally by them. We'll have them destroyed. In turn, we're going to build you a school or do something for you," depending on the community. One man found out, came down, and he said he'd been a Hazara mujahedin chief, commander, and he wanted some food for his village and he was willing to turn over weapons to get it.

We gave him a truck full of rice and sugar and salt, American rations, and some fuel. He gave us a bunch of heavy weapons. They always hold on to some. Everybody there is not 100 percent warm, fuzzy, that everything's going to be good. They expect that someday it's going to kick off again, and they're going to stay ready.[13]

The Thunder Brigade commander stressed the need to keep working to win over the local population:[14]

The challenge in Afghanistan is not just to find and neutralize the enemy; it is to keep the enemy from generating new recruits. The US message should be positive: we build schools while al Qaeda and the Taliban destroy them. The Afghanis have a natural affinity to America, given our shared fight against the Soviets and because the Afghanis recognize that the US is, like Afghanistan, a "religious country." At the same time, it should be remembered that few people hold a grudge longer than the Afghanis; successive unfortunate developments, such as the accidental death of innocent civilians, have a cumulative effect on public opinion."

Very few conventional-forces personnel had experience in counterinsurgency operations, but they learned quickly. At times individual units pitched in on their own to help a local village. Hopkins' unit was one of them.

The unit started focusing on how we could help these people here. So a humanitarian aid project was started. We're making trips in there with Chinooks, dropping off coats, blankets, shoes, gloves, baby supplies, medical supplies, school supplies and helping them, educating them as best as we can. They had nothing. There's no electricity, there's no sewer system. So I went on one of those trips and got out, and it was very interesting. But they had land mines right there in the little village and had them marked, so they made sure that you walked a certain way. So all the little children know where the landmines are that are there, which surprised me.

CJSOTF-A teams were trained for and experienced in COIN operations. Headquartered at Bagram Airfield, CJSOTF-A operated out of a series of small bases spread through much of Afghanistan and along the Afghan–Pakistan border. Along with intelligence gathering and Force Protection Patrols, ODAs conducted medical civil actions (MEDCAPS), which provided limited treatment to Afghans. Sergeant Major Utley relates:

> The most memorable MEDCAP that we went on was on the top of a mountain about 12km west of our firebase. Our task organization was ODA 364 and a USMC platoon, along with tough boxes of Class VIII, and a 6-wheel ATV with medical supplies, water, and ammo. We INFILed [infiltrated] on a CH-47 and the villagers were amazed to see a helicopter land at their village, which was at 9,500ft. Upon our arrival we linked up with a village elder and set up a patrol base behind his house.
>
> The next day we had a huge turnout for the MEDCAP: over 400 people. We treated everything from scabies to sinus infections to burns. The funniest thing was a 50-year-old man who told me that his knees hurt. I told him he needed to move out of the mountains of Afghanistan if he wanted his knees to stop hurting. We gave every child a hygiene bag and a toy.
>
> We EXFILed the next day. The team was frustrated; we had done a low-priority humanitarian while other teams were killing bad guys. I felt that the mission was a huge flop because we had not received any actionable intelligence, and to make matters worse the rooms that we used to treat the patients were not properly ventilated and 75 percent of the team got sick the day after EXFIL. My interpreter told me to wait five days before passing judgment on the mission.
>
> He was right, after about a week people from the villages surrounding the MEDCAP site started coming in and sending messages with runners about caches and personalities. We were able to interdict some al Qaeda operatives transporting explosives and blasting caps from Pakistan to Afghanistan as a result of the information some of the villagers provided. The lesson learned was that nothing happens fast in Afghanistan, and that an enduring presence is necessary to accomplish the mission.[15]

COIN operations were integrated into combat operations, which continued without let up. On June 1, the 1/6 Battalion Landing Team, 22nd MEU (SOC) entered the Daychopan district, Uruzgan province, for Operation

Asbury Park to "Find/Fix/Finish" Taliban and ACM forces in the area and then follow up with medical, educational, and quality-of-life support to the local villages. Instead of using hit-and-run tactics, laying IEDs, or sniping at passing convoys, the Taliban and ACM elements decided to stand their ground and fight.

A sizable number of AMF fighters also accompanied the Marine task force, and mid-way through the operation a second unit was inserted, which set up blocking positions to deny the enemy a path of escape.

Beginning on June 2, the Marines and sailors participating in the mission engaged in pitched battles each day that culminated on June 8 when scores of enemy terrorists, including foreign fighters, ambushed the MEU task force from entrenched and mutually supporting fighting positions. During the operation Marine Super Cobra helicopter gunships, Harrier jets, Apaches, A-10s, and B-1B bombers flew CAS. The last of the fighting took place near Dai Chopan on June 8 and broke the back of enemy resistance in the region. No further contact was made as the MEU task force conducted operations until June 17. More than 85 enemy fighters were confirmed killed and as many as 40 others estimated killed. A handful of Marines were wounded by enemy fire.

In early July, 2nd Battalion, 5th Infantry Regiment, 25th Infantry Division, along with attached Marines and ANA troops, went back into the Daychopan region on Operation *Asbury Park II*. Again Taliban and ACM forces stayed to fight, and again they suffered significant losses.[16]

As Operation *Asbury Park II* got underway, C "Cacti" Company, 2nd Battalion, 35th Infantry Regiment, began the ten-day Operation *Dragon Tree* to the south in the Arghandab Valley, Kunar province. In other villages the people Captain Mike Berdy (C Company commanding officer) interacted with liked the American presence. Operation *Dragon Tree*, however, was in a relatively isolated region with a strong connection to the former Taliban regime, creating sympathies for the anti-coalition movement.

Berdy felt that Afghan locals help the Taliban as a matter of necessity, a reality of life in a mountainous Afghan village. Some of the villagers are "probably 'pro-Taliban' whether it's through coercion or they actually sympathize with them," he said. The operation, as had most of the preceding ones, found large weapons caches but no ACM or Taliban. Berdy summed it up: "This country is one big cache."[17]

Above: Darunta guerrilla training camps. Satellite imagery from clearly shows cave entrances and training camps. The digital imaging sensor is designed to produce images with superior contrast, spectral resolution, and accuracy. (Space Imaging)

Below: The Twin Towers of the World Trade Center smoking on 9/11. The al Qaeda sponsored assault on targets in the United States was the instigator of the US attacks on Afghanistan in Operation *Enduring Freedom*. (Michael Foran)

Above: A view of the damage done to the Western Ring of the Pentagon after American Airlines Flight 77 was piloted by terrorists into the building on 9/11. (US Navy)

Below: Donald H. Rumsfeld (left), US Secretary of Defense, greets Hamid Karzai (right), chairman of the Afghan Interim Administration, at the Pentagon on January 28, 2002. (DOD, photo by Robert D. Ward)

A Tomahawk cruise missile is launched from USS *Philippine Sea* in a strike against al Qaeda terrorist training camps and military installations of the Taliban regime in Afghanistan on October 7, 2001. The carefully targeted actions were designed to disrupt the use of Afghanistan as a base for terrorist operations and to attack the military capability of the Taliban regime. (DOD photo by Master Chief Petty Officer T. Cosgrove)

Above: ODA operators meet with General Tommy Franks in October 2001. Note the pakol hats, Mk 11 sniper rifle (left), and M4A1 carbine fitted with a sound suppressor and the ACOG 4x optical sight. (USSOCOM/DOD)

Below: An iconic image of Special Forces in Afghanistan. From the Harley Davidson merchandize Realtree hunting jacket, and Confederate flag, it is safe to assume a southern ODA. (Courtesy "JZW" c/o Leigh Neville)

Above: US Army Special Forces troops ride horseback alongside Afghan Northern Alliance horse cavalry on December 11, 2001. The deployment of these SF teams was a key element in the early success of *Enduring Freedom*, as they coordinated massive air attacks on Taliban and al Qaeda positions. (US Army)

Below left: Women in burkas in Mazar-e-Sharif on December 15, 2001. Mazar-e Sharif was the first major center to fall to the Northern Alliance forces of General Dostum, backed by US Special Forces. (USAF)

Below right: Local Afghanis ride a taxi at the Mazar-e-Sharif airfield during Operation *Enduring Freedom*, December 15, 2001. (USAF)

Above: A lead element of more than 45 Jordanian Special Forces soldiers stationed outside of Aman, Jordan, arrived in Mazar-e Sharif, Afghanistan, in support of Operation *Enduring Freedom*, December 24, 2001. (USAF)

Below: Northern Alliance troops under General Dostum's command in Mazar-e-Sharif take a break on a wall in the median of the town's busiest street. (USAF, photo by Staff Sergeant Cecilio Ricardo)

Above left: During a search and destroy mission in the Zhawar Kili area on January 14, 2002, US Navy SEALs found valuable intelligence information, including this Osama bin Laden propaganda poster. In addition to detaining several suspected al Qaeda and Taliban members, SEALs also found a large cache of munitions. (US Navy)

Above right: A poster depicting General Ahmed Shah Massoud overlooks the Olympic Stadium in Kabul during a football match between a local team, Kabul United, and ISAF, February 15, 2002. It was the first international sporting event to take place in Afghanistan in five years. (Imperial War Museum, LAND-02-012-0293)

Below: March 2002: the rugged summit of Takur Ghar, with the snow-covered floor of the Shah-i-Kot Valley beyond. It is possible to make out, on the streak of snow at 4 o'clock from the single cross-shaped tree on the center skyline, "Razor 01," the abandoned MH-47E Chinook of the Ranger QRF. (USSOCOM/DOD)

Above: Soldiers from Bravo Company, 101st Airborne Division (Air Assault) prepare to move out after having been dropped by a Chinook helicopters during Operation *Anaconda* on March 5, 2002. (US Army, photo by Sergeant Keith D. McGrew)

Below: A Marine AH-1W Cobra takes off from USS *Bonhomme Richard* in support of Operation *Anaconda* on March 4. At times the number of CAS assets over Takur Ghar created severe command-and-control difficulties. (USMC)

An aerial view of a rugged mountain pass near Gardez. The mountainous terrain provided many hiding places for groups like al Qaeda and the Taliban. (US Army)

Above: Members of the 2nd Battalion, 187th Infantry conduct a dismounted sweep and clear during Operation *Mountain Lion*, a follow-up operation to *Anaconda* in April 2002. This clearly shows the type of terrain Coalition forces were forced tonavigate. (US Army)

Below: Two MH-47E Chinooks of the 160th SOAR launching on a mission somewhere in Afghanistan. (DOD)

Above: A member of the Afghanistan Military Forces has a cigarette while on guard. The AMF were responsible for keeping the locals away while coalition forces, headed by the US Army Criminal Investigation Division (CID), unearth graves in the village of Markhanai on May 5, 2002 in Tora Bora, for Operation *Torii*. (USAF)

Below: US Army soldiers assigned to the 82nd Airborne Division prepare to enter and clear a room while searching for weapons in Paktika province during Operation *Mountain Sweep* on August 21, 2002. They are armed with 5.56mm M4 carbines and an M136 light anti-armor weapon (US Army).

Above: A UH-60Q Blackhawk from the 717th Medical Company flies through the scenic mountains of the Gardez Pass returning from FOB Salerno after an equipment change over on January 25, 2004. (US Army)

Below: This view from the crew door of a UH-60Q Blackhawk, from the 717th Medical Company (Air Ambulance), shows the rough terrain of northeastern Afghanistan on the route back from FOB Salerno on January 25, 2004. (US Army)

Above: US Marines patrol through a dry creek bed while they search caves in Khost on August 18, 2004. The Marines were conducting vehicle checkpoints and village assessments while maintaining an offensive presence throughout the region in support of Operation *Enduring Freedom*. (DOD, photo by Lance Corporal Justin M. Mason)

Below: A US Army soldier provides security as a gun team moves down a mountain after making contact with the enemy near Ganjgal on October 16, 2004. (DOD, photo by Specialist Harold Fields)

Above: US Marines conduct a mounted patrol in the cold and snowy weather of the Khost–Gardez Pass in Afghanistan on December 30, 2004. The mountainous region, not far from the Pakistan border, would be a constant thorn in the side of Coalition forces. (DOD, photo by Corporal James L. Yarboro)

Below: A soldier from the 29th Infantry Division of the Virginia National Guard stoops to enter and search the home of a suspected Taliban member in Afghanistan on June 4, 2005. (DOD, photo by Staff Sergeant Joseph P. Collins Jr.)

Above: An AC-130U gunship from the 4th Special Operations Squadron jettisons flares. The flares are a countermeasure for heat seeking missiles that may be aimed at the planes real-world missions. (USAF)

Below: RQ-1 Predator UAVs, like this one, have been used to increase battlefield awareness at operating locations in support of Operation *Enduring Freedom*. Intelligence, surveillance, and reconnaissance (ISR) assets, including UAVs, have flown more than 325 missions to provide battlefield awareness in support of *Enduring Freedom*. (USAF)

Above: The HH-60 Pave Hawk is the Air Force's primary search and rescue helicopter. It has an 8,000lb capacity two cargo hook pylons for mounting crew-served 7.62 or .50 caliber machine guns for protection. Operationally, Pave Hawks work in pairs for mutual fire support and suppression in kinetic situations. (DVIDS photo)

Below: The AH-64D Apache Longbow attack helicopter's weapons package includes a 30mm automatic Boeing M230 chain gun located under the fuselage with a rate of fire of 625 rounds a minute. It also has four hardpoints mounted on stub-wing pylons, typically carrying a mixture of AGM-114 Hellfire missiles and Hydra 70 rocket pods. (DVIDS photo)

The first national presidential election was scheduled for October 9. In addition to searching for weapons and ACM fighters, all operations had a secondary purpose of registering voters. Along with operations *Asbury Park II* and *Dragon Tree*, *Lightning Resolve* and *Flashman* were others conducted in July, designed to destroy terrorist organizations and their infrastructure while continuing to focus on national stability and support in Afghanistan's south, southeast, and eastern regions according to Brigadier General David Rodriquez. "The objective of this mission was to interdict al Qaeda and Taliban forces who are trying to prevent the Afghan national elections from taking place in the coming months," he said in a press briefing on July 14. The UN and coalition forces were part of the operation, which hoped to register seven million voters.

Forming the environment needed to create a stable Afghan government was difficult. Warlords who worked together ousting the Taliban retained power in several provinces, and maintained well-armed militias to enforce their rule. The major clash between rival warlords took place in Herat.

On September 12 the Afghan Government replaced Ismail Khan as governor of the province with Sayed Muhammad Khairkhwa. Citizens loyal to Ismail Khan rioted when the announcement was made. Armed with Molotov cocktails, stones, and small arms, they burned aid offices and battled government security forces. Major General Olson, the commander of CJTF-76, decided to intervene by sending CTF Saber (3-4 CAV), two SF ODAs, and an ANA company to the area to evacuate nongovernment aid workers and UN employees.[18]

"I never expected to end up in the middle of a riot," said Specialist Matthew Moritz, a member of Combined Task Force Saber's Quick Reaction Force. He and the rest of his team evacuated UN personnel to a safe haven secured by Herat PRT soldiers. Once there, aircrews of UH-60 Blackhawk helicopters 701 and 704 moved in. The aircrews took turns maneuvering their aircraft in and out of the confined space of the courtyard, landing on the basketball court to pick up personnel and evacuate them to a safe location.

Despite the internecine warfare the election was held as scheduled, with President Karzai receiving 55.4 percent of the votes. Voting security was provided by 9,000 ISAF forces, 15,000 ANA, 50,000 Afghan national police, and 18,000 US forces, reinforced by several hundred additional troops. Even with 92,000 security forces spread across the country, the election was marked by violence.

Five ANA soldiers died in skirmishes and from landmines, 15 staff of the Joint Electoral Management Body were killed and a further 46 were injured in various attacks, and two international subcontractors working in Nuristan in support of the electoral process were killed. On the positive side, voter turnout was high, at about 80 percent. Some eight million votes were cast. Of these, it was reported that 41 percent of voters were women.[19]

Relieved of their election security duties, US forces went back on the offensive with a series of operations. Operating out of FOB Cobra in Uruzgan province, units of the 25th ID (Light) ran operations *Outlaw* and *Crackdown* as well as raids in the Daychopan district of Zabul province and the Cehar Cineh area in October. The security patrols also helped reinforce Afghan government forces and gave additional justification for the coalition forces' presence in the country. In keeping with COIN, the soldiers distributed food and bottled water, ran MEDCAPS, and veterinarians from TF Victory examined animals.[20]

On December 11, four days after President Karzai was inaugurated, CJTF-76 troops began Operation *Lightning Freedom*, with the objective of searching out and destroying insurgent forces, which traditionally didn't fight during winter months. The 25th Infantry Division Commander, Major General Eric Olson, reportedly stated that US forces would also be redeployed to tighten border security with Pakistan and that US Special Forces would conduct raids to capture insurgent leaders.[21]

In conjunction with Operation *Lightning*, CTF Thunder[22] launched Operation *Thunder Freedom*. Major Duke Davis, operations officer for CTF Thunder, said:

> It's not all about killing the bad guys. Traditionally, fighters in Afghanistan lay low during the harsh winter months and come back out strong in the spring. I would expect that next spring, when the snow melts, that we will see an attempt to increase activity. But it will be interesting to see how much

better our police and Kandaks [Afghan National Army unit similar to a battalion of infantry, totaling about 3,000 men] are, how much more the people are in support of what we're trying to do, and how much they push away the enemy's ability to initiate actions. The election was successful. *Thunder Freedom* is an attempt to exploit the successes of the elections focused on the opportunities that present themselves to continue in assisting this new, democratically elected government in any capacity necessary. We believe that continuing that press throughout the winter will make the enemy that much less capable of an effective spring offensive."[23]

Conducting part of Operation *Thunder Freedom* fell to TF Trinity (3rd Battalion, 3rd Marines, 3rd Marine Regiment, 3rd Marine Division) in the Korengal Valley, Kunar province. Throughout December they conducted operations *Fairbanks*, *Cornhuskers*, *Saratoga*, *Badgers*, *Golden Gophers*, and *Beaver*. The operations didn't go unnoticed by the Taliban, which struck back.

The day before Christmas, India Company's Combined Anti-Armor Team (CAAT) went to retrieve the Marines who were maintaining an overwatch position in the Korengal Valley. On their way back to camp they were ambushed by heavily armed forces using fortified fighting positions.

"We heard muted gunfire, RPGs exploding, and the sound of rounds hitting the trucks," said Marine Corporal Josh Burgbacher, an India Company machine gunner from Lima, Ohio. "That lasted for maybe half of a second and then you could hear every single gun in the convoy open up. Everyone just reacted with their training." Other Marines said that Burgbacher calmly helped fix a jammed MK19 automatic grenade launcher while rounds were impacting around him.

The ambush was a well-planned attack, according to CAAT platoon commander Lieutenant Jonathan Frangakis. He said the enemy had a pile of rocks marking the start of the kill zone. "We thought at first it was an improvised explosive device, but they knew how many vehicles we had, and as soon as the first vehicle got near the marker, they opened up on us," Frangakis said. "I heard the rounds impacting," relates Lance Corporal Daniel Alfieri, India Company's machine gunner. "I just thought 'here we go again.'"

The Marines assaulted through to the village where much of the fire had originated. They confirmed two enemy killed and captured eight men who they believed were involved in the attack.[24] India Company rested on December 26 then ran Operation *Badgers* through heavy snowstorms and over mountainous terrain until New Year's Eve. It was the last operation by US forces in 2004.

Operations during that year in the contested provinces had made limited headway in disrupting ACM efforts to regain control, at least by the end of the fighting season. The national presidential elections were considered a success and open conflict between warlords had been curbed.

Counterinsurgency efforts gained momentum across the country. However, there were no measurable results in the curtailment of poppy cultivation and drug trafficking. Drug money provided financial support to warlords, criminal organizations such as HIG and the Haqqani Network, corrupt government officials, the Taliban, al Qaeda, and extremist groups operating in and around Afghanistan.[25]

The US lost 52 troops killed in action, bringing the total to 161 since October 2001. IED attacks had killed 12, up from three the year before. Another 217 military personnel had been wounded. Early in 2005 the number and frequency of attacks against US forces reportedly dropped significantly, with Americans being welcomed in areas that had previously been openly hostile. Part of this trend was attributed to Afghan Security Forces' increasing presence and effectiveness. However, the Taliban held a different view. In a press release one of its spokesmen said winter weather was the reason for the inaction, and promised renewed attacks in the spring.[26]

To keep the pressure on, in January 2005 TF Trinity conducted patrols and operations. According to Lieutenant Colonel Norm Cooling, 3rd Battalion, 3rd Marines Commander, "We are not going to sit around and worry about them exploiting the local populace and attacking us. We are going to keep them worried about us bringing the attack to them."

What was reportedly the worst winter in recent history blanketed mountain passes with low clouds and buried the ground under feet of snow. Temperatures dropped below -10 degrees Fahrenheit in some areas, affecting both gear and equipment. Undeterred by the weather, 1st Platoon,

Weapons Company, on patrol on January 11 in the northern village of Zambar, was hit by AK-47s, RPGs, and Russian machine guns fired by a squad-sized ACM element.

On another patrol, Lima Company pushed deep into the border region in the southern area of Nangarhar province, at the foothills of the Tora Bora mountain range. One night, 1st Platoon received information about a weapons cache. On the morning of 17 January, the platoon moved to cordon off the suspected compound and conducted a search with the local ANP. As they arrived at the compound, they started taking small-arms fire from two guards protecting a weapons and drug cache inside. Following the contact, the weapons were confiscated and the opium destroyed.

The large Operation *Spurs* started on January 27 as part of Operation *Thunder Freedom*. Task Force Pirate, the aviation task force, inserted two reinforced platoons from Lima Company and one reinforced platoon from India Company, along with NAVSOF and the ANA 23rd Kandak Battalion into the Korengal, Pech, and Rechah Lam valleys, either by hovering tail down or with troops fast-roping off the ramps into terrain covered in deep snow.

"We flew in fast and low and jumped off just outside the house of one of our main targets," said 2nd Lieutenant Caleb Weiss, a Lima Company platoon commander. "They couldn't have had more than a few moments to react before having entire platoons dropped on their heads."

After the initial insertions came Civil Military Operations (CMO), which conducted three separate MEDCAPS and winter supply distribution missions. With the assistance of Afghan doctors, soldiers from the Asadabad PRT and female military police officers from the 58th MP Company, 25th Infantry Division, distributed winter coats and medication and offered medical help to nearly 500 sick villagers and their children throughout the Korengal area.

"It's great to be able to help the people by giving them medicine and supplies they need," said Army MP Specialist Dayna Urbank. "We're not here just to search houses and detain people. If we show them respect and help them, they'll see that their government can offer them a much better way of life than any of the terrorist groups can."

In February 2005, Major General Jason Kamiya, commander of the Southern European Task Force (Airborne) (SETAF), relieved Major General Olson as CJTF-76 commander. The 173rd Airborne Brigade, the main element within SETAF, took the designation CTF Bayonet, deployed to RC-South at Kandahar Airfield, and then into most of the bases previously established by CTF Bronco. US Army Colonel Kevin Owens, who commanded the 173rd Airborne Brigade, became the commander of RC-South. CTF Bayonet was comprised of 2nd Battalion, 503rd Parachute Infantry Regiment (2-503 PIR); 74th Infantry Detachment (Long Range Surveillance); 173rd Support Battalion (Airborne); elements of 3rd Battalion, 319th Field Artillery Regiment (3-319 FA); and additional coalition elements from Romania and Canada.[27]

Major General Jason Kamiya recognized that the Operation *Enduring Freedom* mission was a COIN campaign, and emphasized a balance between combat and stability operations. The enemy forces in Afghanistan were mounting a classic insurgency, intent on deposing President Karzai's government.[28] A different, but essential, part of COIN operations involved training reliable Afghan National Police (ANP) and Afghan Border Police (ABP) forces.[29] In 2003, the United States, working with the previously led German efforts, began a police training mission using State Department/ INL (Bureau of International Narcotics and Law Enforcement Affairs) contract advisors to train and equip the police, advise the Ministry of Interior, and provide infrastructure assistance, including constructing several police training centers.

By January 2005, 35,000 police had been trained, but corruption, desertion, and drug abuse were serious problems. To help correct the situation, the DOD took the lead in US police reform efforts from State/ INL in April 2005.[30] The 58th Military Police Company, 728th MP Battalion, 8th MP Brigade, deployed Police Technical Advisory Teams to assist and train ANP personnel. One three-man team led by Staff Sergeant William Kegley operating out of Jalalabad was tasked to work with over 3,300 Afghan police in 31 districts spanning three provinces. Kegley and Specialist Joe Ferlicka did an assessment of the situation in Kama on February 9. "During the assessment, it is my job to gather all the facts that are pertinent to the police [Afghan National Police] in the area, to include statistical, biographical, and demographical data, to assess structures they have and their conditions, and identify training needs," Kegley said.

Illiteracy was a major problem with ANP personnel, which included female recruits. During their time in Afghanistan, the advisor system also did its part to advance the role of women in the ANP. There were three female police officers in Nangarhar province, and when Kegley found out that none of them were literate he wanted to change that. Kegley said he wanted to do this because literacy is a necessity for law enforcement at every level. "It entails a great deal of report writing, a great deal of interpersonal communication skills," he said. "If you can't read or write, chances are you probably can't talk to people either. You certainly can't write a report and you can't testify in court if need be."

The ANP were also to provide security for NGO personnel in the area. This last point was of particular significance, since 24 NGO staff members were killed in 2004, and regardless of the risks several NGOs preferred to work without military security for protection. "Without security, NGOs in particular cannot help reconstruct the nation, and the Afghan National Police plays a vital role in security," Kegley said.

Ferlicka said, "Every time we go out and we see it, it brings a smile to our face. You couldn't ask for anything better because our training is getting out there, people understand it, and they're using it."[31]

Kinetic operations continued, with patrols along the Pakistan border where ACM leaders in northern Laghman were believed to have no specific loyalty to the Taliban, Hezb-e-Islami Gulbuddin (HIG), or al Qaeda. Information indicated that they believed other tribes had received preferential treatment and government positions in the Karzai government. Due to this sentiment of "disenfranchisement" they conducted anti-government activity and leveraged organized crime as necessary to support those efforts. The Taliban and al Qaeda took advantage of the situation by providing funding and materials to these gangs to enable them to attack coalition and government forces.[32]

These rogue forces attacked targets of convenience wherever they found them. In this geographic area, that meant the Marines. On February 15, 3/3 Marine Lima Company was ambushed by approximately 20–25 ACM in the Alishang District, coming under fire from RPGs and small arms.

Acting on reports indicating that insurgent activity was increasing in the Khost-Gardez (K-G) Pass, a narrow mountainous road linking Khost and Paktia provinces, the Marines began executing Operation *Mavericks*. Kilo Company pushed 3rd Platoon to the area to investigate the reports. On February 26, after recovering a fairly large weapons cache in the area, 3rd Platoon received machine-gun and small-arms fire from an unknown number of ACM at their patrol base near the village of Waza, in the Jadran district of Paktia province.

Kilo and Lima companies combined their efforts during the battalion operation, simultaneously pursuing several targets they believed were hiding in the Alishang district of Laghman province. Kilo also worked with Navy SEALS who shared a third of their objective among the hilltop villages.

"Working with NAVSOF was great," said 2nd Lieutenant Michael Poliquin, Kilo Company platoon commander, adding, "We do business in a very similar manner. We're both very methodical and detail-oriented with mission-accomplishment being the top priority."

"I've never seen something go as 'according-to-plan' as this did, with as many variables as we had," said Captain Skyler Mallicoat, Kilo Company commander.

The Marines were the first coalition forces many of the villagers had ever encountered. Dealing with the culture shock and keeping everyone calm was essential to the success of the mission.

"There are some uncertainties on both sides, among the young Marines who have never experienced this culture before and from the Afghans who see us swoop in on these huge machines and walk around with all our gear," explained Sergeant Michael Villanueva, Kilo Company squad leader. "Things became heated between one of the Marines and a man whose house we needed to search. Afterwards, though, when everything had calmed down, the Marine and the Afghan man shook hands. I think seeing that, everyone understands we're not here to disrupt anyone's way of life or hurt anyone who isn't out to hurt other people. Maybe an Afghan child seeing that will get the right idea about who we are and why we're here instead of believing whatever stories they are told about us."[33]

Throughout March, India Company continued to focus its presence and security operations in the Korengal Valley and Sarkani areas of Kunar in close coordination with ANA and Army SF ODA-166. Kilo Company focused on keeping the K-G Pass free of IEDs and ambushes.[34]

Sergeant Major Keith A. Looker was ODA-166 Team Sergeant during these operations.

> The overall environment in the Area of Operations was passive, so we initially planned these missions as "soft knocks." Of course, we were always prepared to go 'hard' if the situation dictated. These raids were necessary to prevent the insurgents from establishing a foothold in our AO. Our first raid netted three IED bomb makers and four caches of explosives. After that raid, the insurgents never regained a presence in the area.
>
> We conducted numerous mounted and dismounted presence patrols. By maintaining a presence throughout the area, we soon became part of the community. By remaining firm in our resolve to keep the peace and treating the locals as equals, we soon developed many close friends throughout the area. These friendships were essential in convincing them to take responsibility for their own security.[35]

Heavy patrolling and friendly relations with the Afghans in the border provinces did not prevent the Taliban from launching its spring offensive on March 27, killing four US soldiers when a mine blew up under their vehicle south of Kabul. On April 12, Afghan forces were ambushed by about 30–35 insurgents near Khost, resulting in two US wounded and about 12 insurgents killed. US and local Afghan forces came under attack on May 4 in Zabul province, resulting in six US soldiers wounded and approximately 45 insurgents killed.

Two Marines from 2nd Platoon, Kilo Company, were killed in an ambush on May 8. The ambush occurred in the Mayl Valley, a center of poppy cultivation that hadn't been patrolled before. As the Marines moved into the area, radio intercepts alerted them that an ambush was being set up.[36] "We could hear them discussing how many of us there were, and how we would never make it out alive," said 1st Lieutenant Stephen J. Boada, Fire Direction Officer, 1st Battalion, 12th Marine Regiment. "So from there we set up a satellite communications antenna and called back to higher. We requested close-air support to sweep the hills but the poor weather wouldn't allow it."

While one squad moved up the valley, 1st Lieutenant Sam A. Monte, leader of 2nd Platoon, Kilo Company, sent his machine-gun squad to a ridge overlooking the area. The squad saw 11 people with AK-47s and

RPGs moving along a ridge. The squad took cover and began to close in. There were no helicopters because of the bad weather, so they pulled A-10s out of the stack to provide air support. While two squads moved in the enemy broke into two groups, and one moved into a cave complex. The A-10s pounded the caves without result. Boada relates: "During that time, we could hear the enemy over the radio making exclaims such as, 'That went just by my head,' so they were indirectly helping us adjust our fire."

The A-10s put down suppression fire while the Marines moved in on the caves. Close to the mouth of the caves, Lance Corporal Nick Kirven and Corporal Rich Schoener came upon what appeared to be a dead enemy combatant. Kirven bent down to check if he was dead, while Schoener covered him.

Sergeant Robert R. Campbell recalled what happened: "As Lance Corporal Kirven and Corporal Schoener moved on the cave, there were two three-to-five-round bursts of AK fire from the cave. Kirven and Schoener were hit. They continued to fire as they went down. Lance Corporal Loren Lynch and Lance Corporal Matthew Reynolds, behind them, fired and ... moved toward the cave. A grenade came out of the cave, landed between Kirven and Schoener. The grenade went off. I moved Reynolds and Lynch back, provided cover fire. Lieutenant Boada and Corporal Arndt moved on the cave to eliminate the enemy. I made the call to move up closer so we could see where the fire was coming from and attempt to grab the downed Marines." Boada popped a smoke grenade as he and Corporal Arndt made their way to a position very close to the Marines. He relates what happened next:

> The fire was still coming as we popped more smoke and kind of leap frogged from rock to rock. Corporal Arndt attempted to grab one of the Marines by the sappy plate carrier, but the gear ripped and he fell. By that time the smoke was clearing up and I grabbed him and we got to cover again. I could reach out and touch the downed Marines because they were so close. I then grabbed a fragmentation grenade and threw it, although fire was still coming.
>
> I ended up repeating the process about four times. Corporal Arndt would prep the grenades for me, I would shout "Cover and fire!" and throw the grenades. Corporal Arndt did some amazing things out there as a young corporal, I hope he gets recognized for something.

Several attempts were made to regain the lives of Schoener and Kirven, but CPR was useless. They had passed away. Boada says: "By that time, it was about 1800 and getting dark. We weren't prepared for a night operation and there was a lack of both food and water. We set up an LZ to try to get a MEDEVAC for the Marines, but they couldn't send one to us because of the weather."

That firefight lasted three hours, but the ordeal for Kilo Company's 2nd Platoon was far from over. The Marines had to carry their dead comrades between 9 and 12 miles down steep mountain terrain in the dark, with no food or water, little ammunition, and with the enemy closing in from two directions.

"As the crow flies, it was 5km, but in steps, 15 to 20km. We tried donkey, wheelbarrows, litters – nothing worked," recalls Sergeant Benjamin "Benny" Upton. "Everybody was beat. Sergeant Campbell's squad was in shock. The terrain was so steep. Litter, wheelbarrows, donkey, hand – everybody was beat. Third Squad showing up was a godsend. We had no food or water for 16 hours, we were tired, that was a hard night. The donkeys couldn't carry the weight; they lay down. The wheelbarrows broke. The litters – the wood broke and the ponchos let go. We carried 'em – four to a Marine – and traded off every 10 minutes."

In exchange for two American dead, 14 enemy were confirmed killed (aerial BDA [Battle Damage Assessment] and enemy radio traffic estimated 23 total enemy killed) through coordinated ground/air attacks.

After the ambush, Operation *Celtics* at the end of May provided a much-needed positive impact on the Marines. The operation began as an offensive in the rugged Tora Bora mountain sanctuary, and ANA soldiers also took part. Lima Company Marines were prepared for a fight, but found themselves sipping tea with village elders. "It was a sign of success that we were not getting shot at," said Captain Eric Kelly, Company L commander.

After assessing the needs of villagers in the area, Kelly called in the order. Chinooks from the US Army's Company F, 3rd Battalion, 159th "Big Windy" Aviation Regiment Chinooks flew in eight tons of blankets, rugs, food, and medicine. "When fighting an insurgency, the way to win is to get the people on your side," said 1st Lieutenant J.P. Sienicki. "When you're handing out food and blankets to help people in this rugged, austere landscape, you're helping out on the most personal level."

As what was now a part of every operation, Navy Corpsman Daniel Mayberry treated ailments and injuries in a makeshift clinic. "We're trying to better this country's problems and let them know we care. The local people are trying to get on with their everyday lives, and there's people – Taliban and al Qaeda – threatening their lives. If we show them that we're here to help, they may tell us where's the bad guys with the weapons."[37]

Through the summer, US and coalition forces worked aggressively to blunt the Taliban and ACM, with Operation *Diablo* in May and Operation *Diablo Reach Back* in June both conducted by elements of TF Bayonet. The operations took place in northern Kandahar province, undertaken in response to renewed insurgent attacks.

In the 20-day Operation *Diablo Reach Back*, combined TF Bayonet forces engaged Taliban forces in some of the fiercest fighting seen that year. There was significant enemy contact made by Delta Company, 2nd Battalion, 504th Parachute Infantry Regiment on June 14 in the vicinity of Takht Kalay and on June 17 in the vicinity of Gumbad.

"The men that we are fighting now have been around for a while," said Lieutenant Colonel Bert Ges. "They know how we fight, so we have to be very quick and aggressive. For the most part, the people out here are tired of the Taliban. Because there is no government representation out here, the Taliban come out of the hills and take their food, beat on them, harass them and then leave,"[38]

The heavy fighting resulted in as many as 178 insurgents killed, primarily from US military aircraft attacks.

Not all operations went well. In June, Operation *Red Wings* was mounted to eliminate the ACM led by Ahmad Shah. The operation failed and resulted in the deaths of 11 SEALS and eight 160th SOAR Army Night Stalkers east of Asadabad in the Hindu Kush.[39]

In response to the losses, 2nd Battalion, 3rd Marine Regiment organized and executed Operation *Whalers* on August 11. As had been the case with other operations in 2005, Ahmad Shah and his militia fought back instead of retreating. In firefights ranging across the Shuryek, Chowkay, and Narang valleys, Shah's forces were destroyed. Shah himself was wounded, and he retreated across the border into Pakistan with the remnants of his force. A US military spokesman claimed that during the week-long operation, US forces had been in 29 separate engagements and had killed more than 40 insurgents.

The operations tempo did not slow down. Elements of the 1-325 AIR, 82nd Airborne Division's Task Force Red Falcon along with units from the ANA and ANP ran Operation *Neptune* in eastern Ghazni from August 8–12. IEDs were the major threat to the convoy as it traveled the dirt roads toward its objective. The first IED destroyed a Humvee and left scrap metal and pieces of equipment strewn across the road.

"I thought we had hit a huge bump," said Private Chris Stroklund of D Company. "Then we went up in the air and I saw this black cloud of smoke go over my head and my .50-cal came flying off. I'll never forget that."

Captain Jeff Burgoyne's B Company soon had the area cordoned off. He and his men stalked through the village until they found the elder in charge. Suspecting the elder was concealing information, Burgoyne made sure he understood what was at stake. "I'm holding you responsible for the attacks because they happened in this area. You know who did it, and until we find out who they are, we can't help you," he told the man.

The unit was on its way back to base late the next night when the second IED attack occurred. The blast was part of an ambush by approximately seven militants using small-arms fire and RPGs. Paratroopers forced back the attack, killing one of the ambushers. Luckily no coalition forces were hurt in either attack.[40]

Others weren't so lucky. On August 18 two US soldiers were killed by a roadside bomb in Kandahar province. Three days later an IED planted under a wooden bridge detonated as a US convoy was crossing, killing four US soldiers.

War along the border moved on relentlessly. An eight-Humvee convoy with Marines from Company E, 2nd Battalion, 3rd Marine Regiment, 3rd Marine Division came under ambush near Kandagl on the night of October 17 during Operation *Pil*. Lance Corporal Nathan Davenport, was manning an MK-19 grenade launcher in a Humvee turret when the convoy came under attack. "It was the first time I've been scared," he said. The Marines returned fire, shooting about 1,200 rounds from an M-240 machine gun, 100 rounds out of the MK-19 grenade launcher, and 1,200 rounds from a .50-cal machine gun. The enemy was still shooting at them as the Marines drove away.

Davenport made it through the engagement unscathed, but three Marines were wounded in the incident. Two Marines were hit with shrapnel and a third suffered a gunshot wound to the arm. This was one of 21 firefights during the seven-day operation.

"We've been very lucky that way," said US Marine Corps Lieutenant Colonel Rob Scott, executive officer for 2nd Battalion, 3rd Marine Regiment. "We were able to work hand-in-hand with ANSF and the Government of Afghanistan through religious and cultural sensitivities to have a successful operation. Cordon-and-knock missions are more civil and encourage good relations with the people. At the same time, we're putting more pressure on the enemy so he knows he won't have a safe area."[41]

Operation *Pizmah*, the year's last big operation, finished on December 15. B Company, 2nd Battalion, 503rd PIR had been working in the Dey Chopan district for several months. The goal of Operation *Pizmah* was for elements of B Company to reestablish a coalition presence in the districts of Dey Chopan, Arghandab, and Khaki. "This area was pretty much neglected by the government," said US Army Sergeant 1st Class Julio Nazario, 1st Platoon sergeant. "Most of what the government has seen here is due to my platoon."

The 503rd worked out of FOB Baylough starting on November 30. Previous to the 503rd's arrival the FOB had been the target of the most intense anti-coalition activity of the year. Between June and September it had been attacked by 48 107mm rockets, 39 60mm mortars, and numerous RPGs.

"The reception of the people was not too soldier-friendly initially," Nazario said. "We started our mission by conducting patrols and encouraging support for the government with the people." As part of the long-term mission the 503rd helped to open two schools and a district headquarters for the ANP, and worked to train police and ANA soldiers. "[The people] can sleep relaxed and not worry about Taliban coming in and harassing them," Nazario said. "The government's here to help them out, and if they ever need us, we're just a few kilometers away."[42]

However, no matter how secure an area was when US forces left, the Taliban would filter back into the area, as proven by the number of missions run in the same area over the previous three years.

At the end of 2005 the war had been going on for 51 months. In that time the US and coalition forces achieved a lot of positive work. Training the ANA and ANP was progressing, PRTs and NGOs were making a difference in the lives of many Afghans, a number of legacy militia forces had been disarmed, and a president had been elected with minimum strife.

On the negative side, the Taliban and ACM had neither been defeated nor effectively suppressed. These forces operated openly along the border from sanctuaries in Pakistan, where they were free from fear of attack by coalition forces.

Opium production had risen substantially since the war began. To help counter this, the Department of Defense significantly increased counter-narcotics supporting efforts by Afghan and US agencies such as the Drug Enforcement Agency (DEA) during the year. However, the US military did not become directly involved in counter-drug operations, even though many of its operations were in areas of poppy production.

In 2005, 98 US military personnel had been killed in Afghanistan, and 268 had been wounded.[43] The fighting season was over, and, for the first time since 2001, no major operations were in the works for the following January.

Chapter 7
RESURGENCE, 2006–07

By the beginning of 2006, ISAF command had expanded outward from Kabul to include western Afghanistan. Plans were in place for adding southern Afghanistan to ISAF control by the end of July, leaving the US in control of eastern provinces.

Insurgent activity continued to grow stronger through the refinement of existing tactics and the employment of new ones. Foreign support intensified, and the number of foreign fighters also increased, among them al Qaeda, Pakistani Islamic militants, and Chechnyans. The foreigners brought tactics that had been used in Iraq, Israel, and Chechnya, including kidnappings, assassinations, suicide attacks, beheadings, and remote-controlled bombings. Older tactics were refined. Instead of fighting superior forces, insurgents focused on "soft" targets such as NGO personnel, religious leaders, teachers, and government officials.

NGO staffs were among the hardest hit, with casualties greater than sustained in Angola, Somalia, and Liberia. These losses forced the NGOs to either leave the country or retreat to Kabul, where they attempted to run operations using local Afghans, who in turn became targets.

What made the foreign forces more dangerous was that they were fulltime fighters, whereas Taliban fighters included ordinary Afghan citizens who might participate in the insurgency on a specific operation or attack and then resume their civilian occupations.[1]

The Taliban spring offensive gave an indication of how strong they had become when it launched major attacks in Helmand and Kandahar provinces. The attacks included temporarily taking control of Helmand's Baghran district and threatening Sangin, Now Zad, Musa Qala, and the hydroelectric installations at Kajaki. NATO outposts throughout northern Helmand were kept under attack for long periods of time.

On the evening of February 2, approximately 200 Taliban fighters ambushed a police convoy in the Sangin district in southern Helmand. Reinforcements were sent to support the ANP forces. CAS was supplied by A-10s, B-52s, and British Harrier jets over two days of fighting, which resulted in about 20 Taliban deaths and seven Afghan police and soldiers killed.[2] This was the largest battle in Afghanistan in several months, and one initiated by the Taliban instead of coalition forces, as had been more common.

Drug trafficking remained a major concern. According to reports, Afghan poppy production was on track to increase by 40 percent from 2005 levels, which, when refined, equated to approximately 90 percent of the world's opium. US and NATO senior leadership have characterized Afghanistan's illegal narcotics trade as the number one threat in Afghanistan. The country was in danger of becoming a "narco-state" unless the opium trade was significantly reduced. However, at the beginning of 2006 US military counter-narcotics operations were limited to providing transportation and intelligence to ANP forces.[3] At this time, US drug-eradication efforts were overseen by the Department of State Bureau of International Narcotics and Law Enforcement (INL). This was changing after visits in the early fall of 2005 by Secretary of State Condoleezza Rice, Vice President Cheney, and, later, President Bush, as well as pressure from Congress.

To deal with threats, ISAF and the US focused on the COIN strategy of "Clear, Hold, Build" as laid out in US Field Manual (FM) 3-24, published in December 2006. FM 3-24 was based on US experiences in Iraq but was adapted for use in Afghanistan. Each part is broken down as follows:

Clear – Physically remove / separate insurgents from target area
Hold – Establish the Government of Afghanistan (GOA) as a permanent presence
Build – Build support / protect the population[4]

Master Sergeant Michael Threatt, an ODA team sergeant in 2nd Battalion, 3rd Special Forces Group (Airborne), summarized the COIN core strategy:

"America is all about taking terrain. But in today's world, especially in Afghanistan, that population is the terrain because the bad guys can't operate without them. So every good gesture you do towards the population, you win them over a little more to the coalition side and you take them away from the bad guys."[5]

The US recognized that a more structured approach was needed if the PRTs were to be successful. The teams had three objectives: to promote progress in governance, security, and reconstruction. To that end, 12 PRTs consisting of between 50 and 100 military and civilian personnel were established. Civilian personnel usually consisted of a US State Department representative, a US Agency for International Development (USAID) representative, and a representative from the US Department of Agriculture (USDA). There is also usually an Afghan representative from the Ministry of the Interior on the PRT. In terms of military personnel, each PRT had a commander, two Army civil affairs teams with four members each, a three-man Military Police Unit, operational and administrative staff, and force-protection elements – usually a platoon-sized (40-soldier) force.[6]

The PRTs, commanded by US Navy and US Air Force officers, received extensive training by teams from the 4th Brigade, 78th Training Division at Fort Bragg. Reserve component soldiers were also a part of these teams, integrated from both the US Army National Guard and Reserves. The Department of State, USAID, and USDA representatives were also part of the PRTs. For three and a half months these teams absorbed tactics, techniques, and procedures from individual to team level, and learned from one another the differences and similarities between "aye-aye, sir," and "hooah."[7]

Admiral Mike Mullen, the Chief of Naval Operations at the time, believed the Navy could support at least six teams of the 12 teams. Commander Mike Vaney and Commander John Wade were two of the Navy PRT commanders hand-selected by Admiral Mullen. Commander Wade recalled:

> It was late November, early December. I was sitting at my desk in the late afternoon, and I received a phone call from my detailer. It was not odd for me to receive a phone call from my detailer, since I was working with Navy headquarters and the Bureau of Naval Personnel to work my next job, which was hopefully going to be at the Pentagon on the Joint Staff. So he

opens up the conversation by saying, "Hey John, this is Ken, are you sitting down?"

Normally when you hear something like that from a detailer, you expect to hear something that will be unusual and often out of the ordinary, and boy was it. He told me I was headed to Afghanistan. Long story short, I was in shock. He told me I was going to command some sort of Army unit but he had no details. He told me it was a Provincial Reconstruction Team. I asked him a lot of questions but he had no answers. I tried to assess a timeline. He didn't really have one, and it became then, at that moment, a quest and a thirst for information to try and figure out what the heck I was getting into.[8]

Commander Vaney was another of the six Navy commanders selected:

I found out with a phone call on, I think, December 20, 2005, that I was going to go command one of these PRTs. Surprisingly, another O5, also working the QDR [Navy Quadrennial Defense Review], was selected also. He had been told a week earlier. So, I had spent a week already making fun of him and buying him little toy plastic guns and things like that, only to be told myself that I was going, too. I was surprised. It was an unexpected thing. I was headed out to command a submarine at the time.[9]

The Navy commanders had different skill sets than those of the Army. Commander Wade sums the differences.

You put a Navy commander out at sea in the middle of the night, the ship moves a certain way, you hear a particular noise, you walk into the combat information center where you fuse all the tactical information, you look at a radar screen – you're familiar with that because you've grown up in that environment. You know whether to ask a question, if it's right or wrong, if you need to apply manpower or resources to it. That's part of your experience, so you have a gut feeling, you have a sense.

Well, a Navy commander doesn't have that sense or that feeling on the ground, and that was my biggest concern. I was always amazed by the maneuver battalion commander who I coordinated with very closely. He became my trusted advisor and very, very close friend. He could look at the intelligence and receive the reports from his platoons and my civil affairs [units] engaging with the populace. He could look at the terrain, he could look at the weather, he could just look at the mission as we were proposing and he could determine whether or not the enemy would attack, and if they were going to attack, how they would do it and where.

Then he'd apply that feedback into the planning process and reduce risk. Well, a Navy commander doesn't have that skill set, just because we have not served on the ground, and that was apparent to me. I thought about that while I was training, but it was very clear to me as soon as I reported on the ground.

Commander Wade also worked with Army Reserve and National Guard for the first time, which was another unique experience:

The team composition was about 60 percent Active and 40 percent Reserve and National Guard. I bring this up because I don't think we could have done the mission without the Reserves and the National Guard. I'm ashamed to say that, up until this point, I had really never operated with the Reserves or the National Guard. I really never understood their value. For me, I might find on a Friday afternoon as an XO on a cruiser that the reservist is going to show up on the Quarterdeck in 10 minutes. "It wasn't planned, sorry, but you need to find something for him or her to do for the next weekend." That was my only experience.

But what the Reserves and the National Guard brought to the table was that not only do they have their military skills, they have skill sets from corporate America, whether blue collar or white collar; and when you look at what we were trying to do with building governance and reconstruction/development, there wasn't a challenge either on the FOB or outside the FOB that we weren't able to overcome because of the inherent skills.

In April the PRT commanded by Commander Vaney deployed to Paktika, the most dangerous province in Afghanistan. Commander Vaney describes what it was like:

One of the unique things about having a submarine officer command a PRT is that I know how to avoid the enemy. It's what I've spent my last 20 years doing, going out and nobody knowing I was there. That's the philosophy I took and that's how I trained my infantry platoon. Our objective is to go down to this district and I don't want the enemy to know that we went. That served us well.

There were no roads in Paktika. In fact, the year I was there was the first time they ever saw a paved road, because we built it. This was hard-going, multi-day missions out, but that was one of our things. My philosophy was that our job wasn't to be in the forward operating base; our job was to be out there, so we pushed out. But it was continual training on how to do that. We used intel to avoid the enemy. From a force-protection standpoint, we didn't want to find the enemy, so one of the things we started doing is that if you want to avoid IEDs, don't drive where they think you're going to drive. We avoided the dirt trails and we drove across the desert, and everywhere we could find instead of driving the main routes, which succeeded.

One of my primary goals was to extend the reach of the provincial government. The provincial government wasn't getting out there, so I saw myself as kind of the catalyst to make that happen – and it turned out to be true. If I invited the governor to go down to a far-reaching district and we were going, he would go. We set about doing that; we just forged out.

It's very tribally oriented in Paktika and the key was the tribal elders – people hadn't done that before. We always talked about connecting the people up with the government. Well, we realized that you couldn't connect the people up with the government. What you had to do was to connect the tribal elders up with the government officials and then let the tribal elders deal with the people. Once you figured that out, then it was easy to sit around, drink gallons of tea, and talk to them about what's important, what they are concerned about. Developing those district development plans and provincial development plans was a lot of the work, which we did.

NGOs and Private Voluntary Organizations (PVOs) along with the United Nations Assistance Mission in Afghanistan (UNAMA) were also key components of COIN. However, Commander Vaney had to convince UNAMA that some areas of Paktika were safe.

One of my goals was to get them there and convince UNAMA that the security situation was not as bad. The problem was that they've painted the entire province. Well, that's not specific enough. There are districts in Paktika that are much more secure than other districts, and so we went

> straight to the NGOs and tried to convince them of that. Our huge success was with the medical NGOs.
>
> We managed to get four medical NGOs down into Paktika. Some of them were already working there, but we brought them together with the director of health in the provincial government and his team set up weekly meetings with them. By the time I left we had organized Paktika into four quadrants, and there was an NGO assigned to each quadrant. They were working with the provincial government and those district governments to provide health facilities in each one of those quadrants. Some were more successful than others. We had the International Medical Corps [IMC] there, which was doing great things.

US PRT security detachments usually consisted of a National Guard rifle platoon. Among these were three rifle platoons of the 1-102nd Infantry Battalion (Mountain), Connecticut ARNG, tasked to support PRTs in Qalat, Zabul province; Kala Gush, Takhar province; and Farah City, Farah province.

However, maintaining security was complicated by the fact that ISAF had taken control of RC-West and RC-North. Each RC was under the command of a different country. 1st Sergeant Arthur L. Fredericks, assigned as the operations NCO for the platoon assigned to PRT Farah, mentions some of the problems he encountered:

> Our nearest US command was Task Force Grizzly out of Kandahar Airfield. We had placed our supply cell there to support PRT Farah as well as the other two platoons in Qalat and Kala Gush. The majority of our missions originated out of our ISAF command in Herat. A visit by the Italian general commanding western Afghanistan as well as the US theater commander acknowledged our need and request for more troops.
>
> The Italian general sent us an Italian Alpine Ranger Platoon, as well as an Italian Special Forces team, while the US commander sent us a field surgical team and the scout platoon from the 102nd Infantry. Air support in western Afghanistan was a conglomeration of Italian and Spanish, although we still relied on the US for emergency close air and close air support.
>
> Using the Italians proved to be a challenge, as they could not do any offensive operations and all missions had to be approved by the Italian command.

FOB Farah had been attacked by direct fire, rockets, and a suicide bomber. The Taliban operated extensively in the province with the Gulistan district to the east, which was one of the more troublesome areas. The district was remote to Farah, requiring an eight-hour drive over bad, mountainous roads. Fredericks tells of one operation that illustrates this:

> We planned with the Special Forces Operational Detachment to conduct a key leader engagement as well as locate and destroy a large Taliban cache of explosives and ordinance. We brought our Air Force Explosive Ordinance Disposal Team [EOD] along with the Italian Joint Tactical Air Control Team [JTAC]. We located and blew the ordinance and met with local elders.
>
> We planned to stay overnight but after receiving intelligence indicating the Taliban was massing on our approach route we decided to move out. We chose an alternate route down a dried riverbed and we broke our convoy up into three groups. The ODA team would take the lead with the JTAC team in the center and the infantry platoon in the rear allowing for maneuverability. It was an incredibly dark night, making it a serious challenge for drivers in such restrictive terrain. The driver of my vehicle was having difficulty seeing, so I took over. I routinely went out on all major operations and would go along with my mortar team and radio telephone operator.
>
> We made it approximately one third of the way back where we received heavy machine-gun fire from an elevated position overlooking the riverbed. It was estimated that there were ten to 15 insurgents. The enemy fire seemed to be concentrated on the JTAC team's vehicles, as they were lightly armored. We had no room to maneuver because on both sides of the 150ft riverbed were walls rising about 75ft. The convoy immediately returned fire and gained instant fire superiority. We notified the ODA team so they could attempt to maneuver while the JTAC team coordinated close air support. The gunner in my vehicle had expended a can of MK19 [grenade launcher] ammunition and was loading another when the enemy ceased to fire. The concentration of fire that we placed on the enemy was insurmountable. We had defeated their ambush with no casualties save for a few damaged vehicles.[10]

On April 11, CJTF-76[11] launched Operation *Mountain Lion*, not in the heavily contested southern provinces but in Kunar, Nuristan, and

Nangarhar east of Kabul, known hotspots of Taliban activity.[12] It was a three-phase operation based on the COIN "Clear, Hold, Build" framework. Operational planning began in February, laying the groundwork for the "Clear" phase, consisting of lethal and nonlethal actions. Special-operations forces neutralized several high-value targets, enemy IED cells, and weapons caches, thus disrupting enemy operations before the main assault.

The "Hold" part comprised two objectives. First, the counterinsurgency effort had to dominate the physical terrain by creating permanent or semi-permanent facilities. Second, CJTF-76 had to dominate the human terrain. This kind of dominance required capable internal security forces and reasonably effective government agencies. Achieving it required substantial investments of $5 billion and sustained effort.

Finally, the "Build" stage of operations planned to transform the physical and human terrain by showing the tangible benefits that come from supporting government operations. To accomplish this, CJTF-76 leveraged Commanders Emergency Response Program (CERP) funds to improve the infrastructure and economic environment. CJTF-76 acquired $82 million in CERP money in 2006 for construction and rehabilitation of the economy, which improved living conditions and bolstered the government's credibility.

"This operation is helping the government of Afghanistan set the security conditions so democratic processes can take root," Major General Allen Peck, deputy Combined Forces Air Component commander, said in an Air Force news release. "Our job is to bring airpower to bear on the anti-Afghan forces and support the coalition troops on the ground."

The operation began with night air assaults by US and Afghan troops in CH-47 Chinooks and UH-60 Blackhawks, escorted by AH-64 Apaches. US Air Force F-15s, A-10s, and B-52s, and Royal Air Force GR-7 Harriers, flew CAS. Global Hawk and Predator drones provided intelligence and reconnaissance, with KC-135 and KC-10 aircraft provided refueling support.

"The enemy had very few options," said Marine Lieutenant Colonel James Bierman, commanding officer of 1st Battalion, 3rd Marine Regiment. "The first option he had was to run. If he runs, he leaves the safety and sanctuary of the villages where he's mixed with the local population, and he now becomes detectable by air support."

Command Sergeant Major James Redmore adds: "They gave their victims no sanctuary. They'll receive none from us. However long it takes to rid this area of extremist activity, we'll be there."

Army Colonel John Nicholson, Task Force Spartan's commander, emphasized the joint nature of the operation: "Together, with our ANA brothers-in-arms, we were eliminating the enemy's remaining sanctuaries in Kunar province," he said.

There were skirmishes with the remaining enemies, and the ones that were left were "just stubborn," according to Marine Sergeant Michael Chambers, platoon sergeant for 3rd Platoon, Company C. "They pop off a couple rounds at us and then run back along the ridgeline, trying to get away."

"There have been dozens of firefights so far, but the enemy is finding out that they pretty much can't do anything effective against us," added Marine Staff Sergeant Jason Butler.

During the combat phase of the operation, over 650 patrols were conducted, killing up to 80 Taliban insurgents. A total of 12 significant weapons and ammunition caches were discovered.

The medical mission was conducted under Operation *Lion's Pride*, which provided medical assistance to Afghans with supplies airdropped in 24 containerized systems.

"We hired local Afghans from the surrounding communities to help set up the drop zone by painting the [drop zone] with the letter "A" on the ground, and we waited for the supplies to be dropped," reported US Marine Captain Timothy Kelly. "Local Afghans were hired to climb the hills and carry the supplies down into the villages for distribution."

"Our Navy corpsmen have treated over 3,000 Afghan locals in the Korengal Valley since the start of Operation *Mountain Lion*," said Marine 1st Sergeant John Armstead, of Headquarters and Service Company of the 1/3. ."We are here to help make their lives better and to provide whatever support and assistance we can."

"These events allow us to make a solid connection with the local population in order to gain their support and keep this area from reverting back to a terrorist haven," added Kelly.

Coalition engineer units worked alongside ANSF engineer units constructing bridges and clearing mines and IEDs. The task force built nine bridges and 13 new district centers, built or refurbished seven schools, and constructed or paved nearly 400km of road. These projects put over

1,800 potential insurgents to work and infused millions of dollars into the local economy.

"Operation *Mountain Lion* has put us five to ten years ahead of where we were before the operation started," concluded Major Michael Miller, USMC.

The 10th Mountain Division was also involved in the operation. Sergeant 1st Class Connors tells what his experiences were with the opposition:

> We took part in *Mountain Lion* in April; that's when we got in our first big engagement, on the 29th of April. We were up on the Chaliz ridgeline in the Showikat Valley, and our commander had just come back from a shura [a meeting of village elders] in the town, and when he got up to the command post [CP] on top of the ridgeline we got ambushed by DShK heavy machine guns, small arms, and RPG fire. Half of my platoon was centralized there at the platoon CP, with myself. My platoon leader was about a klick [1km] around the mountain, set up in an OP over watching the town, and had eyes on my CP also. It was a pretty long firefight, went on for quite a few hours. We were pretty successful that night, we took no casualties. The enemy reported over 17 KIA and 23 wounded, coming over the integrated communications [ICOM] scanner.
>
> We were supposed to be wrapping it up pretty soon, and they made the decision that we'd stay there for a little while longer, a few days longer, to see if we could drum up any more action from the local area there, and they never came back. Never came back into attack. We actually did a patrol over to the mountain where they attacked us from. Took an eight-man team up there and basically looked around for any evidence, anything we could find as far as battle damage assessment. Pretty much all we found was a lot of blood splatter, a lot of debris, very little trash. They're really good about cleaning up their brass and ammo; after a firefight they'll pretty much take everything.[13]

Although the Taliban hadn't put up much resistance, on May 5 a CH-47 Chinook helicopter (from Company B, 3rd Battalion, 10th Aviation Regiment, 10th Mountain Division) crashed, killing six crewmen and four 10th Mountain Division soldiers. It happened at night in the 10th Mountain Division area of operations. The helicopter's call sign was "Colossal 31." It had made one pickup in twilight conditions before reaching the next 10th Mountain unit.

Lieutenant Jorgensen remembers what happened that night:

It was supposed to be a day exfil, then twilight extended into the night, by the time that the helicopters finally got on station it was an all-night exfil. The LZ that I used in our area wasn't very large, and right at the end of it there was another terrace. So there wasn't a whole lot of room around it, but we had helicopters land there probably about a dozen times at that point, and at LZ Red where the accident happened we had probably had helicopters land six or seven times there too.

We had had almost no water for two days at that point, and we had burned our trash so that we wouldn't have crap everywhere that would attract rodents and things like that, so we had burned some trash earlier that day, and without water we basically covered it up with dirt. So when the helicopter landed it blew off the dirt, and then stoked up the coals that had been burning in there.

Now at night, through NVGs, to the pilots at first it looked like tracer firing. With the downdraft it blew the stuff back up at the bottom of the aircraft, so if you're a pilot there are just little things that look like tracers coming at your aircraft. So he bugged out quick. It took us about five minutes of him circling... And then the Apache that was with him... I was telling him, trash fire, nothing to worry about.

They got the fire pit covered as best they could, so that the helicopter could come back in. It kind of touched down, it touched off, and it touched down the third time, and it just came too close to the tree and the tree and the debris, and it hit.

It kind of touched down, it touched off, and it touched down the third time, and it just came too close to the tree, and the tree and the debris and it hit. I'll remember this as long as I live. On the NVGs you could see the blade strike, the static electricity on the rotor blades is very bright and it's something that you look for, and I suddenly saw it get very white, and then a piece go this way and a piece go that way and a piece go that way.

You just heard this sickening crunch, this metal shattering sound, and then you heard the helicopter throttle up to try to get out of there. Then it just flipped over, it fell into ... it fell down this cliff, about 300–400ft, and exploded.[14]

Staff Sergeant Anthony Nilon later recalled:

We had a lot of night missions going on, we were moving people from OP to OP. We could get the air in, that's the reason. We were standing there waiting on OP Red, that's what they were calling it. They were getting them first, I was standing there watching as they were trying to upload those guys. It took like three, it took three ... he tried it two times, three times. On the third attempt is when it happened.

On the second attempt he saw he couldn't make it, he rose up, tried to regroup, as he came back he hovered for a little bit, he didn't take back off, he just went up and he came back.

As he came down on that last one, he went down real low, he came up a little bit, it seemed like he popped up, and as he popped up it was like a white flame came up from the top of the blades, once that happened, it immediately went down in a ball of fire, flames came up. It went down, Lieutenant Jorgensen right there, all I heard him say was, "Oh my God, they're going down."

You could hear the pilots over the radio saying "We're going down," and that was pretty much it. At that point when the bird went down we immediately got one of our sections to go and secure it. That was led by Staff Sergeant Harris. He went down, but the flames were too high and a lot of rounds were cooking off, and we couldn't get close to it, so we secured the bird as best we could. The next day the Marines came up and helped us secure it. We got down to the bird and then we went and got all the remains from the soldiers that had fallen.[15]

In May, the number of insurgent attacks significantly increased, mostly in the Kandahar, Helmand, and Uruzgan provinces. Operation *Mountain Thrust* was launched to counter the rising violence and to break the Taliban's hold on the region before ISAF took control of the area. In an operation scheduled to last six weeks, approximately 11,000 US, British, Canadian, coalition, Australian, Romanian, Czech, Dutch, and ANA hit the three provinces with strong air support. The heaviest attack concentrated on a mountain spanning northeastern Helmand and western Uruzgan provinces.

"They'll be in one area, they'll move out of that area, they'll conduct an attack in another area, then move back to a safe haven," according to Major General Benjamin Freakley. "This is our approach to put simultaneous pressure on the enemy's networks, to cause their leaders to make mistakes, and to attack those leaders."

In reality the operation was a series of siege and counter-siege, ambush and counter-ambush by the opposing forces, focusing on key villages in each province. After six weeks of fighting, when the main body of troops withdrew the situation remained largely unchanged, with the Taliban still the dominant force in the region.

By the end of July coalition casualties stood at 155 killed, 106 wounded, and 43 captured. The opposition lost an estimated 1,134 killed. However, the almost ten-to-one kill ratio doesn't tell the whole story, as noted by Tom Koenigs, UN envoy to Afghanistan: "The Taliban fighters reservoir is practically limitless. The movement will not be overcome by high casualty figures."

As the fighting intensified in RC-South, ACM forces continued smaller-scale operations in RC-East. One of these was an ambush on a 10th Mountain Division patrol in one of what was considered a historic ambush site: Hill 2566. The hill is near Spera, approximately 40–50km southwest of Khost. Lieutenant Justin L. Sax and his four up-armored Humvees were running security for an eight-to-ten-vehicle convoy when the attack took place in mid-July:

> We moved past the area where previous units had been ambushed, but we don't get ambushed. We turned around and came back. I'm the lead element of the company movement, and prior to moving through the ambush area I stop my convoy literally 500m before [the site], and I reconfigure my trucks [with] my best gunners to get in there and my best drivers. I literally want to be ready to shoot as I go through there. We do our first bound through this ambush area and on our first bound we make heavy contact.
>
> I come under heavy contact from PKM machine guns, rocket-propelled grenades, AK-47s, and DShK fire. We started taking heavy fire, and we make our first bound. I call up, "Hey, we're under contact, heavy contact from the hill to the east."
>
> At that time we try to move out the kill zone, my soldiers start shooting back, we start gaining fire superiority because I have four heavy machine guns [.50-cal M2 machine guns] and we start laying down heavy fire with them. We keep bounding through the area, it takes a direct hit, and they kill my lead vehicle so we can't move that vehicle. We go around to the front of it, we stop, we're in the middle of the kill zone, getting shot at, we have to stop and I have to personally get out. We hook up our tow strap to pull our

vehicle out. We are under a devastating barrage of fire coming from an elevated position.

We pull our vehicle out of the kill zone, and my gunners have killed approximately 20 to 30 of the enemy. They have such overwhelming fire superiority, and [the enemy] start breaking contact. My gunners are doing a good job and they're laying down an enormous amount of fire in a short period of time. We're in the kill zone approximately five to ten minutes.

So the enemy is breaking contact because my gunners are literally killing everybody coming towards us, which is a good thing. And then my platoon leads, the rest of the company started bounding forward, they get stuck behind us, they're coming forward to support us, everybody got backed up basically once my lead vehicle got hit, so everybody is stuck in this kill zone which is about one kilometer long. We are stuck in this kill zone, with about 70–80 bad guys in an elevated position shooting down at us. I come up, we get there, and we hook up our tow strap, I lead us out of there, out of the engagement area to a place where my company can reorganize and consolidate. When I get there basically over half the tires on my vehicles are blown out, my lead vehicle is completely destroyed, so we had to hook up our tow bar, so we fixed our vehicles enough to roll out, at the same time we pulled everybody back and started dropping in artillery and bombs on the hill with fast movers.

So that was our biggest engagement to that time. One of my gunners got injured. We got several really close calls, where the gun got shot; some of my gunners came within half a centimeter of dying when the machine gun was shot, or the gunner protective kits [GPKs] or armored gunner stations and turrets on top of the vehicles stopped something. Our whole vehicles, windows, doors, vehicles were completely pelted with gunfire – definitely my doors stopped several rounds, both the windows on my side were all shot out.

I had one of my gunners, one of my .50 cal gunners get hit in the middle of the engagement, shot through the hand. When he got hit, he just looked at his wound, decided, "hey, it's now or never," and then he just popped up there and started returning fire. Shot almost 1,000 rounds of .50-cal in that short period of time, which is amazing.

We got intelligence back that we killed the commander of the attack. Supposedly the guys were lying on the hillside crying. According to the intel, we gave a devastating blow to their morale.[16]

All was not going well in RC-South. The heavy Taliban opposition encountered in Operation *Mountain Thrust* continued all of the follow-on operations for the rest of the year. Since ISAF now had command of RC-South, the burden of the fighting fell predominantly to British and Canadian forces, with US and other coalition forces in support.

To the north and east, the four-month-long Operation *Mountain Fury* struck Paktika, Khost, Paktia, and Logar on September 16. These provinces, like those subjected to *Mountain Thrust*, were centers of opium production and Taliban strongholds. The Taliban forces were strong enough to repel an all-out British Royal Marines assault on a valley near Garmsir in Helmand.

During operations *Mountain Thrust* and *Mountain Fury* two major battles were fought in Panjwayi district, Kandahar province alone. Operations subsequent to *Mountain Fury* included *Medusa*, *Wyconda Pincer*, *Sledgehammer Hit*, *Zahara*, and *Falcon Summit* among others. Along with Panjwayi, hard-fought and costly battles took place in Lashkagar, and Now Zad and Sangin were besieged. The two operations cost the ANA and coalition 262 dead and over 300 wounded, while the opposition paid for the battles with an estimated 2,265 killed. Although tactical victories for the ANA and coalition forces, neither major operation nor the small ones succeeded in clearing the Taliban and its allies from the contested regions.

Despite the increased fighting, US casualties for the year were 98 killed and 401 wounded, which was no increase from the number of deaths in 2005. However, there were an additional 134 wounded, many attributable to the increased use of IEDs. Unlike the end of 2005, when no one was involved in major operations and none were planned for the immediate future, the fighting continued into 2007 unabated in a large part of the country.

On February 15, 2007, President Bush announced the administration's plans to deploy an additional 3,200 US troops to Afghanistan. The total at the end of March was 24,845, of which 21,581 were active duty and 3,264 were Reserve or National Guard, not including 12,000 military support personnel in Kuwait or naval personnel aboard ships patrolling through the Persian Gulf.[17]

NATO forces (primarily British and Dutch) fought a series of small battles in RC-South through the winter to keep the opposition off balance.

Operation *Achilles* was the first major offensive of the year involving US forces. Beginning on March 6, it was intended to preempt the Taliban spring offensive in the northern Helmand districts of Musa Qala and Washir. It was the largest NATO-led operation to date, deploying over 4,500 NATO troops, including the 1-508 PIR, 82nd Airborne Division, and close to 1,000 ANSF troops against an estimated 4,000 Taliban.

Achilles was divided into subsidiary operations *Silver* and *Silicon*. Operation *Silver* fell to the 1-508 along with an armored column of 250 Royal Marines. The 1-508 air assaulted into the oft fought-over town of Sangin only to find that most of the Taliban had withdrawn. However, on April 30, ISAF and ANA forces fighting to drive Taliban forces from Gereshk in the Sangin Valley met a stronger response, and killed 130 of the enemy.

RC-South, where Taliban resistance was strongest, became the heart of the war. The reasons for this were not only to break the Taliban's hold on the area but also to suppress poppy production. Helmand province alone furnished close to 40 per cent of the world's supply of heroin. If production was not stopped, US aid funds would be withheld.

Both destruction of the Taliban and suppressing drug production necessitated the need for operations to clear new areas or retake ones cleared in previous operations. Often the insurgents would be back as soon as ISAF troops left. A resident of Sangin summed up the situation. "The Taliban are all over the place," said Abdul Hakim. "The British will never be able to get rid of them. We now have troops from 35 countries. They could make it 70 countries, and still they wouldn't succeed."

Efforts to improve roads, build schools, and improve the life of Afghans were part of every operation. However, without the forces to maintain security these efforts were often for naught. Attempts to suppress poppy production also proved futile. One such attempt by Canadian forces actually increased resentment against both ISAF and the Afghan government. According to one local shura member: "We will never stop cultivating poppy. This is our land and our livelihood. If we stop planting poppy life will get much harder."

ISAF and Afghan forces did not relent in the face of these problems. As soon as Operation *Achilles* concluded in the northern Helmand districts, the British-led Operation *Lastay Kulang* (Pashto for pickaxe-handle) began to clear Sangin and Gereshk and secure the Kajaki district.

It started on May 30 when an 82nd Airborne unit air assaulted a Taliban compound. During the assault one Chinook was shot down by an RPG, killing five Americans, one Briton, and one Canadian on board.

Operation *Lastay Kulang* ended on June 14. When it was over Lieutenant Colonel Charlie Mayo, a spokesman for ISAF, said: "From Sangin to Gereshk, the entire area is under government and ISAF control. The Taliban are weak. They are not able to fight with ISAF and the Afghan government."[18]

ISAF considered Operation *Lastay Kulang* a victory. However, neither the aftermath of the operation nor the Taliban's purported inability to fight reflected the true situation on the ground. Residents had a different view. "At ten in the evening on Thursday [June 14], NATO took its soldiers away by helicopter," said Mahmadullah, a resident of Kajaki. "Then the Taliban came back. They took over those areas that NATO and the Afghan government captured two weeks ago, called Kata-Kajaki [lower Kajaki]."[19]

Helmand wasn't the only hot spot. In Kandahar province the Taliban launched Operation *Kamin* ("Ambush" in Persian) on May 27. A Taliban spokesman named Ahmadi stated the operation's objective: "In this operation, we will target our enemies and use our tactics – suicide bombs, remote-controlled [roadside bombs], and ambushes – against occupying forces and the government. We start this operation today in all of Afghanistan."

An ANP convoy was the first target. An ambush killed two officers and wounded three others. Next, ANA and coalition forces near the village of Chenar were hit by rocket and small-arms fire. In a four-hour firefight that included close air support an estimated 24 enemy fighters were killed.

The attacks continued. On June 5, Afghan troops were ambushed in Kandahar province. The soldiers called in airstrikes that killed an estimated 20–40 Taliban, but two Afghan soldiers were killed and three others wounded over 24 hours.

A four-day battle for control of the small town of Chora, Uruzgan province, and its vital road junction erupted on June 15. It started with an attack on a Dutch convoy in Tarin Kowt and escalated to one of the most brutal battles fought by the Taliban. The enemy quickly overran the three ANP posts at Kala Kala, Nyazi, and Sarab. Reportedly, at the Sarab police post, after killing two brothers of the commander, they also cut off the hands of the wife of a captured policeman, who was forced to watch her mutilation before being beheaded himself.

After the Sarab police station was overrun, hundreds of Taliban slipped into Chora and the Dutch troops got involved in fierce street fighting. In the evening the situation worsened, and the Dutch commander of Chora asked what the coalition could do to keep the town in allied hands.

In response, US A-10s and Apache gunships along with Dutch F-16s were sent to provide close air support while Australian troops deployed in Baluchi Valley, between Tarin Kowt and Chora, and secured the key road into town. One Apache strike was against 30 Taliban volunteers led by Bosnians nicknamed Kaka and Sadam, who had gathered inside a farm at the village of Qual Eh-Ye-Ragh. Two Hellfire missiles killed not only the Taliban, but also civilian hostages held inside.

When the battle ended the Taliban had suffered about 70 casualties, including one of their top mullahs called Mutalib. Reportedly, at least 60 civilians were killed by the Taliban. Two Dutch, an Australian, 16 Afghan police, and US Army Staff Sergeant Roy P. Lewsader Jr., part of the transition team assigned to 1st Brigade, 1st Infantry Division, died in the attacks. The Taliban did not gain control of Chora.[20]

Because of the Taliban's tactics, civilian casualties caused by air strikes were difficult to avoid. Air Force Staff Sergeant Benjamin Narro, an AC-130 gunner with the 4th Special Operations Squadron, explains the rules of engagement (ROE) in place at the time and his take on them:

> As soon as we get into country we go through a brief from the previous crews as to what they experienced regarding the rules of engagement. This is what you can do this is what you can't do. This is what we encountered and this is where it gets gray and what JAG [Judge Advocate General] said was okay. When you're up there you don't have time to think about whether this is what I can or can't do.
>
> Then we sit down with the JAG so there is no question as to what can happen, and the ground guys know, too. When they're getting shot at they try to lead you down a bad path, but we're there to back them up as to what can be done. We actually erred more on the side of safety.
>
> Especially if you're on the ground taking fire you push the panic button, but we're up above and can see what's happening. We can tell them, "Hey you're here and they're over there. If you go behind this building they're not even going to see you."

> It's better to take out the building when you know who is inside. Our biggest thing is to try to break contact. We'll go down to let the enemy know we're here and they need to stop. If they keep shooting, we put rounds closer and closer. If they still keep shooting and they have our guys pinned down and there's no other alternative, we will go ahead and take them out.
>
> One of the insurgents' tactics was to force civilians to shoot at Americans, so typically when you start putting down rounds they stop.
>
> We record everything to protect us, and at the end of an engagement it's reviewed.
>
> A lot of guys were angry at the fact they couldn't shoot as much. To me it does help a lot more in a war like this. People dislike us out of ignorance; they don't know us and that's all it is. Once we're out there and they see their father shoot an RPG at an American and he's not killed, he's detained and released back to his community. So the community members say, "Hey, this guy shot an RPG at them and they didn't kill him. Or, they wounded him to take him out, but didn't kill him, and then brought the medics in to fix him up. So who's the bad guy here?"
>
> So you stop that chain right there. It puts a question in their minds about Americans by not doing so much harm.[21]

Besides using human shields, taking cover in civilian homes, and forcing civilians to shoot, all of which had been done in other wars, the insurgents didn't honor the international convention about not firing on MEDEVAC helicopters marked with a Red Cross.[22]

Major Gary Means served as a flight surgeon with the 82nd Airborne Combat Aviation Brigade (CAB) in Kandahar. His unit's mission was to provide MEDEVAC support, and he had oversight of MEDEVAC for all of RC-South. He talks about how the Army handled this problem.

> We had a MEDEVAC detachment of three Blackhawk helicopters, a lift platoon of four Chinooks, and then a company of Apaches. I don't recall exactly how many Apaches we had, something like six. Basically what this allowed us to do is give general support to the forces in RC-South. We were expected to do rotary wing lift of personnel and equipment, and we were expected to do MEDEVAC support with the MEDEVAC detachment. We did heavy lift transportation operations with the Chinook helicopters, and then also had a close-combat attack mission with the Apache helicopters.

My piece of this mission as the flight surgeon was to take care of the soldiers in my battalion, of which there were almost 500 soldiers with the maintenance people and other attached personnel.

One of the big challenges that we had was that we had only three aircraft and three aircrews to provide MEDEVAC support to the entire southern region of Afghanistan.

The helicopters within our detachment were all marked with a red cross, and they were not armed. The crew onboard carried their own personal weapons, but there were no crew-served weapons mounted to that aircraft. If there was a high risk of enemy threat in the area, we would launch with one or even two Apache aircraft as escort and those Apache helicopters would eliminate the threat in the area. If the threat couldn't be mitigated with that type of support, then I would imagine the mission wouldn't launch until that threat had been mitigated.

I don't believe the red crosses were respected as a non-combat target; they routinely received fire from the enemy. Thank goodness we didn't lose any aircraft during my time there, but the aircraft received effective fire on many occasions.[23]

Although RC-South was the heart of the war, ISAF and US forces in RC-East faced their own challenges to security. Here the opposition was from the Haqqani Network and Hezb-e Islami Gulbuddin (HIG). Fighters from Pakistani Islamist groups such as Lashkar-e-Taiba (LeT) and Tehreek-e Nafaz-e-Shariat-e-Mohammadi (TNSM) also operated in the area, especially in Kunar and Nuristan. The region was also the main area of operations for remaining al Qaeda fighters operating in Afghanistan. Added to this mix were local warlords, drug smugglers, and local criminal gangs.[24]

After months of almost daily firefights with Taliban fighters in Chapa Dara, Korengal, Shuryak, and Pech river valleys, Operation *Rock Avalanche* kicked off on October 21 to counter the problem. It began with an pre-dawn air assault by Company A ("Able"), 2-503rd PIR, 82nd Airborne Division, about three miles south of their forward operating bases in the Pech River Valley.

B ("Battle") and C ("Chosen") companies joined Bravo Company, 1-508 PIR, 82nd Airborne Division; Air Force JTACs; and a Low-Level

Voice Intercept (LLVI) team from the 513th Military Intelligence Brigade, along with ANA 201st Corps in different areas of Kunar province at different times, hoping to flush insurgents out of one area and into another, where US and Afghan forces would be waiting for them.[25]

There were several skirmishes early in the operation, ultimately leading to AC-130 and Apache gunships firing into the village, resulting in some civilian casualties.

The LLVI team monitored insurgent communications and passed information on to the combat commanders. Captain Louis Frketic Able Company commander, 2-503rd, told how important that information can be. "A lot of times we started getting locations and then we picked up names," he said. "It is usually specific to that cell what kind of things they are talking about. Sometimes they will start talking about people, fighters, locations, ammo, or weapons systems that they have."

His men were atop a 7,500ft mountain in Kunar's Watapur Valley, another restive area close to the Korengal Valley. "Our area comprised mainly of hidden Taliban," Frketic said. "The problem was that you get these huge ACM on the high ground, and getting control of that high ground is crucial."

Around noon October 24, Frketic put that information to use and launched soldiers from 1st Platoon, Company D, into action. The platoon was a heavy-weapons platoon attached to Able Company for the deployment, and commonly referred to as the Dragon Platoon. They had air-assaulted onto the ridgeline with their MK19 grenade launchers and 7.62mm M2 machine guns. An 81mm mortar team from Headquarters Company, 2-503rd, was also put into action. Their fire destroyed one command-and-control node operating in the Shuryak Valley.

But it wasn't all one sided. On October 23, Taliban forces overran a US machine-gun position, killing Staff Sergeant Larry Rougle and wounding two more soldiers before a counterattack drove them off. Before withdrawing, Taliban forces captured several weapons and items of equipment from the Americans. US and Afghan forces continued to patrol the area, resulting in several more firefights. CAS from F-15 Strike Eagles, AC-130s, and Apache gunships, along with artillery support, helped beat off the attackers.[26]

Early on the morning of October 25, US and ANA forces began trekking down the mountains to their extraction points. Although they had finished the operation, the Taliban hadn't finished with them.

That evening, Specialist Salvatore A. Giunta's platoon was conducting a movement to interdict enemy forces on the Gatigal Spur in order to provide overwatch for 2nd and 3rd platoon's exfil back to Combat Outpost Vimot, and the Korengal Outpost. While conducting their exfil from the platoon's blocking position, Specialist Giunta's platoon was ambushed by 10–15 enemy personnel, who utilized an "L"-shaped, close-range ambush within 10m of the platoon's main body. The enemy initiated the ambush with sudden and intense RPG and PKM fire. They fired ten RPGs and three PKM machine guns from the apex of the ambush, and AK-47s from throughout the ambush line.

Sergeant Brennan and Specialist Eckrode, walking at the front of the single-file formation, were wounded in the initial onslaught. The enemy used an uncharacteristically high ratio of tracer rounds to normal rounds, which created a wall of fire to the left of the squad. The squad members dropped to the ground and sought cover within a couple of feet of where they had been standing to return effective, controlled fire from prone positions.

At the initial barrage of enemy fire, Specialist Giunta sought cover and brought his team online to begin returning fire. At some point in the battle, Specialist Giunta left cover to assist Staff Sergeant Gallardo back to their cover position. While exposed, the enemy shot Specialist Giunta multiple times, but the rounds were all stopped by his body armor. After numerous grenade volleys, Specialist Giunta, Staff Sergeant Gallardo, Private Casey, and Private Clary linked up with Specialist Eckrode. Specialist Giunta continued on toward Sergeant Brennan's last known position. Upon reaching it, Specialist Giunta identified the injured Sergeant Brennan being carried away by two insurgents.

Giunta, seeing that Eckrode was tended to, continued with Private Clary to advance over the exposed, open ground of the ridge in the dark, looking for Brennan. When they could not locate him where they expected to find him, they ran after the retreating Taliban. The ACM covered their rear with effective small-arms fire, but the Americans ran after them.

Giunta saw three individuals and then recognized that two of them were Afghans dragging Sergeant Brennan, one by the legs and one by his arms. Giunta pursued them, firing his M4 carbine as he ran, killing one. The second Afghan dropped Brennan and fled. A Spectre AC-130 gunship shortly afterward spotted someone carrying Brennan's rucksack, and killed him. Giunta said, "I ran through fire to see what was going on with

[Brennan] and thought maybe we could hide behind the same rock and shoot together… He was still conscious. He was breathing. He was asking for morphine."

The ambush had lasted three minutes. The next day, Brennan died while in surgery.[27]

The majority of US Air Force fighters and Special Operation Squadron aircraft used for CAS across Afghanistan were stationed at Bagram. Among these was the 336th "Rocketeers" Fighter Squadron, flying F-15E Strike Eagles. The maintenance officer for the squadron was Captain Angelina Stephens. She tells about base security and the deadly cost of one time when CAS wasn't available:

> The work was very difficult and exhausting, but when you see the jets come back empty and they're dropping the bombs where we could hear them, it's hard not to have high morale just because we know we're making a difference. It was pretty easy to keep people focused as to what we're doing and why we were doing it.
>
> People were dying; you see that coming through the base. It's crystal clear. We were talking to folks on the ground who yesterday lost people, or they were coming over to thank us because they didn't lose anybody. The sense of purpose is impossible to ignore; our job is keeping the guys on the ground safe.
>
> One incident sticks out in my mind. In November there was an F-15C crash, which grounded both the F-15Cs and the F-15E Strike Eagles. Our aircraft were included in that. It was a very hot time and there were a lot of troops in contact. We were scrambling on a daily basis. All of a sudden we were grounded and not allowed to fly. There was a lot of back and forth at levels way higher than us about whether or not we could stay on alert status. We couldn't; we were grounded.
>
> There was no word about what happened, but pictures circulated that looked like the aircraft just broke apart. We couldn't do anything. All this happened in a span of four days but it felt like weeks and weeks.
>
> The third night there was some pretty heavy fighting and the weather was bad. There weren't many people who could react to it. We were not released to fly to react to it. I was standing there with the aircrew from the

Rocketeers and one of them was on the IRC CHAT with the JTAC on the ground. It had always been exciting because you knew we could go help them. But as they're typing back and forth, the guys on the ground are getting shot at thinking, "it's okay because the horn's going to blow and we'll get covered."

It went on and on and we couldn't do anything. My master chief and others are standing around getting angry because they wouldn't release us. There was nobody else who could go, and they never release us. That night we lost eight people.

All the human remains come through Bagram at night to be flown home. They make an announcement and a lot of people wake up, put their clothes on, and line the roads as the bodies are driven all through the base and out to the Flight Line. Later that night we were across the Flight Line from the aircraft and we saw the eight coffins. Every one of our people stood there saluting. People were crying, angry, just incredibly emotional. Never had there been a moment when we realized more, "If we're not there, what would happen?"

That was a very difficult night. I have airmen who are 17, 18 years old who deploy into those kinds of situations, but they're not carrying a gun or dealing with the kinds of tragedy our ground forces do. It shocked them because they realized what can happen.

The next day some Army folks came over and they didn't blame us. We blamed ourselves a hundred percent, all of us did, the aircrews did, the guys sitting there in their gear ready to scramble did. It was gut wrenching for everybody.

The following night almost the exact same thing happened. Similar time of night. The conflict was again significant. We were standing there, emotions incredibly high because of the previous night. This time they released us. I don't think anybody ever ran so hard getting the jets ready to launch. It was the fastest scramble that happened on my shift. Everyone who had lined up the previous night lined up now. We all got emotional when the jets took off. It was the polar opposite of the night before. It was the proudest moment of my life.

The firefight was close enough we heard the booms. The jets came back empty. There was not a single coffin that night.[28]

The last major offensive of the year, Operation *Snakepit*, once again targeted Musa Qala in Helmand province on December 7. After a series of airstrikes, once more the 1-508th PIR led the way, with a night air assault rolling up Taliban defensive positions, clearing a path for TF Helmand's Scots Guards, Household Cavalry, Royal Marines, and ANA forces.

By December 10, after fierce fighting, the Taliban withdrew, leaving ANA and ISAF forces in control, at least for the time being. Lieutenant Colonel Richard Eaton, spokesman for TF Helmand, described the retaking of the town: "The current situation in Musa Qaleh is that it is underneath the Afghan flag… Midmorning today [December 12, 2007] our operations to relieve and recapture Musa Qaleh were concluded with the final phase being an assault into Musa Qaleh by the Afghan Army."[29]

Even though the fighting ended in Musa Qala, it continued elsewhere. On December 11–12, Taliban forces attacked a government center in Sangin, losing 50 killed to Afghan forces and air strikes.

For US forces the year ended with 117 killed in action (KIA) and 752 wounded in action (WIA). These numbers were up from 98 KIA and 401 WIA the year before. The increased operations tempo and proliferation of IEDs drove the numbers upward. The number and size of ISAF, US, and ANA operations against the Taliban and other anti-government forces had an impact on enhancing stability and security in eastern and southern Afghanistan, but not enough of one to ensure it. The Taliban and other anti-government/coalition forces remained well organized, well armed, and well-funded.

Chapter 8
REASSESSMENT, 2008

The war was at a stalemate. Multiple operations in 2007 had failed to defeat the Taliban and remaining al Qaeda, or weaken their ability to conduct major operations from bases in eastern and southern Afghanistan and sanctuaries in Pakistan. Increasing operations by HIG, the Haqqani Network Pakistan Islamist groups LeT and TNSM, and other heavily armed groups often linked to drug networks, along with corrupt Afghan officials, undermined the security situation.

There were still two distinct commands in Afghanistan: the NATO-led ISAF, which focused on stabilization, and the US Operation *Enduring Freedom*, which was combat-oriented. US Army General Dan K. McNeill assumed command of ISAF in February 2007 and had seen it through the year's hard fighting. Because of the command structure in place, General McNeill did not have control over US forces in RC-East. He also had to work within varying national rules of engagement.

Several NATO nations imposed restrictions ("national caveats"), which prevented their forces from conducting combat operations or permitting their forces from being transferred to different areas in Afghanistan to help balance force levels.[1] The five regional commands were each controlled by a different nation, without a unified plan for stabilization, reconstruction, or counter-narcotics operations.[2]

The lack of consistency in combat operations carried over to the PRTs. US PRTs moved throughout their territories with the focus on engaging local populations and government to bring about tangible results. They also had the ability to respond to attacks against them. ISAF PRTs consisting of coalition personnel had the same resources, but were hesitant to engage the local population in combat operations.

Instead of set-piece fights against US, ISAF, and coalition forces, the insurgents increasing relied on suicide bombers and IEDs to inflict casualties. The first Taliban attack of the year occurred at 6:30pm on January 14, 2008, when four men wearing police uniforms over suicide vests attacked the heavily guarded Kabul Serena Hotel. After a car bomb was detonated outside, a guard shot and killed one attacker at the gate to the hotel's parking lot, which triggered the attacker's suicide vest. A second attacker blew himself up near the entrance to the hotel's lobby, and the third attacker made it inside the hotel, shooting his way through the lobby and toward the gym, killing a number of guests before blowing himself up. The fourth didn't trigger his vest, but rather changed clothes in an attempt to escape. Security forces searched the premises and found him on the roof. The attack killed six and wounded six others. It was the deadliest attack on a Kabul hotel since 2001.[3]

Just over a month later, a suicide bomber detonated himself among a densely packed crowd in southern Afghanistan during a dog-fighting match, killing at least 55 people and injuring 80 others. Abdul Hakim Jan, an anti-Taliban militia leader and leader of the auxiliary police force, who was in attendance at the event, was believed to be the intended target. The Taliban denied responsibility, and intelligence indicated it may have been HIG who set up the attack, the worst such attack in Afghan history.

The Taliban claimed responsibility for another incident the next day, February 18, when a car bomb exploded near a Canadian forces convoy in a busy market area in Spin Boldak, about 75km south of Kandahar city. The blast killed 38 Afghans, wounded dozens more, and four Canadian soldiers received minor wounds.

Commando Wrath, the first major operation of the year, launched on April 6. The mission targeted the HIG terrorist group meeting in a village located in the Shok Valley, Nuristan province, just north of the Khyber Pass. The provincial governor had been tipped off that Gulbuddin Hekmatyar, the founder of HIG, would be there. The village was accessible only by foot or pack mule. In April, a fast-moving river, fed by melting snow, ran down the middle of the ravine with cliffs rising to 160ft on either side. The intelligence estimate said there were about 70 combatants in the village.

US Army 3rd Special Forces Group Captain Kyle M. Walton commanded the assault force, which consisted of three 12-man ODA teams and the ANA 201st Commando Kandak.

Walton led ODA 3336 and its part of the Afghan commandos against the village while the other two ODAs secured secondary objectives scattered more than a mile up and down the valley.

Each ODA had its own Air Force JTAC qualified to direct supporting air strikes. Senior Airman Zachary J. Rhyner, 21st Special Tactics Squadron, was embedded with ODA 3336. Staff Sergeant Robert Gutierrez Jr. was JTAC for ODA 3312, assigned to an objective farther down the valley. The third combat controller with the force was Senior Airman Cory Madonna, attached to an ODA that would attack an insurgent position a kilometer to the north of the main assault. Specialist Michael Carter (55th Signal Company Combat Camera) was also assigned to ODA 3336.

Six CH-47 Chinook helicopters inserted ODA 3336 and the Wolves in the objective area in the morning. Captain Kyle M. Walton said that many of the men were carrying 60lb packs and that "they jumped off [the helicopter] into jagged rocks, running water, and 40-degree temperatures at approximately 10,000ft elevation."

The noise of the approaching helicopters ruled out any possibility of surprise, but Walton and his troops hoped they could catch the insurgents before they were fully prepared. As the Chinooks descended toward the landing zone at the bottom of the cliffs, insurgents scurried for firing positions in stone houses and holes dug into the canyon walls. Apache attack helicopters, A-10 Warthogs, and two F-15E fighters from the 335th Tactical Fighter Squadron circled overhead.

Walton took advantage of the view provided by the F-15E's targeting pod. "They asked me to get them the best route of ingress from the riverbed to the village itself," said Captain Prichard Keeley, weapons system officer (WSO) on one of the F-15s. "I chose the terrain that was least exposed to enemy gunfire and the easiest point of ingress, while avoiding the most mountain climbing."

The team separated into three groups, six Afghan commandos and an interpreter with each element. The plan was to get to the village up the mountain, enter the village by surprise, take on any insurgents in the village, and then fight their way downhill to the extraction point. Walton said: "We didn't want to fight uphill."

Since they were at the base of the valley, their plan was to get to a village perched strategically above the valley on top of the mountain, so right away they had to climb. Rhyner described the climb up: "Initial infiltration began … with snow on the ground, jagged rocks, a fast-moving river, and a cliff. There was a 5ft wall you had to pull yourself up. The ridgeline trail was out of control." As they climbed up about 1,000ft, they could see enemy scurrying about to get into position. Master Sergeant Scott Ford said the time from when they were inserted until the first shots were fired spanned about 30 minutes.

"The buildings in the village are built one on top of the other, on top of a slope thousands of feet in the air," said Walton. "So we started the climb. The insurgents waited until the lead element was within a couple hundred meters of the compound before they initiated contact. As soon as the shooting started, we realized that they had their defensive positions dug in, and they were occupying buildings 360 degrees all around us." Staff Sergeant Rob Gutierrez said: "We were caught off guard as 200 enemy fighters approached. Within 10 minutes, we were ambushed with heavy fire from 50m. The teams were split by a river 100–200m apart, north to south."

The first burst of fire killed the interpreter, 23-year-old "CK," standing beside Walton. CK, an orphan, had hoped to one day come and live in America. "He has six years of combat experience. He's been with six SF teams and been in hundreds of firefights – but he doesn't get the six-month break," said Staff Sergeant Luis Morales.

Moments later, Staff Sergeant Dillon Behr was shot in the leg. Behr, a communications sergeant, stayed in the fight and sustained another wound before he became unable to continue the fight.

The only protection was a shallow wadi in the rock. "When the enemy opened fire, I was on a narrow terrace, about 60ft up from the bottom of the valley and 6ft wide, with little to no cover," said Rhyner. He was shot in the leg. "The rounds hit my left thigh and went through my leg and hit another guy in the foot," he said. Walton treated Rhyner's injury as Rhyner called in air strikes. The Apaches and the F-15s swept down with rockets and strafing runs to hold the insurgents back.

Walton said Sanders was the first person he thought of who might be able to identify where the insurgents were. "I was standing next to the combat controller, and when we got to a place where we could talk, he called in close air support, and two F-15s from the 335th Fighter Squadron rolled in immediately. I knew my guys were up there, and I know that when you call in danger-close air, you are probably going to get injured or killed. I called back to Sanders and asked if he was too close. He said, 'Bring it anyway.' Bombs started exploding everywhere. When I called to see if he was still alive, all I could hear him saying was, 'Hit them again.'" Walton said that it is rare to call in danger-close air even once during a firefight. Throughout the afternoon, the team called it in 70 times.

Captain Prichard Keely, USAF, was a weapons system officer (WSO – "Whiz-oh") aboard one of the Eagles, responsible for firing the weapons. He was the lead WSO, and was responsible for finding and verifying targets and determining which weapons were needed for each situation. Keely's later comment was: "It was a great feeling. Those guys were in the heat of it. It was the least we could do."

"We did take some casualties from the danger-close air," said Staff Sergeant Seth Howard. "A lot of the commandos got injured from falling debris. The bombs were throwing full trees and boulders at them – they were flying hundreds of meters."

At one point in the battle, when it looked as if the C2 element would be overrun, Sanders called for the bombing to come closer. "They dropped a 2,000lb bomb right on top of our position," said Walton. "Because of the elevation, the bomb blew upward rather than down. It just didn't seem like we had much of a decision. Our guys were wounded, and we couldn't go back the way we came." Sanders commented: "We knew we might get hurt, but we really didn't think about it."

Walton knew that time was running out. Reports from the air said more insurgents were moving in their direction. Everyone on the team had sustained some sort of injury, four of them critical, and the commandos had their share of injuries, as well. "Everyone kept fighting, but there was a window closing on us," said Walton. "We knew we had to get out."

With their backs literally against a wall, and recognizing that they couldn't go down the same way they came up – the switchbacks they had climbed up were the primary focus of the insurgent fire – they began assessing another route for exfil. "We knew we couldn't go back the way we came, so our only option was going down the cliff," said Walton. "We were completely pinned down. There was intense fire all around us. We couldn't leave the casualties. We were prepared to sit there and die with them, but we decided we were going to get them out of there."

Sanders made the first climb down the mountain by himself. When he climbed back up the sheer face of the cliff, Walton had one question: "Do you think we can make it down?"

Sanders' reply put the climb in perspective, "Does it matter if they have broken necks or backs?"

"My question was: will they live?" said Walton. With Sanders' assurance that they would live, the team began the treacherous climb.

Master Sergeant Scott Ford, the team sergeant, set up the MEDEVAC and organized the less seriously wounded to carry the more critically injured down. While organizing the commandos, Ford was shot in his chest armor plate by sniper fire. He immediately got to his feet and continued to lay down suppressive fire. One of the insurgent snipers had Ford in his sights, and shot him in the upper left arm, nearly severing it. With a tourniquet around his arm, Ford climbed down the mountain and continued to organize the MEDEVAC.

Morales said that the team made its way down the cliff hanging onto branches and rocks. Near the bottom of the cliff, most made a 20ft drop. He remembered seeing John (Walding) carrying his leg down. (Walding's leg had been almost amputated by sniper fire.)

As the wounded made their way down the cliff, Howard, Walton, and Specialist Michael Carter, a combat cameraman assigned to the unit, remained behind to lay down suppressive fire and retrieve equipment. "There were a lot of guns around where everybody had been shot," said Howard. "It kind of became an issue that there were too many guns up there, and we didn't want to leave them in enemy hands."

Carter ran through a hail of fire to retrieve the guns and other equipment. His own cameras had been shot up during the initial hours of the battle. He gathered equipment and began throwing it off the cliff, while Howard continued to pick off enemy combatants.

"The stars really aligned," said Walton. "Bullets were coming down from the side and behind us, and we could hear guys yelling above us. An element that came to reinforce the team that was on the ground stepped out into the open and started firing, which gave us the chance to get out. Seth was crazy enough to stay up there and cover us while we made the climb down."

Alone, with less than a magazine of ammunition left, Howard covered his team as they made their way down, and only after they were safe did he leave the mountain.[4]

In the six-and-a half-hour-firefight more than 150 insurgents were killed. There were two ANA casualties.[5] The mission failed to capture Gulbuddin Hekmatyar or impact HIG operations in the region.

Operation *Mouje Sealam* on April 21–24, conducted by the ANA's 207th Commando Kandak along with their US SOF trainers, captured one insurgent, killed another who tried to mount an attack against them, and recovered weapons, IED material, and rockets.

US and Afghan forces conducted a search of several compounds in the Tag Ab Valley on April 26 in an effort to locate a Taliban leader suspected of facilitating a number of deadly attacks against security forces. The raid also aimed to disrupt local insurgent roadside-bomb cells. A suicide bomb vest was discovered during the search and removed from the area. Shortly after searching the compounds, gunmen ambushed the patrol from neighboring buildings, sparking a massive gun battle that lasted until coalition forces unleashed a hail of artillery fire and called in CAS. Several gunmen were killed in the bombardment and a number of civilians were wounded. The suspected Taliban mastermind is believed to have been killed during the battle.

Despite efforts to thwart it, the Mujahdeen victory parade attack came off on April 27 when six snipers opened fire on hundreds of journalists, dignitaries, and government officials gathered to observe the national holiday. Four people, including a member of parliament from Paktia province and a ten-year-old boy, were killed in the attack. Three of the attackers were shot dead by police and the remaining three were arrested. The attack was believed to have been carried out by the Haqqani Network in conjunction with HIG. The attack was a major propaganda coup for the Taliban, who previously claimed they could launch an attack anywhere in Afghanistan at a time of their choosing. There was little that ISAF, US, and Afghan security forces could do to stop them.[6]

The Marines got back into the fight in RC-South on April 28 when 1st Battalion, 6th Marines, 24th MEU started an attack on the Taliban stronghold town of Garmsir in Helmand province.

The British-led forces in the area were outnumbered by the larger Taliban presence, which was held in check by aircraft and heavy artillery. Territorial gains were measured in yards. When US Marines arrived in Kandahar, General Dan K. McNeill, ISAF commander, was adamant that the Marines were not "the cavalry" coming to the rescue of British, Dutch, Canadian, and other allied forces in southern Afghanistan. However, it was the Marines who took the initiative to shift the balance of power in the region.

Operation *Azada Wosa* ("Be Free" or "Live Free" in the Pashtu language) was to last ten days, with the objective of enhancing security for the Afghan citizens of a district in Helmand province, and engage leaders to determine what would be required to bring stability to their district.

The key was control of the Helmand River, which runs north to south through the center of the province and provided easy access for the insurgents' logistics. "Fighters and weapons funneled through there, it was a stop along the way to other locations in and out of Afghanistan," said Major Carl McCleod, intelligence officer, 24th MEU.

According to Major Tom Clinton, "The Marines are entering an area lush with opium poppies. The Marines don't want to antagonize the local population by joining US-backed efforts to destroy the crop. We're not coming to eradicate poppy. We're coming to clear the Taliban."

The plan was for Charlie Company to create a diversion in the north and Alpha and Bravo companies to insert into their objectives to the south. The plan was that insurgents could not react to a three-pronged attack, and that they would certainly not be ready for the Marines when they woke up in the morning, explained Major Mark D. McCarroll, battery commander, Battalion Landing Team 1st Battalion, 6th Marine Regiment, 24th MEU, ISAF.

"They had no idea we were going to land that far south. They weren't prepared for us. We literally dropped in behind them," said McCleod. "It took them a few days to realize we were there in that size of force behind them."

In less than 12 hours the Marines penetrated into the enemy-held territory of the Snake's Head and seized key crossing points and terrain.

For the next 35 days, the Marines and insurgents engaged in approximately 170 engagements.

"We were told that the insurgents would fight for a few days and then they would scatter," McCleod said, "but that's not what happened. The Taliban aren't giving up… In groups of three and four, they open fire at the Marines with assault rifles or rockets, then flee. Sometimes they attempt infantry maneuvers, trying to draw the Marines in one direction with a feint, then attacking from another direction."

"They were tactically sound," said Charlie Company commander Captain John Moder. "It shows that they've done it before, that they might have been trained."

"The enemy consistently fought from fortified positions to include the hardened structures they evicted the civilians from," said Major Todd Mahar, operations officer, BLT 1/6, 24th MEU, ISAF. "They dug textbook trench lines and bunker systems and at times had mutually supporting positions. In some areas, within days of the initial assault, we began to see civilians repopulating areas that we had just cleared. They wanted to work their fields and live under the security of the Marines."

On May 28, two Marine companies pushed from their eastern positions to the Helmand River, disrupting insurgent strongholds in between the two and essentially ending the combat phase of operations.

One of the objectives incorporated in this push included the insurgent base known as Jugroom Fort – the British objective in an attack that took place on January 15 2013.

"Much like we did on the initial assault, the insurgents were oriented to one direction. We went up around them and dropped in behind them … again," said McCleod. "Within 48 hours of us pushing down on them there was a mass exodus of insurgents."

Even as the fighting continued, the Marines launched a major COIN operation in Garmsir. "The key to holding any area is the elimination of safe havens," said Colonel Peter Petronzio, commanding officer, 24th MEU. "Eliminating their ability to have a place where everybody can work, meet, plan, and prepare unopposed is very important to their defeat. The insurgents must be denied the ability to establish these new locations but not at the expense of leaving what has already been cleared. I don't see them as phases [in the COIN doctrine of clear-hold-build]. I think of them as a circle and they run continuously: we're constantly clearing, we're constantly holding, and constantly building."

On June 5, Garmsir held its first shura in nearly three years – with not only village elders, but the district governor and chief of police in attendance. In less than a month more than 70 shops opened.

"It shows that people feel safe enough in their own community to come back out," said Master Gunnery Sergeant John Garth, civil affairs chief, 24th MEU, ISAF. "It's a feeling that is shared by more than Sunday shoppers. You see a lot more of them on the side of the road, more people out playing in the canal." A local merchant gave one reason for the bolstered confidence of the locals. "Before, everything was bad," an interpreter relayed. "Since you guys got here the Taliban are not here."

Major Mark McCarroll, battery commander, Alpha Battery, Battalion Landing Team 1st Battalion, 6th Marine Regiment, was in charge of efforts in the district to make payments in compensation for the damage done to homes during the operation. He listened to one man's claim about damage to his house. When the man showed a drawing of his house, McCarroll recognized it instantly. "Yep, that's the spot," he said to himself. "We dropped a couple of bombs on it, we did a helicopter run on it and we shot artillery on it. It was uncomfortable and strange."

Garth said: "A lot of people told me they lived in the desert for 18 months. On the edge of the desert, the adult males, at least the working males, came back to their house every day to work their fields, harvest their poppy or wheat, then they went back to the desert. Why? Because the Taliban didn't want them living in their houses, but they would let them come back and farm their fields every day – part of that was so the Taliban would have a food source. Had we not come, their houses wouldn't have been destroyed, but they still would have been living on the edge of the desert under Taliban control. So when you look at it from that perspective they didn't have a home to begin with. We are now giving them a chance to move back home and rebuild."

It wasn't until September 8 that the Marines turned over responsibility for the region's security to the British and ANSF.[7]

US General David D. McKiernan assumed command of ISAF from General Dan McNeill during a handover ceremony held on June 3, 2008, in Kabul. This was significant, as the two men had served together during their careers and it was the first time successive commanders had been from the same country since 2003. It also provided a continuity of command and control within the NATO-led ISAF forces. It is important to note that both generals were NATO commanders and did not have command of US regular forces in RC-East or access to information about US Special Operations activities. General McKiernan began a push to bring US forces under the ISAF four-star commander for better command and control of everything that was going on on the ground. This he accomplished in October. The RC-East commander became the US Forces Deputy Commander under General McKiernan. One of the big advantages of the change was that ISAF was better able to support the efforts in the south by now having control over assets in RC-East.

One problem in attempting to coordinate combat actions was that under ISAF there was no US intelligence leadership – it was all ISAF. The commander lacked direct intelligence knowledge at all levels. To counter this lack of intelligence about the enemy's intentions there was a push for additional ISR assets. The available ISR was focused in RC-East and was controlled by the US Central Command. Forces up north had little to none, and the "Center of Gravity" RC-South had very little. To the west there was basically no ISR. Because of the US commitment in Iraq there were not a lot of ISR resources available to deploy in Afghanistan.

General McKiernan has said:

> In 2008 we had five regional commands and unless there is an American presence there is little combat operations. There were regional campaign plans that weren't tied in with the other regions.
>
> I went down to RC-South to discuss the national campaigns within a region. The situation was the Australians with US support were in Arghistan, the British in "Helmandshire", Canadians in Kandahar, and the Romanians with US support in Zabul. Four different campaigns with four different political guidance streams. Not coordinated, not synchronized. It was a highly decentralized fight. One of the main things I found was unless we did something different with the security forces in the south we're stalemated.

> The only way to create some momentum in the south is to get more forces. We don't have enough Afghan forces yet. NATO wasn't going to provide any additional forces. We had to go back to the US. My initial request was for an additional 30,000 of which the Bush administration approved a small part and, in 2009, the Obama administration approved about 22,000.
>
> We also needed to shift resources from Iraq to Afghanistan. Specifically enablers, not large manpower units but [units with] key capabilities. For example, we probably had two Predator lines a day, while in Iraq they had about 15. We needed more route clearance companies. At the time there were about three in Afghanistan and 80 in Iraq. Other areas that needed additional resources were signal intelligence, engineers, and counter-IED. This caused some friction in Washington.[8]

The situation for ISAF and US forces continued to deteriorate through the summer. On June 13 Taliban insurgents attacked the Sarposa Prison in Kandahar, killing 15 police officers and freeing more than 1,200 prisoners. In the following days insurgents captured 18 towns around Kandahar while several hundred more infiltrated into the neighboring Arghandab district. These movements were preliminary to an effort to recapture Kandahar. The insurgents destroyed culverts and bridges and planted mines to hamper ISAF and Afghan forces' mobility, as well as driving local civilians away from their homes. To preempt the attack, large Canadian and ANA forces swept the area, entering Arghandab on June 18. The effort was successful in preventing the planned Taliban assault, but did not inflict significant casualties on the enemy.

The Taliban struck again when a car bomb was detonated in front of the Indian Embassy in Kabul on July 7, killing 58 and injuring over 150 more.

In RC-West the 2nd Battalion, 7th Marines Division occupied FOB Leimbach in the Farah province close to the Afghan–Iran border. RC-West, under command of Italian Army Brigadier General Francesco Arena, was not experiencing the intense fighting seen in RC-East and RC-South. It was, however, a major supply and logistical staging area for the Taliban as well as providing secure transit routes for drug trafficking.

Within RC-West was the town of Shewan, a known Taliban and al Qaeda base used to launch attacks against US Marines and Afghan forces.

For months, Marine patrols based out of FOB Leimbach had been ambushed, and suffered one of the highest casualty rates of any Marine unit deployed in Iran or Afghanistan.

On August 8 a force assaulted Shewan, comprising two squads of US Marines from Golf Company, 2nd Platoon, 2nd Battalion, 7th Marines; one 81mm mortar team, an element from 1st Reconnaissance Battalion, three squads of ANP led by Police Sergeant Major Hadji-Kadadoud, one US Army Police Mentor Team (PMT) Advisor, and a DynCorp advisor. The objective was to secure the town as a base of operations and block the road between Herat to the north and the town of Farah to the south.

The Marines set out onto Highway 1, splitting into two groups. 2nd Platoon (call sign Golf 2) and the ANP would circle around Saffarak Mountain and attack the city from the north, while "Recon" unit, commanded by Captain Byron Owen, would travel up Highway 517 directly into Shewan and then dismount and clear the city on foot. Golf 2 was to set up to the north of the city with the 81mm mortar team to provide support for Recon, and to serve as a QRF.

2nd Platoon (call sign Golf 2) moved around Saffarak Mountain as the Recon unit drove up Highway 517. Golf 2 began receiving reports from the ANP that there was movement to their north, and many policemen began firing into the trees in front of them.

As they approached Shewan, Recon began taking small-arms fire from a tree line and the town in a place called Si-Jangal. Their vehicles were hit by a volley of RPGs, and a Humvee was set on fire. The crew suffered minor shrapnel wounds, and other Marines quickly returned fire and rushed to the wounded Marines aid, retrieving them from the vehicle. "The enemy fired over 40 RPGs from the tree line but were unable to effectively engage the Marines trapped in the kill zone because of the high amount of accurate fire being directed at them," Owen said. "The enemy was reinforcing the tree line and replacing fighters as quickly as we were killing them."

Golf 2, seeing the smoke from the Humvee, pulled off the road on line and sped towards the berm that ran parallel to the city, firing their crew-served weapons into the Taliban positions. "It turned out later that there was a big meeting of enemy leaders in the town that we had interrupted and we inadvertently trapped them inside of their compound," the platoon commander wrote later. "They must have thought that if they ambushed us we would cut and run. This was not the case."

"There's smoke and fire everywhere, so you can't tell where the smoke and fire is coming from. A lot of guys, they can't actually see what to hit," Owen said. "At this point, there are 100 to 150 Taliban on scene; we're outnumbered five-to-one. It's becoming a dire situation where you are firing for your own individual survival."

The Forward Air Controller with Golf Company called in a pair of F-18s. After making strafing runs they circled back and dropped several 2,000lb bombs, which didn't discourage the Taliban, who were fighting from well-fortified positions.

What started as an ambush by 30 insurgent fighters had now swelled to a full-fledged assault by an estimated 250 enemy fighters. "We knew it was bad, but we had no idea how bad it was going to be. We stayed on the battlefield and they left. It was clear cut," Owen said. "There were dead bodies all over the place, and that never happens. The Taliban recover their dead. They retreated, they fled. We fired the last shot."

The battle lasted eight hours. After the action ended, more than 50 insurgents had been killed according to Marine Corps intelligence estimates. Only two Marines had been wounded. However, the Marines didn't take the town before returning to FOB Leimbach.[9]

The pace of attack and counterattack didn't slacken. A convoy of French and Afghan forces with a US special forces CAS team and its escort was ambushed by 140 HIG fighters in the Uzbin Valley northeast of Kabul on August 18. When the firefight ended the French had lost ten killed and had suffered 21 wounded.

US forces at Camp Salerno, Khost province, in RC-East, were attacked twice in two days, first on August 18 and again on August 19. At least 30 Taliban fighters assaulted the base on the 19th but were stopped by a wall of small-arms fire and Apache gunships. According to reports, seven Taliban fighters were killed, six of whom were suicide bombers. In Laghman province the next day, US-led coalition forces killed more than 30 insurgents.

Throughout the fall, Afghanistan was wracked by attacks on government officials, ASF, coalition troops, foreign aid workers, and international businessmen. Enhanced security was no assurance of surviving an attack.

US ground forces didn't mount any major operations during the final months of the year, but Air Force and Army Aviation units provided CAS for the British, Canadian, and Australian forces in RC-South as well as covering US forces spread over RC-East.

By the end of 2008 another 155 US troops had been killed and 793 wounded.[10] The Taliban, HIG, Haqqani, and other anti-government forces had not been significantly reduced despite heavy losses, and had returned to areas that had been cleared, but not held, by US, NATO, coalition, or ANSF troops.

This increased enemy resistance required a larger commitment of forces to overcome the increasing hostile activity. In a counter move, the US increased its troop levels by 80 percent between January and June, with additional forces added later in the year. Finding the forces needed presented a problem to US and NATO planners, since most, especially the US, were committed to the war in Iraq. At the end of December there were 234,851 US forces in Iraq versus only 44,393 in Afghanistan.[11] ANA and ANP units were proving effective when teamed with US or coalition forces, but there were not enough to effectively occupy all of the territory cleared.

Tensions between the US and Pakistan also increased as US-led Special Forces conducted raids attacking houses in a Pakistan village close to a known Taliban and al Qaeda stronghold. The year ended with several major Taliban and criminal thefts and acts of arson against NATO convoys in Pakistan.

So the year ended as it began: in stalemate.

Chapter 9
SURGE, 2009

The majority of the insurgency now centered on three distinct but overlapping geographic fronts: northern, central, and southern. The northern front encompassed Pakistan's North West Frontier province and northern parts of the FATA, to such Afghan provinces as Nuristan, Kunar, and Nangarhar. Gulbuddin Hekmatyar's Hezb-e-Islami was the predominant militant group in the area. In addition, criminal organizations were also very active and not reluctant to engage in combat operations to protect their smuggling operations.

The central front was further south along the border from Pakistan's FATA to eastern Afghan provinces including Paktika, Khost, and Lowgar. Sirajuddin Haqqani's network had reported links to Pakistan's Directorate for Inter-Services Intelligence, from which it received aid, and had become lethal at conducting attacks deep into Afghanistan. Another group on this front was Hezb-e-Islami Khalis, which was led by Anwar ul Haq Mujahid. Al Qaeda was also active in the region.

Mullah Omar's Taliban based in the vicinity of Quetta, Pakistan, operated in the southern front, including Kandahar and Helmand provinces. Working with the Taliban were criminal groups, primarily drug traffickers who ran operations on both sides of the Afghanistan–Pakistan border and ran criminal networks through Iran and Central Asia.

Although not a threat to US, NATO, or coalition forces, Abdul Rashid Dostum and Atta Mohammad established strong power bases and controlled significant resources and militia forces in the north. These forces weakened the central government's power and drew off money and assets needed in other areas for stability operations.[1] With increasing numbers and groups of hostile forces, 2009 was shaping up to be a bloody year.

Map 3: Major Enemy Groups, 2009

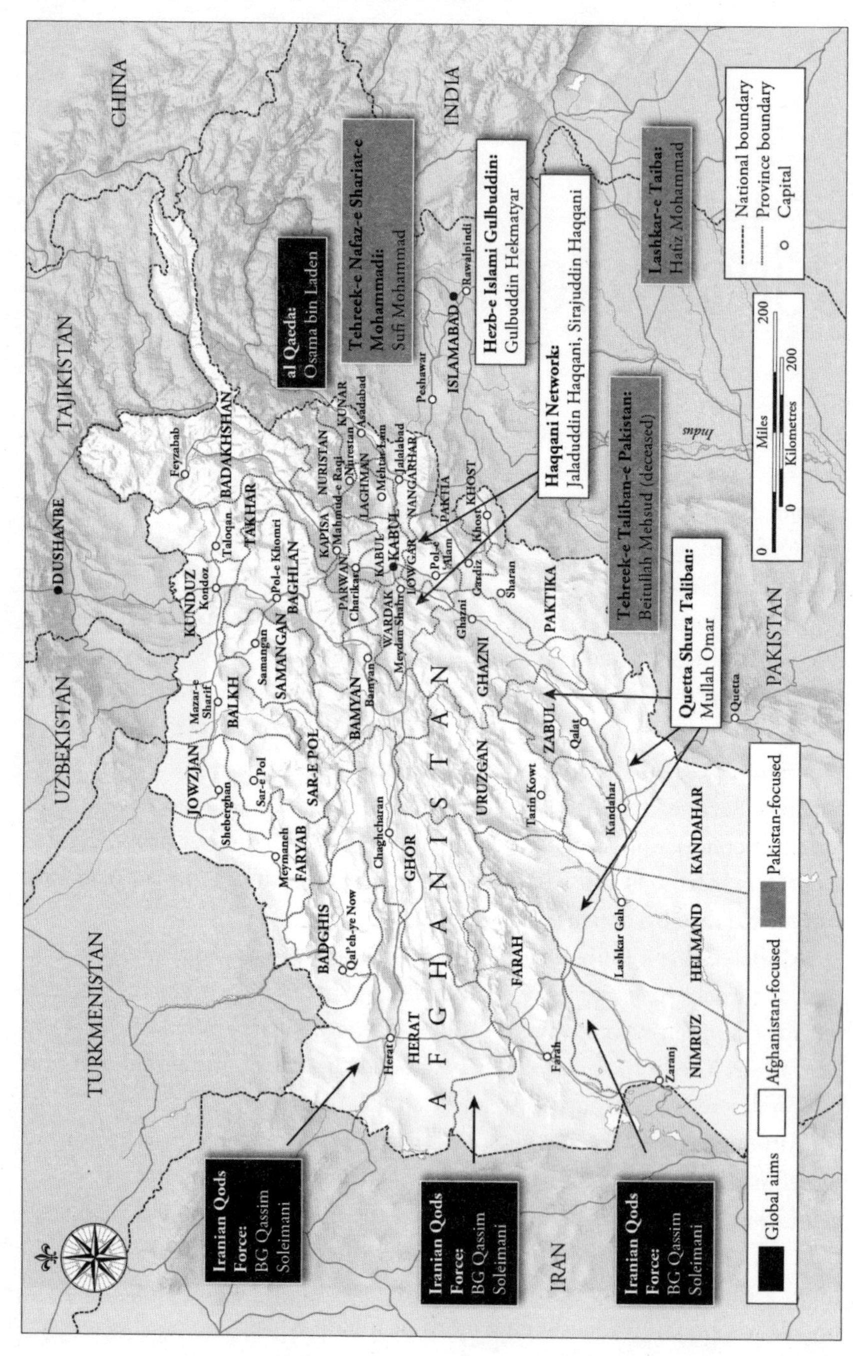

On January 1, Taliban insurgents attacked a US base in Helmand province, losing three men and failing to breach the base defenses. In Shah Wali Khot district of Kandahar province Canadian troops killed the driver of an explosive-laden vehicle before he could reach his target. Afghan troops in Herat province weren't so fortune, losing one man to a suicide bomber.[2]

There was no lull in the fighting. Although not leading any major, named operations through the late winter and into spring, US forces supported NATO forces throughout Afghanistan. All of the operations included ANSF.

On January 7, US and ANSF forces moved into the Alishang district in the northeastern province of Laghman to disrupt the Taliban's IED construction. "During the operation, as many as 75 armed militants exited their compounds and attempted to converge on the force," the US military statement said. "Shooting from rooftops and alleyways, the militants engaged coalition forces with small-arms fire in the village."

In the resulting firefight 32 insurgents were killed, one suspected militant was detained, and two large caches of weapons and explosives were destroyed.[3] Another six militants were killed in an operation involving Afghan soldiers and US-led forces in Farah province.

The same day, the British-led Operation *Shahi Tandar* (aka Operation *Atal*) moved into the Khakrez and Shah Wali Khot districts of Kandahar in RC-South. Focusing on destroying IED production capability, the operation involved the British 42 Commando Royal Marines, 24 Commando Engineers Regiment, Canadian 3rd Battalion, Royal 22e Régiment, 2-2 US Infantry, units of the Royal Danish Army, and ANA troops, all of which extensively combed the areas.[4]

According to Lieutenant Colonel Roger Barrett, Commanding Officer of the 3rd Battalion, The Royal Canadian Regiment Battle Group: "The purpose of the operation was to disrupt terrorists in the Western Panjwayi and Western Zhari districts, and specifically target areas where the enemies of Afghanistan make and store explosive materials, weapons, and equipment."

When the operation was over on January 31, the forces had seized six large caches of explosives, 38 pressure plates used to detonate hidden mines, 3,000 rounds of ammunition, AK-47s, anti-personnel mines, 22 RPGs, and 20kg of opium. They had captured eight Taliban bomb-makers, and killed several senior Taliban commanders. One key success was the destruction of a facility used to produce vehicles packed with explosives (Vehicle Borne Improvised Explosive Devices – VBIEDs).

Starting in April, RC-North and RC-West were the focus of Taliban campaigns after having been comparatively quiet since 2002. The attacks threatened key supply routes coming out of Uzbekistan, and regional stability for the upcoming Afghan presidential election in August 2009.

Living conditions for US troops in RC-East stationed at remote combat outposts and isolated observation posts were austere.

Major Dave Lamborn, a company commander for 4th Brigade, 101st Airborne, discovered this when he took over as company commander. "They weren't getting mail. They were running out of food and water out in the mountains. Of course, they're getting attacked, that's natural. That's par for the course, but it's the other things. They did not feel like they were being supported by anybody, by battalion or by brigade. They had very little contact with family members back in the States – like I said, they weren't getting their mail. When they stopped getting routine shipments of food and water, they really felt like they had been left out there to their own devises. So, morale was really bad."[5]

Major Casey Crowley, Headquarters Troop (HHT) commander for 3/61 CAV [the reconnaissance squadron for 4th Infantry Brigade Combat Team (IBCT) from 4th Infantry Division (ID)] talked about the situation when the unit arrived in RC-East:

> The brigade was going to deploy to what was called Nangarhar province, Nuristan province, Kunar province, and Laghman province in Afghanistan; the brigade footprint was called N2KL. Those are the two Ns, the K, and the L. The brigade headquarters was in Jalalabad and sort of encompasses the Torkham Gate area. That was more in the southern part and we were north of that. For the most part the N2KL is a very, very austere and mountainous region.
>
> I'm never one to complain [about] the living conditions themselves on the FOB. We had hot and cold running water; we had air conditioning and heat. We had electricity and everything else. Once you got to the mountaintops where the guys were it was a lot more austere and some of

these locations are accessible only by helicopters. There was one road that came down from Jalalabad and went a little further from our FOB but not much further. Most of the hilltops we had guys on were helicopter only. We didn't have too many Pathfinder or air-assault-qualified people but when we did resupply those were the ones who had to rig sling loads for the helicopters to get them food, water, and ammunition.

Whether it was the winter (it was harder to fly in the winter) or the summer (they couldn't carry as much in the summer because it was too hot), the weather would come in, aircraft would break, or sometimes the pilots wouldn't want to fly to a location because they thought it was too dangerous. It was prioritizing what those guys got and unfortunately that's always going to be food, fuel, and ammunition. Mail and ice cream didn't always get out to them, which is tough for the guys. That was probably the most difficult challenge we had to deal with.[6]

The 4th IBCT was also tasked with interdicting smuggling along the border with Pakistan, as Major Crowley recalls.

As battle space owners we would meet with our local political counterparts – the police chief, mayor, and that sort of thing – as well as partner with the security forces, and not just the Afghan National Army but also the Afghan Border Police because we were so close to the border with Pakistan.

The police chief in our area was probably one of the most outspoken Afghans I've met. As the police chief he wanted to do tactical missions and go after bad guys. We were like, "No, no. Unfortunately you're not in the Army. You're here to just secure the populace in your district." We had to try and tone him down but he had a really good police force. [In] the ABP corruption is sort of an inherent part of their culture and way of life. The ABP were by far the most corrupt of the organizations. They would take a lot of bribes on the border to let stuff come in and go out or whatever. That was very frustrating. Their battalion commander was a very interesting dude who was Mujahedeen and he was probably the single most responsible person. Although he could have easily doubled for Jerry Garcia – same beard and glasses and everything – I think the Taliban gets to these guys in the leadership positions and puts pressure on them. They threaten their families. We could sort of see that his hands were tied on the ABP side.

> We would see timber smugglers with donkeys loaded with timber coming from Pakistan. Ideally we wanted to see insurgents coming across the border. I think the timber was going into Pakistan and the insurgents were coming in to Afghanistan.
>
> Up in the town of Nuray there was a lumber pile that was probably 3km by 3km. I'm not saying tree trunks; these things were blocks 3ft by 3ft by 30ft. These things were huge and they just stay there; they couldn't do anything with it. That was one of the things we asked them about: "This is just sitting here. You guys can sell it." "No, the Taliban owns this. We can't touch it." The lumber just sat there. It was one of the very interesting political dynamics we were in.[7]

Smuggling wood was a small part of the pandemic lawlessness plaguing the government in the eastern provinces; the major part remained the growing amount of drug trafficking in the southern provinces. It was estimated by United Nations officials that in 2008 the export value of opium poppy crop and its derived opiates reached over $3 billion. Money from the drug trade financed the Taliban, al Qaeda, and other anti-government groups. It also added to the corruption of appointed and elected Afghan officials.[8] In October 2008, President Karzai replaced Interior Minister Zarrar Moqbel (a Tajik) with Muhammad Hanif Atmar (a Pashtun) and tasked Minister Atmar with working to combat corruption in the police forces and ministries.

The key to reducing the trafficking was poppy eradication. To accomplish this, in early 2009 the ANSF fielded Counter Narcotics Infantry Kandaks (CNIK) and ANP units in Helmand province. Each unit had a US Army or Marine Embedded Training Team (ETT) to assist. This was part of a wider program of shifting the responsibility for conducting operations away from coalition forces and onto ANSF. At the time, the Ministries of the Interior and Defense supervised the following counter-narcotics law enforcement and military units: Counternarcotics Police-Afghanistan (CNP-A); National Interdiction Unit (NIU); Sensitive Investigations Unit/ Technical Intercept Unit (TIU); Central Eradication Planning Cell (CPEC); Poppy Eradication Force (PEF); CNIK; Afghan Special Narcotics Force (ASNF); and ABP.[9]

"Whether it's man, train and equip ANSF units ... whether it's ANSF casualties or troop movements; that all falls into our visibility," said Captain

Charles Hayter, the Marine Expeditionary Brigade-Afghanistan ANSF future operations coordinator. "We provide the expertise on ANSF activities."

Not surprisingly, Taliban and criminal networks fought to stop the CNIK. One of the CNIK ETTs was from the Illinois Army National Guard. The following are excerpts from reports written by Major Kurt C. Merseal, team chief, covering the unit's operations from February 1 through March 26 in the vicinity of Nad Ali. The reports show how dangerous it was for both Afghans and Americans.[10]

The ANA's CNIK was tasked with conducting a joint operation with the ANP's Poppy Eradication Force (ANP PEF) and DynCorp (a US contracting firm) in an area north of Nad Ali city.

As the unit moved into position it began taking small-arms and machine-gun fire, along with indirect mortar and RPG fire. One ANA soldier was wounded. Soon afterward another ANA soldier was hit.

The team's medic, Specialist Rowton, then ran to the scene to assess the wounds and provided combat care under fire until the wounded soldier could be transported out of the immediate area. The 3rd Advising Team then attempted to secure transportation for the wounded man through an ANA soldier nearby, but he would not leave his covered position, as he was taking heavy machine-gun fire. Private Garcia, without regard for his own safety, and on his own initiative to secure the life of the soldier, ran to the truck while heavy machine-gun fire was landing near him and over the team's head, and moved a vehicle to their position to provide cover and then transport. Both ANA casualties were safely evacuated, but the unit didn't make it to the poppy fields.

The situation got worse on February 16. At 4:11pm, Major Merseal reported that the CNIK and CNIK ETT began receiving direct small-arms fire from southeast of their positions. On or about 12:38pm Major Merseal then reported that an RPG 7 warhead had been thrown through the window of one of 1st Companies' Ford Rangers and was lodged against the back seat. The warhead had been fired in the vicinity of the 1st and 3rd ANA CNIK companies and their respective advising teams.

DynCorp's Explosive Ordinance Detachment (EOD) was requested, as the warhead was still intact. EOD arrived on the scene, removed the warhead, and detonated it at 1:28pm.

While this was going on 1st and 3rd companies began receiving small-arms and machine-gun fire. Dismounts from the companies and their respective advising teams began to conduct fire and maneuver onto several clots in response to the S3's order. 2nd Platoon, 1st Company was directed to push forward in order to assault enemy forces located to their south. The first house was cleared with little resistance. However, the platoon began to receive fire from a house to the east. Two platoons from the 2nd Company were ordered to move forward to support the 1st Company. These platoons failed to move forward, as the company's Executive Officer reportedly turned his radio off.

As the dismounted ANA force cleared the first clot, enemy fire began from another, and several fighters ran from one clot to another to the east. As two ANA soldiers approached the entrances to two separate clots, they came under machine-gun fire. One soldier was hit in the head and the other was hit in the torso. At this time, the 1st and 3rd Advising Teams were moving forward to the position. Lieutenant Mays pushed forward with his team and determined that the reported wounded ANA soldier was actually KIA. He then moved forward of their position in response to orders, but without regard for his own safety, to throw a fragmentary grenade into the house from which the team was receiving heavy machine-gun fire. Approximately 15 minutes later, Captain McLean (a US Army nurse) arrived to assess the second soldier, and determined that he was KIA. At 1:29pm Major Merseal reported to the Joint Forward CP that two ANA soldiers had been killed in the contact, as their injuries were too extensive for treatment.

The enemy force stayed and continued to fight on in the face of significant firepower by the CNIK, CNIK ETT, and attack-helicopter support (two Hellfire missiles were fired, in addition to 30mm cannon rounds).

This day's operations resulted in two KIAs within the CNIK, five confirmed enemy KIAs (believed to be as high as 12), and with 14 detainees being taken. On February 21 the opposition used a ZSU-23 (a two-barrel 23mm antiaircraft gun) and 107mm rockets to stop the CNIK. And so it continued. Each day the units encountered increasing resistance while only occasionally managing to destroy some of the surrounding poppy fields. At the time of Major Merseal's last report on March 26, the opposition fielded enough fighters to lay siege to ANA patrol bases and sustain attacks over extended periods of time. Poppy production continued, despite the costly efforts in men and equipment by the CNIK, ANP, and their US-led ETTs.

In February and March 2009, President Obama approved an increase of over 17,000 US forces to deploy during the course of the year. By June there were approximately 55,000 US troops in Afghanistan. Some 8,000 came from the 2nd Marine Division and another 4,000 from the 5th Stryker Brigade Combat Team, 2nd Infantry Division, which was the first time the Army had deployed this type of brigade to Afghanistan. The remaining 5,000 were support forces including military police and engineers drawn from regular, reserve, and National Guard units.

The additional US forces deployed in RC-South to stop the influx of foreign fighters coming over the border from Pakistan through an increased number of "seize and hold" operations spread over more territory, helped provide stability, and trained ANSF.[11] Operations included establishing bases, which would provide greater mobility and counterinsurgency efforts.

The Marines were first to strike into enemy territory. On July 2, 4,000 2nd Expeditionary Brigade Marines and 650 ANA troops struck over a 75-mile front into the Helmand River Valley south of Lashkar Gah. Operation *Khanjar* ("Strike of the Sword") was the largest Marine operation since the Vietnam War.

Key targets of the assault included the districts of Garmsir and Nawa near the southern border with Pakistan. One of the immediate goals was to secure the area before the presidential elections. This time, instead of a quick in-and-out, the forces were to remain in place, working with Afghan farmers to develop alternate crops to replace opium poppies. More than 90 percent of Afghanistan's poppy production comes from Helmand province, making the area a major cash supplier for the Taliban. The Marines anticipated a hard fight based on an Afghan Army Intelligence estimate that there were 500 foreign and 1,000 Afghan Taliban fighters in the area.

"This is a big, risky plan," Marine Brigadier General Larry Nicholson told his men at a briefing at Camp Leatherneck in the run up to the launch of the battle. "It involves great risks and amazing opportunities. These are days of immense change for Helmand province. We're going down there, and we're going to stay – that's what is different this time."

The Marines did not employ artillery or bombs from aircraft, in an effort to show that the operation focused more on protecting people than on killing the enemy. "The success of this operation is going to be dependent on how the populace views this, not just in how we deal with the enemy," Captain Pelletier said.

The operation launched at 1:00am local time, July 2, 2009, when Marines from 1st Battalion, 5th Marines (1/5), were dropped by CH-47 and UH-60 helicopters of the 82nd Airborne Division into dirt fields around the town of Nawa-l-Barakzayi, south of Lashkar Gah. Two Marine infantry battalions and one Marine Light Armored Reconnaissance (LAR) battalion led the operation.

In the north, 2nd Battalion, 8th Marines (2/8) pushed into Garmsir district. In central Helmand, 2nd Light Armored Reconnaissance Battalion (2nd LAR) entered Khan Shin in the Khan Neshin district, at the same time as 1-5 Marines pushed into Nawa-l-Barakzayi.

The first shots of the operation were fired at daybreak (around 6:15am) when a Marine unit received small-arms fire from a tree line. Cobra attack helicopters were called in and made strafing runs at the tree line from where the fire was coming from. Simultaneously, Marines from 2nd Battalion, 8th Marines (2/8) were dropped by helicopters just outside the town of Sorkh-Duz. This lies between Nawa-l-Barakzayi and Garmsir (where the unit had fought in 2008). Conditions in the field were hot and dry, with temperatures reaching over 100°F (38°C). Heat stroke was as much a risk for the heavily laden troops as was enemy fire and IEDs.

"We were kind of forging new ground here, going to a place nobody has been before," said Captain Drew Schoenmaker, who commanded Bravo Company of 1st Battalion, 5th Marine Regiment.

The next three hours brought repeated bursts of gunfire and volleys of RPGs. A Cobra helicopter providing CAS fired rockets at a tree line nearby. Other Marines walked through fields of corn and hay. Only a handful of villagers dared to venture outside into the area of crisscrossing canals, mud houses, and lush tree-lined fields.

"It's like when you open up the oven when you're cooking a pizza and you want to see if it's done, you get that blast of hot air. That's how it feels the whole time," said Lance Corporal Charlie Duggan Jr.

By July 3, Marine Colonel Mike Killion reported: "An enemy-controlled baseline just south of Garmsir was crushed yesterday, but that doesn't mean all the enemy have gone." This was proven the next day when Taliban militants shot and damaged two unarmed medical helicopters marked with a red cross, deployed to evacuate Marines suffering from heat stroke.

The stiffest resistance occurred in the district of Garmsir, where Taliban fighters holed up in a walled housing compound engaged in an eight-hour gun battle with troops from 2nd Battalion, 8th Marine Regiment. The Marines eventually requested a Harrier fighter jet to drop a 500lb bomb on the compound. There was no immediate count of insurgents killed, although ground commanders reported that 30–40 were shooting from in and around the compound early in the day. The airstrike also resulted in several secondary explosions, leading Marines at the site to suspect that the house may have contained homemade bombs.

Poppy eradication was not part of the Marines' mission. Brigadier General Nicholson addressed this in his press conference:

> Coalition forces, and particularly US Marines, were not involved in eradication. Eradication is a program that is run by the Afghan Government. So now, if they are somewhere out eradicating and they're in a firefight, will we come to their rescue? Absolutely. Will we MEDEVAC them? Yes, we will. But are we out there? You will never see Marines out there plowing fields, digging – you know, I mean, it's just – that's not why we're here. That's not what we're doing. That's an Afghan program. And so I hope that answers that.
>
> Now, if I find – if our Marines are out there and they find a lab, if they find a drug lab, will they report it to the Afghan officials? Will they cordon off the area and treat it like a crime scene and bring in Afghan Government folks? Absolutely. But are we out there hunting labs? Are the Marines hunting labs or hunting poppy fields? The answer is unequivocally no.

Officially the operation ended on August 20, however, Marines set up several operating and logistics bases throughout the region. For all the combat, only one Marine was killed and several others were injured or wounded on the first full day of the assault. Also on the first day, Lieutenant Colonel Rupert Thorneloe (one of the most senior British Army officers in Afghanistan) and another British soldier were killed when a bomb exploded under their armored vehicle near Lashkar Gah. The ANA lost two men and one interpreter. For all the effort, the confirmed number of Taliban killed was between 49 and 62.[12]

Post-operation intelligence indicated the Taliban escaped the area prior to the start of the operation, rather than choosing to fight. The fighters had moved to German-controlled northern Helmand near Baghran and the eastern edge of Farah province, an area mostly under Italy's control. General Zahir Azami, the Afghan Ministry of Defense spokesman said: "They want to carry on fighting. They don't want to escape during the summer. This is the height of fighting season."

A senior coalition officer who agreed to speak only if he was not identified said: "The sense is that many of the Taliban have left, but they have not gone very far. They are not abandoning the Helmand River valley. They have seen a lot of forces come and go, but we are not going anywhere."[13]

Although Operation *Khanjar* was considered successful, work still needed to be accomplished. Several follow-on clearing operations ensued in some areas to clear out Taliban militants and give Afghan civilians the security and freedom of movement required to participate in the August 20 national and provincial elections.

One of these operations took place on July 18 when Marines with Company F, 2nd Battalion, 8th Marine Regiment (2/8) and ANA soldiers conducted an early-morning raid on a prominent Taliban-controlled bazaar near Mian Poshteh. "The purpose of the raid was to disrupt freedom of movement within the bazaar and to exploit the enemy force logistic base," said Captain Junwei Sun, commander of Company F. "This seizure means we invaded Taliban territory, discovered their caches, disrupted their log operations, and squeezed them out of the area." Just over two months later, 2/8 Marines established a patrol base within close proximity to this bazaar in order to deny the insurgents influence in the area for the long term.

After studying insurgent movements and activities in the Now Zad region, approximately 400 Marines of 2nd Battalion, 3rd Marine Regiment (2/3) along with 100 ANA and British troops supported by Marine Aircraft Group 40 launched Operation *Eastern Resolve II* against the town of Dahaneh, a Taliban stronghold for the past four years. The operation began on August 12. Control of the town was essential to controlling the Now Zad Valley, a major Taliban staging area and large opium market, as well as the best vehicle route connecting Taliban safe havens in northern Helmand. Later that morning a convoy of Marines met heavy resistance as they fought to seize control of the mountains surrounding Dahaneh.

It took three days of heavy fighting to secure the town at a cost of one Marine killed, Lance Corporal Joshua "Bernie" Bernard. Although the Taliban were defeated, the villagers weren't convinced they would not come back. Marine Captian Zachary Martin, operation commander, gave a realistic assessment of the situation: "They're waiting to see what we're going to do. They want to see if we're going to stay the course, if we're going to be the winning side, because they very much want to be on the winning side."[14]

During the operation, which commenced just a few weeks before the national and provincial elections, the Marines established a position between the insurgents and the village of Dahanna. Another achievement in the operation was establishing a presence in the Dahanna Pass, which served as a logistical resupply route for the insurgency. The Marines' intense efforts provided the security required to allow people to vote in the August 20 elections.

Other significant accomplishments for 2/3 include the compacting of Route 515, which was initially cleared by 3/8 to connect the districts of Deleram and Bakwa. After the route was cleared, it continued to be plagued with IEDs. Today, the road is still dangerous, but much safer due to the project 2/3 facilitated.[15]

The loss of a friend is hard, as is the loss of a man under your command. Army Major Louis Gianoulakis tells what it was like.

> I served at Contingency Outpost [COP] Michigan. It's a COP in the Dari-Pesh district in Kunar province within RC-East. It's at the mouth of the Korengal Valley and the Pesh River, which snaked through my area of operations [AO]. On the west side Sundri was the border and on the east side Metina and Cara were the borders. I lost three Soldiers from my company; two while I was in command and one a month after I left command.
>
> Making that phone call to speak to the mother of the first Soldier was probably one of the most difficult things I'd ever done in my whole life. I'd been a casualty assistance officer before, I've been an escort officer before to bring a Soldier home, but making that phone call and talking to the Soldier's mother [was hard]. It turned out to be a wonderful experience and we had a great conversation, but just the initial opening of the conversation, talking to her – even though I knew she'd been notified, even though I knew

she'd spoken to other people – just to be the guy who was responsible for her son. It was hard to talk to her.

The first Soldier [who died] was a very vibrant and energetic Soldier who could turn a very drab, boring day into a very exciting event. He just had that personality. He died doing exactly what you would want a Soldier to be doing: trying to get his weapon back into operation so he could continue to lay suppressive fire for his element – he was a Mk-19 gunner – so they could call for some indirect fire and hopefully kill the enemy, but at a minimum suppress the enemy and get them out of the kill zone without anybody getting injured. His Mk-19 [grenade launcher] malfunctioned; he switched to his 240Bravo [machine gun] and then deemed it would be more effective if he got back on the Mk-19, and that's when he took a round to his head.

Dealing with the casualties was by far the hardest thing I had to do, and it's something you cannot make a mistake with anywhere in the process. There are no-fail missions at the tactical and operational level, but I would say it is more important to ensure that that Soldier and his family are taken care of the right way, because without those Soldiers you'll never accomplish any other mission. If you fail to do that, your men will see it.[16]

The men and women who lost their lives were flown home out of Bagram Airfield. A ramp ceremony was held for each one as their coffin was loaded on board the aircraft. People stood at attention, holding a salute until the last coffin passed.

Major Melvin Porter, 3-61 Cavalry company commander, and his unit had just arrived. He relates: "After we got off the plane, they told us to drop our bags and run back to the ramp, so my guys had just hit the ground and now they have to do a ramp ceremony where they drive the [HMMWVs] with the coffins of three soldiers past them. That was really sobering for them, too, especially for some of the younger guys, who had never deployed at all. As soon as they hit the ground the first thing they see are three American bodies."

It didn't get easier for him or his troops when they flew into their COP in RC-East.

It took us maybe two to three days to get from Bagram to our actual COP. Then we were on the ground for a couple of hours and we get into our first firefight. We landed on the COP probably about 0230 to 0300, and about

> 0700 there was an enemy attack. The COP sat in a depressed low area with high ground all around it, so it was interesting to get there and know that you were going to be fighting from a bowl for a year. That was a daunting task to look at going ahead. One of the Soldiers for the unit that we were replacing was injured pretty badly, so it was really an eye-opening experience for my Soldiers, and even prior to that, as soon as we landed in Afghanistan at Bagram, there had been an attack and some Soldiers had been killed.

While the major fighting was taking place in RC-South, two small operations were run in RC-East to enhance security for the presidential elections. The 2nd Battalion, 377th Parachute Field Artillery Regiment, 4th Brigade Combat Team (Airborne), 25th Infantry Division, along with ISAF and ANA forces, ran the week-long Operation *Champion Sword* at the end of July against insurgent safe havens in the Sabari and Tirazayi districts of Khost province. The operation netted 14 militants captured with no casualties.

In the first week of August Operation *Silver Creek* was kicked off with the same mission of enhancing security before the elections in Nuristan province on August 20. The 2nd Battalion, 77th Field Artillery Regiment, 4th Brigade Combat Team, 4th Infantry Division and ANA forces with the Marine Embedded Training Team 4-4 from the 3rd Marine Division were the units assigned to this operation.

Back on June 15, General Stanley L. McChrystal relieved General David D. McKiernan as ISAF Commander and Commander of US Forces – Afghanistan. It was the routine annual change and, at the time, did not alter operational planning. The first indication of General McChrystal's views on how the war should be fought was stated in "Commander's Initial Assessment" submitted to Secretary of Defense Robert M. Gates on August 30.[17] In the opening paragraph General McChrystal wrote: "Stability in Afghanistan is an imperative; if the Afghan government falls to the Taliban – or has insufficient capability to counter transnational terrorists – Afghanistan could again become a base for terrorism, with obvious implications for regional stability."

He then redefined the fight as one not "focused on seizing territory or destroying insurgent forces" but rather stated the need to conduct "classic counterinsurgency operations in an environment that is uniquely complex."

Success, he contended, "demands a comprehensive counterinsurgency campaign." Accomplishing the mission required a "change in operational culture" and a new strategy focused on the population. There was also the acknowledgement that time was critical. After almost eight years of war McChrystal believed that "failure to gain the initiative and reverse insurgent momentum in the near-term (next 12 months) – while Afghan security capacity matures – risks an outcome where defeating the insurgency is no longer possible."

One of the strongest points in the summary was the need for more troops. In public statements he suggested an additional 30,000–40,000 US forces were needed in addition to the 65,000 already in country.

The offensive went on. In RC-East Operation *Buri Booza II* on September 8 had ANA and ABP forces moving into Ganjgal village in Kunar province. With the ANA was the Marine ETT 2-8 (Major Kevin Williams, Lieutenant Ademola D. Fabayo, 1st Lieutenant Michael Johnson, Gunnery Sergeant Edwin Johnson, First Sergeant Christopher Garza, Staff Sergeant Aaron Kenefick, Corporal Dakota Meyer, and Navy Hospital Corpsman 3rd Class James Layton). Captain William D. Swenson and Sergeant 1st Class Kenneth Westbrook from the 10th Mountain Division were with the ABP.[18]

This was supposed to be a routine operation similar to ones the units had run before. "We were not there to fight, we were there to have the Afghan forces prove to an unreceptive audience that the government was fair, professional, responsible, and most importantly, it was Afghan," said Captain Swenson.

Intelligence sources hadn't reported any heavy concentration of anti-government forces in the area. "The valley is notorious for welcoming you in, and your farewell present is always fire – always," Swenson said.

But this time an RPG hit the front of the column as the lead Marines moved within 100m of the village. Then the entire force was hit by heavy machine-gun fire, RPGs, and AK-47s from the valley to the east. "We're surrounded!" Gunnery Sergeant Edwin Johnson yelled into his radio. "They're moving in on us!"

An estimated 60 insurgents had infiltrated and maneuvered into Ganjgal from the north and south through unseen trenches. Heavy fire spewed from houses and buildings. According to eyewitnesses, village women and children could be seen shuttling ammunition and supplies to the Taliban fighters.

In the first attack, Johnson, Kenefick, Johnson, Layton, and an Afghan soldier they were training were killed.

At least twice, a two-man team attempted to rescue their buddies, using an armored vehicle mounted with a .50-cal machine gun to fight their way toward them. They were forced back each time by a hail of bullets, RPGs, and mortars. A bullet hit the vehicle's gun turret, piercing Meyer's elbow with shrapnel. Eventually, Meyer reached the trapped men. He found them spread out in the ditch, dead and bloody from gunshot wounds. Their weapons and radios had been stolen.

"I checked them all for a pulse. Their bodies were already stiff. I found Staff Sergeant Kenefick face down in the trench. His face appeared as if he was screaming. He had been shot in the head."

Bleeding from his shrapnel wound and still under fire, he carried their bodies back to a Humvee with the help of Afghan troops and escorted them to the nearby Forward Operating Base Joyce, about a mile to the northeast of Ganjgal.

Coalition forces had been flanked and were taking rocket and artillery fire on three sides from multiple angles and elevations by the advancing Taliban. "The enemy realized they were gaining the initiative and that our fires were ineffective," Swenson said. "We called in artillery, but we couldn't put it where we wanted to, and they saw that as a deficiency on our part and exploited it. This was a maneuvering enemy, a thinking enemy, an aggressive enemy, and a new enemy."

Swenson called repeatedly for white phosphorous smoke to shield the coalition and allow them to withdraw. He was repeatedly denied the incendiary rounds on the basis that the drop would be too close to a populated civilian area. The closest obscuring effect of the White Phosphorous shells shells was 400m away, too far away to be effective as cover for the withdrawal.

"A difficult decision was reached that we were no longer combat effective. We were going to be overrun, so we started a controlled withdrawal, but it was not the decision we wanted to make because we still knew we had the Marines up ahead," Swenson said. "We didn't know where and were hoping, just hoping they'd taken cover inside a building and stayed there, thus the break in communication. We just didn't know, but what we did know was that we'd be no good to them where we were, so we began our withdrawal, with additional casualties."

Major Williams had been shot in the arm and Garza's eardrums had been ruptured by an RPG. The wounded were accumulating. Unable to physically evacuate the wounded down the steep terraces and out of the kill zone, Swenson coordinated for combat helicopter support.

Westbrook had been isolated and lay in the open suffering a chest wound.[19] Negotiating 50m of open space, Swenson, Garza, and Fabayo quickly covered ground, zig-zagging and returning fire as they raced for Westbrook. Despite the maelstrom of direct fire, which had killed two ANA soldiers and wounded three others, the team was holding their own in the kill zone.

At about the same time, a team of OH-58D Kiowa Scout helicopters carrying a combination of missiles, rockets, and .50-cal machine guns arrived on the scene.

"We did receive our aviation support, the Kiowas," Swenson recalled. "They're aggressive, like little bees, they swarm all over the place, quick, nimble. The enemy knows when helicopters show up it's in their best interests to find somewhere to hide. If the enemy is out in the open, they'll be found and that will be a bad day for them."

Swenson and Fabayo then manned one of the unarmored ABP trucks and re-entered the kill zone twice to evacuate wounded and bringing them to a casualty collection point. Next, Swenson and Fabayo went in search of the missing Marines, while staying in constant contact with one of the helicopters, which was also trying to locate them.

The arrival of the Kiowas gave them the time needed to move Westbrook and the other wounded down the steep terraces to the ABP trucks, which then carried the wounded to a landing zone where a UH-60 Blackhawk MEDEVAC helicopter waited.

A mission that started as one of good will became a struggle for survival. The immediate cost to the coalition was the loss of four Americans and eight ANA soldiers. Approximately 12 insurgents were killed.

Captain Swenson summed up the operation in just a few words. "There was loss, terrible loss, but we brought forces in to continue that mission, to finish that mission, to clear that village, and to show what our resolve was and what our response would be."[20]

The next major insurgent (referred to as Anti-Afghan Forces, or AAF) attack in RC-East took place against COP Keating near Kamdesh, Nuristan province. The attack was the result of the decision by General McChrystal to withdraw troops from remote outposts and consolidate them around larger population centers. COP Keating, along with several other tiny firebases in eastern Afghanistan, was ordered to shut down. The COP lay in a deep bowl surrounded by high ground, with limited overwatch protection from nearby OP Fritsche.

The COP and OP were manned by 60 men from Bravo Troop, 3rd Squadron, 61st Cavalry Regiment, 4th BCT, 4th Infantry Division, along with two Latvian Army advisors to the ANA forces. During the five months of B Troop's deployment to COP Keating, the enemy launched approximately 47 attacks – three times the rate of attacks experienced by their predecessors. Usually the attacks were made by just a few fighters, and lasted five to ten minutes. This changed on the morning of October 3.

At approximately 5:58am, both the OP and COP were hit with concentrated fire from B10 recoilless rifles, RPGs, DShK heavy machine-gun fire, mortars, and small-arms fire from the heights. This immediately inflicted casualties on the COP's guard force and suppressed COP Keating's primary means of fire support, its 60mm and 120mm mortars. ANA soldiers on the eastern side of the compound failed to hold their position, and within 48 minutes enemy fighters penetrated the perimeter at three locations. Once inside the wire, the attackers burned down most of the barracks and managed to wound 22 soldiers and kill eight, in total half of the approximately 60 Americans there.

Insurgents also captured the outpost's ammunition depot. Eight Afghan soldiers were wounded, along with two Afghan private security guards. Some of the defenders took refuge in armored vehicles, but at least two were killed by shrapnel from RPGs that breached their turrets.

Lieutenant Cason Shrode, fire support officer, said the initial round "didn't seem like anything out of the ordinary." There was a lull and then there was a heavy attack. "We started receiving a heavy volley of fire. Probably 90 seconds into the fight they ended up hitting one of our generators so we lost all power. At that point I knew that this was something bigger than normal."

When the attack started, Staff Sergeant Clinton L. Romesha, a section leader for Bravo Troop, pushed through heavy enemy fire to the Long Range Advanced Scout Surveillance vehicle battle position 1, or LRAS 1, to ensure that the MK-19 automatic grenade launcher and Specialist Zachary S. Koppes were in the proper sector of fire and engaging enemy targets. He then headed to the barracks, grabbed an MK-48 machine gun, and, with assistant gunner Specialist Justin J. Gregory, moved through an open and uncovered avenue that was suppressed with a barrage of RPGs and small-arms fire. Romesha grabbed a limited amount of cover behind a generator and destroyed a machine-gun team that was on the high ground to the west. He then engaged and destroyed a second enemy machine gun.

Continuing to fight under the heavy enemy indirect and direct fire from superior tactical positions, and suffering a loss of power to the tactical operations center (TOC) when enemy forces destroyed the main power generator, B Troop withdrew to a tight internal perimeter. Within 40 minutes, A-10s, F-15s, a B-1 bomber, and Apaches arrived on the scene. Chad Bardwell, an Apache gunner, said he had to confirm the fighters he saw on ridgelines were the enemy because he had never seen such a large group of insurgents. "We tried to stop them as they were coming down the hill... We were taking fire pretty much the entire day." One of the pilots' initial reports described, in laconic terms, flying through gauntlets of fire, and occasionally finding a shooting gallery of insurgent targets.

Chief Warrant Officer Ross Lewallen, the Apache pilot, said a few aircraft were damaged in what was a "time-consuming endeavor" governed by tough terrain. "One of the primary reasons for the fight taking so long is that it is an extreme terrain. There's a lot of cover so you really can't detect the enemy until they start moving again," he said, adding that it was tough for MEDEVAC aircraft to land "because we were still trying to control [the outpost]."

As CAS was raking enemy positions, Romesha engaged multiple enemy positions on the north face, including a machine-gun nest and sniper position. With 3rd Platoon providing a base of fire to cover the assault on the entry control point building, Romesha led a team to secure and reinforce it using an M-203 grenade launcher and a squad automatic weapon (SAW). Once in the building he ascertained that the source of the enemy recoilless rifle fire and RPGs was originating from the village of Urmul and the ANP checkpoint directly to the front of the entry control point. He then called in CAS and heavy mortar fire to take care of the problem; air support neutralized AAF positions in the local ANP station and mosque in the nearby village of Urmol, as well as in the surrounding hills.

The fighting died down at 5:10pm when the last of the AAF withdrew. The Quick Reaction Force was delayed by bad weather and didn't reach the COP until 7:00pm.

During the attack eight US soldiers were killed and 27 wounded; eight Afghan soldiers were wounded, along with two Afghan private security guards.[21] The US military estimated that 150 Taliban militants were also killed as a result of repulsing the assault. One of the defenders, Staff Sergeant Clinton L. Romesha, was awarded the Congressional Medal of Honor for his actions during the attack.[22, 23]

In the days following, B Troop withdrew from COP Keating, but, the Americans left so quickly that they did not carry out all of their stored ammunition. The outpost's depot was promptly looted by the insurgents.

In RC-South, Marines continued operations to clear the Taliban out of the region. From October 6–10, 200 Marines from 2nd Battalion, 3rd Marine Regiment along with the Afghan 2nd Battalion, 2nd Brigade, 207th Corps conducted Operation *Germinate* to clear Taliban insurgents out of a pass through the Buji Bhast Mountains in Farah province. Company F traveled into the dangerous pass to clear the route connecting the population centers of Golestan and Delaram in order to allow freedom of movement for local Afghans in the area. Along the route through the pass, Taliban-planted IEDs had killed more civilians than Marines.

"I figured it was either going to be a ghost town or it was going to be a significant battle," said Captain Francisco X. Zavala, Company F's commanding officer. "Unfortunately, there was some battle, but it was nothing my Marines couldn't handle." As the ground element rolled through the pass, the rest of the Marines and ANA soldiers who had been inserted via helicopter blocked the eastern and northern exit routes. Their supporting mission was to stop and search Afghans fleeing the area and prevent any possible insurgent support from reinforcing their comrades.

"We saw spotters throughout the hills, and we were just waiting for something to happen," said Staff Sergeant Luke N. Medlin, the engineer platoon sergeant and part of the eastern blocking position.

A few hours after they assumed these blocking positions, the Marines and Afghan soldiers started receiving fire from machine guns, rifles, and mortars from enemy positions in the surrounding hills. The Marines quickly dispatched the initial attackers and called in a UH-1N Huey, an AH-1W Super Cobra, and an F/A-18 Hornet to destroy the enemy position farther uphill. "We were attacked from a well-fortified fighting position in the hills," Medlin said. "My Marines quickly returned fire, giving us time to maneuver and overwhelm the position with fire until air support got there."

The only other excitement during the operation came two days later. "During the clearing of one compound, a woman drew a pistol, aiming it at one of the Marines," said Lieutenant Shane Harden, weapons platoon commander, F Company. "Lance Corporal Justin B. Basham demonstrated extreme composure and great fire discipline not to shoot her. Within a split second he realized that he could use a non-lethal method to disarm her."[24]

Marines and sailors from India Company, 3rd Battalion, 4th Marine Regiment returned to towns surrounding the Buji Bhast Pass area as part of Operation *North Star* from November 15–17. They found the Taliban reasserting its influence by shooting at the Marines. The patrol attended a shura in the town of Gund, and the Taliban responded to the meeting with small-arms fire from the surrounding hills.

"[The Taliban] responding to the shura in that manner. [By] shooting at us, they're just trying to reinforce their presence there to the locals. They wanted to let [the locals] know, 'Hey, we're still here, we see you talking to the coalition forces, and we don't like it,'" said 1st Lieutenant Scott Riley.

Taliban fighters increased their efforts to reinforce their influence over the region later in the day. This third attempt targeted the Marines, using an IED. "We turned around to look at how beautiful the valley was up there with all the mountains, when we saw a huge plume of smoke and dirt shoot up. Then we waited and eventually heard the explosion," said 2nd Lieutenant Robert Fafinski, a platoon commander with India Company. "We were pretty sure somebody had died, and eventually we were able to learn from the locals that it was the IED emplacers."[25]

Although no villagers or Marines were hurt during the operation, it was obvious that efforts to eliminate the Taliban's influence had not yet been successful.

Operation *Cobra's Anger* targeting the Nawzad District in the volatile Helmand province was more rewarding. The three-day operation ran from December 4–7, where members of 3rd Battalion, 4th Marine Regiment returned to the town of Now Zad. Alpha Company, 2nd Combat Engineer Battalion traveled by road while other units air assaulted using via CH-53E helicopters and V-22 Osprey aircraft. After clearing multiple IEDs the Marines entered the town and came under fire.

"An insurgent shot at us and we saw him peeking from behind a corner shooting rounds at us," said Corporal Trevor W. Curtis, a vehicle gunner for Lima Company. "Once we had him spotted, one of our gunners shot at him with a .50-cal machine gun and I unloaded my Mark-19 on him. After we shot, a tank fired at his building and all that was left was rubble."

"I thought they'd put up more of a fight," said Corporal Cody P. McGuire, a combat engineer for Alpha Company, 2nd Combat Engineer Battalion. "This was a hot spot, but there was very little resistance, except for IEDs. I was there three days and found three IEDs. They have the capability to put up a good fight. But we rolled in with assault breacher vehicles, tanks, and air support. I think they were intimidated."

After the operation ended, Navy medical personnel assigned to the Marines treated about 300 people while Lieutenant Colonel Patrick J. Cashman, the Marine CO, and Lieutenant Colonel Sakhra, commander of the ANA 207th, met with tribal elders to build rapport with the locals scattered along the route to the pass and the ANA forces in the area.

"As far as bringing the people back into the city, we are about 50 percent, because we have to de-mine the place and clean it up," said 1st Lieutenant Mathew M. Digiambattista, 1st Platoon commander, Alpha Company, 2nd Combat Engineer Battalion. "Given the right tools and time, we can accomplish anything."[26]

This post-operation work was part of the overall COIN strategy and, for the immediate future, helped keep the area secure.

In 2009 the US lost 310 people, of which 266 were killed in action. General McChrystal's new policies were being implemented, but it was too early to assess their long-term impact. What was evident was that the Taliban and other anti-government forces had not been brought under control or even seriously weakened in RC-South, even with the heavy concentration of US, ISAF, and ANA forces. In RC-East ISAF and US forces ceded control of the more remote areas in an effort to concentrate forces around population centers. The Haqqani Network and Hezb-e Islami Gulbuddin continued to be the dominant forces in the region, and there was no apparent way to interdict their operations. Germany had command of RC-North. Over the year, German forces, working with Swedish, Norwegian, US, ANA, and local security forces, conducted a series of operations resulting in the death of over 600 insurgents. But the areas outside of the vicinity of major bases remained under the control of the Taliban and its allies. RC-West remained as it had been – dominated by anti-government forces and criminal organizations.

After eight years of war, the end was not yet in sight.

Chapter 10
NEW INITIATIVES, 2010

With the New Year came the continuing deployment of 30,000 additional US troops, 9,000 of these to be in place by the end of March and another 18,000 by June. When completed in August, the total would be approximately 98,000 US forces in Afghanistan. NATO and allied countries pledged over 9,000 additional troops, for a coalition total of about 150,000 personnel.[1]

Along with the increase in troops and US Special Operations Forces in country, General McChrystal requested the CIA to increase the number of Special Activities Division (SAD) paramilitary officers. In Iraq the combination of SOF and SAD teams had been deemed the key to the success of the surge.

ISAF headquarters identified 80 Afghan districts as "key terrain," with another 41 being designated as "Areas of Interest." These were areas of concentrated population and high economic importance, whose stabilization would be the primary focus of ISAF operations.[2]

There were changes on the political front, too. On January 28 an International Conference on Afghanistan was held in London to discuss a new course for the future of the country.[3] Attending the conference was Afghan president Hamid Karzai, the Afghan Minister of Foreign Affairs Spanta, the US Secretary of State Hillary Clinton, UN Secretary General Ban Ki-Moon, UN envoy Kai Eide, British Foreign Secretary David Miliband, the former Afghan Minister of Finance Ashraf Ghani, and the British Prime Minister Gordon Brown. Other attendees included senior representatives and foreign ministers from more than 70 countries as well as members of international organizations.

One purpose of the conference was to formulate plans for transferring responsibility for security from ISAF and NATO to Afghan forces province by province over the next five years, with Afghan forces securing the most volatile provinces within three years.[4]

To accomplish this, in January 2010 the Joint Coordination and Monitoring Board, the formal decision-making body for Afghan and international coordination, endorsed increasing the growth target for the ANA to 134,000 by October 2010 and171,600 by October 2011. It also endorsed the growth target for the ANP to 109,000 by October 2010 and to 134,000 by October 2011 through expansion of training facilities and increased use of contractors to carry out training.[5]

Operation *Moshtarak* (Dari for "Together"), the first major operation of the year, was launched on February 13. The attack force consisted of 8,000 Afghan national security force personnel and 7,000 RC-South units including US, UK, Canadian, Danish, and Estonian forces with a total of 33 coalition nations providing aviation support. Afghan forces consisted of six ANA Kandak battalions, two special commando kandaks, and approximately 1,000 Afghan gendarmerie (ANCOP, special police force nationally recruited).

Also, approximately 1,000 new ANP were inserted into Nad Ali and Marjah once the "Hold" phase of the operation started to become effective. Intelligence estimates on Taliban strength ran from as low as 400 upward to 2,000.

One of the main objectives was to gain control of the Marjah, the center for most of the world's opium, which had been controlled by the Taliban and drug lords for many years.[6] In a briefing on February 18, British Major General Nick Carter, commander of NATO-ISAF Regional Command South, indicated that they expected it to take 25–30 days to complete the military objectives, and another six months to judge the overall success in wresting control of the region from the Taliban. Unlike on previous occasions, following active combat operations ISAF and Afghan military and police forces would remain to provide security for the population, the governmental administration, and those undertaking the economic reconstruction of the region. If operations went as expected, it was anticipated that within the next six months a similar effort would be undertaken in neighboring Kandahar province. The operation was scheduled to last until December 2010.[7, 8, 9]

The Marines of Charlie Company, 1st Battalion, 3rd Marine Regiment, 1st Marine Division were part of the initial air assault on February 9.[10] "I felt the assault went well," said Captain Stephan P. Karabin, commanding officer of Charlie Company, 1/3. "We got in here quickly, under the cover of darkness on the helicopters, moved into position, set everything in place and were able to seize the objective. This area is important because it's the one intersection which links northern Marjeh ... to [eastern Helmand province] and it blocks that supply route. The Five Points intersection and surrounding area is also part of the main route from Marjeh to Lashkar Gah, the Helmand provincial capital."

The Taliban reacted quickly and began firing machine guns at the assault teams. Marines and ANA soldiers fired back with heavy machine guns, rockets, and small-arms fire, wounding and killing several Taliban fighters, forcing them to retreat.

"While we were reinforcing our position on a roof, we came under fire again," said Sergeant Stephen Y. Roberts, Weapons Platoon, Charlie Company, "It was three or four of the same fighters we had seen firing at us earlier."

Roberts responded to the enemy machine-gun fire by launching a Javelin shoulder-fired missile into the position the fighters were firing from, immediately silencing the heavy machine gun. Marine AH-1 Cobra attack helicopters flying over the area followed Roberts' fire to strike with a volley of cannon fire and rockets, putting an end to the engagement.

Five days later Charlie Company finished construction of a new COP and christened it Combat Outpost Reilly, in honor of Lance Corporal Thomas J. Reilly Jr., the only Marine from 1/3 killed in action during the battalion's deployment to Karmah, Iraq, in 2009.

The COP was built near a key intersection Marines called "Five Points," a junction of major roads connecting northern Marjah with eastern Helmand province. Marines of Charlie Company conducted a helicopter-borne assault to seize Five Points and the surrounding area on February 9, days before Operation *Moshtarak* began in Marjah. "We pushed west along Route Olympia and cleared the way for Bravo Company on the ground, clearing IEDs, and bridging gaps to get them out to Five

Points," said Lieutenant Justin P. Murphy, Combat Engineers platoon commander, 1/3.

Approximately 300 Marines and Afghan security forces air assaulted into Marjah, under the hours of darkness on February 13. Twelve UH-60 Blackhawk helicopters and CH-47F Chinook helicopters, command-and-control helicopters, and aerial security provided by AH-64 Apache helicopters from TF Pegasus facilitated the air assault of Kilo Company, 3/6 Marines, in seizing their objective area.

"Protected by Apache air weapons teams, the Marines and their partnered Afghan security forces quickly began moving to their initial objective, seizing key terrain and preparing to link up with their parent headquarters scheduled to begin a ground assault into Marjah [mere hours after the air assault]," according to 82nd Combat Aviation Brigade commander, Colonel Paul Bricker.

Shortly after the Marine insertion, additional TF Pegasus aviation assets concurrently assisted a coalition air assault into nearby objective areas in Nad Ali. Task Force Pegasus's 1st Attack Reconnaissance Battalion, 82nd Aviation Regiment (TF Wolfpack), was one of three rotary wing aviation units involved in the operation in support of the Royal Air Force TF Jaguar's No. 903 Expeditionary Air Wing Sea King Surveillance and Control helicopters.

On February 18 the Afghan national flag was raised over Marjah's bazaar, marking the conclusion of the heaviest fighting. Having lost control of the city, the insurgents turned to IEDs, sniping, and intimidation as a means of continuing the battle, all of which undermined the Afghan government's control.

Ironically, with the center of opium production now in friendly hands, the Marines were ordered to avoid damaging the poppy crop since this was the main source of income for two thirds of the local population. Officially, Operation *Moshtarak* continued through December, at which time US casualties were 45 killed, UK casualties were 13, and ANA over 15. In exchange, intelligence estimated that 120 Taliban had been killed.

USAF Major Robert Lee, an F-15E pilot, flew CAS for the operation:

> We were right in the thick of it. More generally our squadron was supporting the operation in Marjah when they said we were going to plus up troops and go through Marjah. A lot of us were involved in supporting that and of

course, that's always a pretty good feeling because it went off relatively successfully without a whole lot of trouble. That was pretty good. I think the most rewarding event wasn't necessarily a specific mission. As we were redeploying to come home, we were in the staging area just basically waiting for the planes, and of course it's not specifically a USAF transport ride home; you're going to be going with whoever needs to be going from the AOR to home.

There were some Army guys there and we just started talking with them because we had hours to wait. They said, "Oh, yeah. You guys were the Strike Eagle guys. You went by 'Dude' call sign. We remember you guys. You did some great work for us." They told us some stories from their perspective, on how it was just great to hear the Strike Eagles show up and drop munitions.

They said, "One time you dropped a 2,000lb bomb on the hill and it made this huge explosion. We all had to get down." They just had some great stories and they were thankful for all the work we'd done over the past four and a half or five months. I think that was probably the best way you could ever leave; for the guys you've been supporting to come and say, "Hey, I know who you are," maybe not specifically you but, "It was the 'Dude' call signs, the Strike Eagles, the 15Es that we loved to hear overhead." They had some great stories and they even had some pictures.[11]

After more than eight years of war, ISAF and ANSF had yet to gain complete control of Kandahar province and the city of Kandahar. Operation *Omaid*'s ("hope") objective was to change the situation. It was also a key part of General McChrystal's strategy to reverse the Taliban's momentum in RC-South.

It was the largest operation in Kandahar province to date, and consisted of two major offensives, one covering the Panjwayi and Zheray districts, located next to each other, while the second concentrated on the Arghandab district located north of Kandahar. The combined offensives were to clear Taliban forces from major population centers and extend government into the cleared areas consistent with the COIN "shape, clear, hold, and build" strategy.

According to James Appathurai, NATO's chief spokesman, Operation *Omaid* was not about killing Taliban fighters. "It is about protecting the population, about changing the political culture and perception. Kandahar is, from the psychological and communications point of view, the heartland of the Taliban," he said. "The biggest problem in Afghanistan is not the Taliban, but the lack of strong governance and the delivery of services."[12] A nonmilitary priority objective of the operation was to eliminate bribery and corruption in the city, an almost impossible task in and of itself.

Unlike previous operations, information about this was published in advance, which led to a series of deadly Taliban-led bombings in Kandahar on March 13. Countering the Taliban pre-operation offensive, coalition and Afghan forces secured key routes in the province, and as many as 70 significant Taliban commanders were seized or killed ahead of the operation.

The operation was not universally greeted with enthusiasm. "Operation *Omaid* will bring more insecurity, instead of peace," said Salaam, who lives in the Maiwand district of Kandahar province. "We have just seen that the opposition has accelerated its attacks. There are more and more explosions in the province. You cannot bring peace through war."[13]

Launched on March 30, operations started with approximately 8,000 coalition troops and 12,000 ANSF troops and police. Since the operation was planned to extend for several months, coalition strength was to increase by 3,000 in June by adding a US brigade. The operation was timed to be completed shortly before Ramadan started on August 11. No casualty figures were posted when the operation ended.

Operations in RC-South following Operation *Omaid* remained focused primarily on Helmand and Kandahar provinces. Operation *Hamkari* (Dari for "cooperation") in Kandahar began on May 11 and was to run through December.

Major General James L. Terry, Regional Command South commander, summed up the mission this way: "I think we all realize it takes more than knives and guns in this counterinsurgency campaign. It really requires that governance and development aspect that's out there." But knives and guns were still needed to gain control of some Kandahar districts. The Australian SASR and 2nd Commando Regiment, along with ANA forces backed by US helicopters, fought a three-day battle in Shah Wali Kot. No coalition forces were lost in this engagement, but on 21 June three Australian commandos were killed when a US UH-60 Blackhawk helicopter crashed in northern Kandahar province. One of the UH-60 crew chiefs also died, while another seven Australians and a US crewman were seriously injured.

Over in Helmand province, Lima Company, 3rd Battalion, 3rd Marine Regiment, in partnership with the ANA, established an observation post in support of Operation *New Dawn* in Southern Shorshork on June 17.

"We're going to be conducting patrols, vehicle checkpoints and looking at the population, making sure there aren't people from out of the area coming in and causing harm or issues for the local people," said Captain Luke Pernotto, L Company commander and commander for 3/3's ground force in Operation *New Dawn*.[14]

> We want to make sure enemy forces can't be reinforced, and don't fall back to regroup in this area. We've made extreme progress in Nawa, and to have it all go to waste, especially when we're doing our last bit of clean-up in the Trek Nawa area, would be a shame. We're essentially on the line where the desert ends and cultivation and civilization begins. Once the population realizes that a lot of their fears are unwarranted and we really are here to help them, that's when we can begin to work with them and show that the government of Afghanistan, along with the partnership of the Marines, are here to help them and are here to make their lives better.[15]

Up in RC-East, 2nd Battalion, 327th Infantry Regiment, 101st Airborne Division, along with ANA and ANP units, launched Operation *Strong Eagle* on June 27 to take the village of Daridam in the Marawara District, Kunar province. There was a strong insurgent force in the Ghaki Valley, which had occupied local villages and threatened government centers in the district. The plan was to take Daridam, which would block the insurgent advance and eliminate the top commander, Qari Zia ur Rahman, holed up in Chinar, the next village over.

The operation began with an air assault on three peaks along the main road. However, the Taliban retained control of the key ridge overlooking the road and had fortified the village. Headquarters Company Captain Steven Weber and his men staged at the Marawara District Center at the entrance to the Ghaki Valley. Lieutenant Stephen Tangen and 15 men from

Headquarters Company, 1st Platoon, along with 60 Afghan soldiers, would lead Weber's armored vehicles up the valley road on foot, while 1st Lieutenant Doug Jones' 2nd Platoon, teamed up with ABP, walked the ridgeline to the north.

As five ANA troops neared a tree at a bend in the road, the Taliban opened fire from three different ridges. One Afghan soldier was killed and the others wounded. Tangen and his men headed for the tree to reinforce the Afghans. One of Tangen's men, machine gunner Private Stephen Palu, was shot in his arm and leg. "At least we had a little bit of cover," said Specialist Adam Schwichtenberg, a squad point man. "The ANA were pinned down at the tree."

The unit's armored vehicles pushed forward to lend their firepower and provide protection. Staff Sergeant Eric Shaw, one of Tangen's squad leaders, ran up to alert the Afghan soldiers that they were stopping and to find cover. As Shaw maneuvered back behind the truck where Tangen was standing, a bullet found its way under his helmet, shattering his face and killing him instantly.

"There is no way to train for a squad leader that you spent a year of your life with to receive a gunshot wound to his head and die right in front of you," Tangen said. "There is no way to prepare his squad for that... You have to keep moving."

On the road, air support helped suppress the insurgent fire, allowing the men to evacuate their dead and wounded. But the Afghan soldiers had had enough. As the wounded were evacuated, the rest of the Afghans retreated with them.

Up on the ridgelines, men of 2nd Platoon looked on as the battle unfolded below them, too far away for them to effectively contribute. "We saw RPGs hitting Shelton's vehicle," Schwichtenberg said. "We saw smoke everywhere. They were down there getting whupped."

Across the road on the other ridge, Lieutenant Doug Jones divided the 2nd Platoon into two groups to engage several enemy positions. One group took shelter in a small compound a few hundred yards from where the insurgents were dug in. The other group took position behind a wall in the roofless ruins of an old building about 50 yards away. Jones' men battled on the ridge, several men surviving by a hair's breadth. Private Jeremy Impiccini had a bullet come straight for him, but it hit the magazine casing in his bullet pouch instead.

"We were crossing one of the terraces and Impiccini said 'Sergeant, I think I got shot!'" recalled Sergeant Cole McClain. "But we were good." With all his men in heavy contact, Captain Steven Weber was commanding from the rear, working to relay positions to the air assets so they could bomb the enemy positions.

On the ridge, Staff Sergeant Matthew Loheide heard the call for men to take cover ahead of CAS fighters coming in on a bombing run. Loheide was more concerned with the men on the road below. "We thought the bomb was going to hit 200 yards away from us," Loheide said. But something went terribly wrong. Instead of striking the insurgents, a 500lb bomb hit approximately 5m from Loheide's position in the roofless ruins, causing three casualties. Following the blast, Loheide immediately began to assess and take control of the situation, despite his brain being severely injured.

Identifying the three casualties that were not able to move, he quickly called up Lieutenant Jones and led the movement down the mountain, where he established and prepared a hot landing zone. Loheide moved out into the open, with enemy small-arms fire impacting inches from him. Jones and his men made two trips down the mountain under heavy fire to evacuate the wounded. They were all rattled and dazed. Miraculously, not a single man had been killed. Loheide cleared and marked a landing zone with yellow smoke for the MEDEVAC helicopter, then had the rest of the element take cover against the terraces so no more casualties would be sustained by the platoon.[16]

The fight continued in hot temperatures. The Americans ran out of food and water but kept fighting. Finally, as the sun went down, the fighting died away.

At 1:30am the next morning, Afghan commandos pushed into the village of Daridam. The commandos, joined now by the returning ANA, the ANP, and the Americans behind them, walked into the village of Daridam. There was no one there; the insurgents had retreated during the night.

The battle along the road and on the ridgelines lasted 18 hours in blistering heat. US soldiers believed they faced as many as 250 insurgents, and before the fight ended about half were dead.[17]

US and ANSF members cleared the village of Chenar from Taliban control in four hours during Operation *Strong Eagle II*, on July 19. According to Captain Joseph L. Holliday, 2nd Battalion, 327th Infantry Regiment's intelligence officer: "*Strong Eagle I* dealt a strong blow to the

Taliban network in the area. They did not have the ability to mass forces against us." There were no ANSF or US forces reported killed or wounded in action, but four individuals were detained.[18]

When the operations ended, US forces stayed for a month after Afghan police returned to Daridam. The police didn't stay for long on their own before retreating and refusing to go back without US forces to back them up. Without a strong military or police presence, the area slipped back under Taliban control.

As the 101st fought to control RC-East, ISAF made a significant organizational change by dividing RC-South into two parts, establishing RC-Southwest on July 3. The change was made due to the increase of ISAF and US troops from 35,000 in late 2009 to 50,000 by July. RC-Southwest was tasked with the responsibility of overseeing operations in Helmand and Nimruz provinces. Commanded by USMC Major General Richard Mills, the forces assigned included the 1st Marine Expeditionary Force (1 MEF), 2nd Brigade Combat Team of the 101st Airborne Division (Combined Task Force Strike [CTFS]), and ANA 215 Corps, together with British, Norwegian, and Georgian forces for a combined total of approximately 27,000 personnel, with headquarters at Camp Leatherneck.

On June 23 General McChrystal resigned as ISAF and US Forces Commander. His resignation was due to the publication of an article in *Rolling Stone* magazine in which he and his staff made unflattering remarks about Vice President Joe Biden, National Security Advisor James L. Jones, US Ambassador to Afghanistan Karl W. Eikenberry, and Special Representative for Afghanistan and Pakistan Richard Holbrooke, among others. General David H. Petraeus took over the position on July 4.

Operation *Dragon Strike* on September 16 was the first major offensive launched by the RC-Southwest command. At least 8,000 troops were deployed in the traditional Taliban strongholds of Arghandab, Zhari, and Panjwai districts, an area dubbed "The Heart of Darkness."

"Operation *Dragon Strike* is one of many operations designed to secure the majority of the Afghan population in the Zhari and Maiwand districts," said Colonel Arthur Kandarian, CTFS commander. It was also part of the anti-Taliban offensive projected to extend until the US and

NATO forces withdraw in October 2014. German NATO spokesman Brigadier General Josef Blotz believed that Afghan and international forces could anticipate strong battles and that the goal of the operation was to wipe out Taliban positions around Kandahar and force the militants to leave the area.

A point of contention in the operation was that the military push in Kandahar would force insurgents to shift to other provinces, particularly in the northern regions. This was a problem, since the gains from this operation would be limited if it worked only to force insurgents out of Kandahar and into Helmand, northern Afghanistan, or even across the border.

The operation got off to a quiet start with no casualties for the first several days. "Since the Operation *Dragon Strike* began, we have seen an increase in freedom of movement for the Afghan people on Highway One," said Kandarian. "We have also seen an increase in the amount of elders and leaders coming to the district center and we have been able to have the district governor go to more of the villages in the district to conduct shuras with the locals."

"By removing the firing points the Taliban use along Highway One, we remove the Taliban's ability to limit our movement in the area," said Lieutenant Reily McEvoy, platoon leader with Headquarters and Headquarters Troop, 1st Squadron, 75th Cavalry Regiment, one of the units in the operation. "This is what we trained for and this is a classic dismounted fight."

But it wasn't all that simple. The roads, fields, orchards, and seemingly every house were laced with IEDs. By the third week in September the battalion had suffered seven men killed and 14 who have sustained life-changing injuries, including four double leg amputations, and, according to one account, dozens of others had been wounded within a square mile of the "The Gardens" of the Arghandab Valley.

"I have been lying in the middle of a road doing my job, with bullets skipping off the dirt and I'm laughing," said Sergeant Jay Huggins, a Texan who served with one of the US Army bomb disposal teams in the Arghandab. "But, man ... when I step out into those fields ... it's a different matter. My wife gave me a piece of scripture from Isaiah 54:17: 'No weapon that is formed against thee shall prosper.' Thinking about that is how I get through a day in the gardens."

At Strongpoint Lugo, a US manned compound, a 101st Airborne soldier was blown in half by a device on the other side of the compound wall. Another had lost a leg in the assault to take it. Often the only way to clear an area of IEDs was to either bomb it or, if it was a structure, bulldoze it flat. Before the operation began, hundreds of families, and in some cases entire villages, were abandoned due to pressure from insurgents. Taliban militants took over hundreds of deserted homes and other structures, turning some into homemade bomb factories, fighting positions, or weapons stores. Taliban bombs hidden in buildings, ditches, walls, and other structures in the region killed at least 97 Afghan civilians and injured another 167.

When the operation ended on December 31, 34 US soldiers, one Canadian soldier, and more than seven Afghan police had been killed. Another cost of the operation was the $1.4 million in compensation paid to Afghan civilians whose properties were rigged with explosives by Taliban militants and later demolished by Afghan and coalition security forces. General David Petraeus said: "Remember that it is the insurgents who rig these buildings with IEDs and use them as weapon caches that threaten local Afghans. It's that Taliban tactic that has necessitated the targeted destruction of buildings too dangerous to inhabit or rehabilitate."

In January 2011 families began returning to their villages, and each family was greeted by the ANSF with a "welcome home" gift of humanitarian aid supplies. "Helping the residents back into the village is a huge victory," said Captain Walter Tompkins, commander of Company B, 1st Battalion, 66th Armored Regiment. "Not only does it show huge gains in perception of security, but also presents a great opportunity to truly partner with the residents of the village. We want to develop this village and make it a model for the surrounding communities. We want to show them that with improved security comes rapid development."[19]

This was part of "build" phase of COIN. Its success rested on the ANSF's ability to keep the districts secure. Based on previous post-operation experience, reliance on the ANSF to ensure long-term security was not something to be taken as a given.

As the size and tempo of operations increased in RC-Southwest, forces in the mountainous RC-East fought to contain the flow of insurgents coming over the border from Pakistan. The Pech River Valley, in Kunar province in RC-East, was a transit route for insurgent fighters from Pakistan. It was also only five miles from the Korengal Valley, where the US had lost 42 men before shutting down all combat outposts earlier in the year. After the pull back, insurgent activity increased, which, in turn, led to a series of counterinsurgency operations by ANA and US forces.

The first was on October 15 in response to an attack by a number of insurgents, reportedly from the village of Matin, just north of the Shuryak Valley in the central Pech River Valley, that purposefully damaged the road in neighboring Tarale. Tarale elders asked the insurgents from Matin to stop, but their requests had no effect. Local Afghans from Tarale then attempted to forcefully remove the insurgents from their village. The insurgents fired into Tarale and escaped back to Matin. No injuries were reported, and ANSF responded, but could not track down the attackers.[20]

A day later, soldiers from 2nd Company, 1st Commando Kandak, partnered with US Special Forces and elements of the 101st ABD Division (Task Force Bulldog), killed 13 insurgents and recovered and reduced four weapons caches during combat operations in Darah-ye Pech district. The four-day operation was to clear known insurgent strongholds in Tsam, Chenar Now, and Matanga villages. On the last day, CAS aircraft engaged a group of armed men maneuvering toward high ground, killing 13 insurgents with precision-guided munitions.[21]

"[ANSF] have said that they will pursue the insurgents until they can be assured that the security situation in the Pech Valley improves," said US Army Lieutenant Colonel Joe Ryan, 1st Battalion, 327th Infantry Regiment commander. "They have brought the fight to areas where they believe the enemy now feels the safest, but will not feel safe there any longer."[22]

This may have held true for Kunar province, but apparently not for the insurgents over in Paktika. On October 30 soldiers from Company C, 2nd Battalion, 506th Infantry Regiment, 101st Airborne manning COP Margah in Paktika province were attacked by more than 120 Haqqani Network and al Qaeda fighters for the second time that month.

It started at around 1:20am, but before the attackers got to the COP Private James R. Platt, on guard at the northeast corner in the turret of an MRAP (Mine-Resistant Ambush-Protected vehicle) spotted movement and reported it to Sergeant Donald R. Starks, a fire team leader. The insurgents fired an RPG at the vehicle, followed by concentrated small-arms fire.

"I began to lay down suppressive fire, to give Platt a chance to exit the vehicle," said Private Michael T. Landis. "At this time, the enemy had 30-plus men [attacking] the OP," said Landis. "We got into firing positions so the enemy couldn't flank us."

The situation developed so quickly that some of men didn't have time to put on all their battle gear. "Sergeant Starks, even though he didn't have time to put his boots on or find all his gear, still maneuvered through the enemy while being fired on," Landis said. "It was almost unreal for him to keep positions manned and keep in contact with Margah Base while engaging the enemy."

With the observation point under attack, the soldiers down the mountainside at the COP below prepared to defend their outpost. Specialist Matthew D. Keating, a gunner, picks up the story: "Under heavy small-arms fire, my team immediately ran to the rooftop mortar position and started preparing rounds to provide suppressive mortar fire for the soldiers under attack at the observation point."

With the rounds prepared, the soldiers wasted no time and began raining down mortar fire on the enemy. "Shortly after I reached the roof top, Sergeant Reed and Specialist Keating made their way to the roof and manned the 60mm mortar system," said 1st Lieutenant Christopher S. MacGeorge, a platoon leader. "I let them know we were taking contact from the [valleys] to the west and they immediately began dropping mortars in that direction."

Meanwhile, at the OP, the enemy was massing more men for the attack, and the six soldiers were giving their best effort to continue pushing them back. "Private Timothy James had run across open ground under fire to reach the southeast machine-gun position, which ended up being essential to defending our ground," said Starks. "While at that position, he was able to fire the [rocket launcher] as well as throw two grenades in the direction of the enemy."

Landis says: "Sergeant Starks positioned himself on the [light crew-served machine gun], Private James was on the .50-cal on the northwest, and Private Platt and I were behind the bunker waiting on more enemies to come up the road."

With the enemy surging, Starks realigned his men to better defend against the threat. "Private Platt yelled to me that they were coming up on the OP from the road entrance, so I sent Private Morehouse to assist in eliminating the threat by [increasing] fire from the bunker," Starks says. "At that time, I informed Margah Base that our situation was getting worse because they were beginning to rush us and that I had observed more insurgents running up the road to increase their numbers."

"Private Platt and I were both laying down a steady rate of fire, engaging the enemy to the southeast of the OP," said Private Livingston D. Morehouse, an infantryman with C Company. "They were so close we could hear them speak to each other."

Margah Base soldiers at the bottom of the mountainside were on the rooftop doing everything they could to assist their brothers in arms while they battled a surging enemy at the OP above. The insurgents breached the outer defenses, briefly captured an MRAP vehicle and used its weapons against the COP's defenders.

"Sergeant Clifford Edwards was now acquiring enemy targets with the [grenade launcher] from the firing position located on the rooftop directly to our front," Keating said. "I fired one HE round to the northwest and Sergeant Edwards immediately came back with a correction of left 50ft drop 50ft, he was also firing his personal weapon while giving these corrections." Keating said they kept adjusting the mortar fire as they spotted muzzle flashes or enemy movement, and fired rounds to the northwest, south, and southeast.

An OP provides early warning of attacks for the main COP. Since the warning had been provided and the OP was running low on ammo, Starks decided it was the ideal time to withdraw and pull back to Margah Base. "Everyone was reporting that the ammunition was running low so I made an attempt to reach the ammo bunker, which was between our position and the enemy," he said. "Due to heavy small-arms fire and grenades, I was not successful in retrieving any ammunition."

The men continued to stave off enemies coming toward them, but it became increasingly difficult because they were within 15–20ft, so Starks began making preparations to tactically reposition his men back to Margah Base. "Right then we started taking RPG fire again, which had wounded two of my men with shrapnel," Starks said. "All of us took cover behind some cliffs about 100m down and I gave the mortarmen on the roof the signal that we were clear from the OP." Both soldiers, despite their injuries, were able to move down the mountain toward Margah Base.

Once the signal was given that the OP had been repositioned, MacGeorge explained that Specialist Brett Capstick moved off the roof to assist with the 81mm mortar system and the team began to bombard the OP with 155mm mortars from Forward Operating Base Boris, as well as 81mm mortars and 60mm mortars on the roof. "I tried to direct them best I could," Starks said. "I told them they were hitting danger close and that they needed to fire higher up the hill to the east."

Soon after the barrage of mortar and artillery fire was laid, the air-weapons team (AWT) was on site with AH-64 Apache helicopters to finish the job by accurately targeting the enemy from the sky above. "Once the AWT was on station, everything calmed down as they began engaging the enemy," MacGeorge said.

The AWT continued to engage the enemy until 2:00pm. When the dust settled, five soldiers were wounded, but 92 enemy combatants were killed, two were wounded and captured, and numerous enemy weapons and communication systems were confiscated.

With the wounded treated and medical evacuation complete, the complex attack was defeated. It would not have been possible without the bravery of the soldiers involved. "We knew air was red. We knew we were outnumbered, and we knew that the insurgents wanted to take over the COP, but all hands were on deck that night ready to fight, backfill, and give everything we asked of them and more," said Schulz.

More than 90 insurgents died in a counter-barrage of gunfire, helicopter-fired missiles, and bombs. There were no US fatalities.[23]

On the overcast night of November 8, COP Margah was attacked again. "They believed the heavy cloud cover and fog would prevent CAS from blowing them up," Captain DeShane Greaser said. "It did not. There was a VBIED heading to the COP and after the first bombs hit we got reports that the enemy said, 'We're turning around, there are jets overhead.'" No fewer than 70 Taliban dead were counted outside COP Margah when this attack ended.[24]

Major Aaron Ruona, 336th "Rocketeers" Fighter Squadron, an F-15E Weapons Systems Officer (WSO), talks about what it was like flying CAS:

> We flew seven days a week; all the days were the same. Get up, try to get a couple of hours in the gym, get a brief from squadron, a brief from intel, fly from three to six hours depending on the tasking, land, do some paperwork,

go home, watch a movie, repeat day in and day out. Sometimes get food in there at the chow hall. I stopped doing that a couple of months and then ate cereal at the squadron the last four months.

On my first mission I was recovering from food poisoning so I threw up a few times before the mission and a couple of times during the flight. It was a real eye opener. First sortie, talking to four or five different JTACs, being sick at the same time was pretty interesting.

You could write a whole novel for everyday missions covering the guys on the ground. Even when nothing happens or they don't get shot at, just talking with them. The tenseness that can be in the air when they're concerned about a particular person walking down the road, that alone could be a novel – 50 of them are all the same but two that stand out were in the fall of my deployment. There wasn't snow on the ground yet and it wasn't all that cold.

In one a group of JTACs got stranded out in the middle of a patrol somewhere, low on food, low on bullets up in the mountains. They had taken some casualties so they were bringing some helos in to get those guys MEDEVACed out while they were still under fire. We were the only two planes on station. The helicopters were rolling in dropping speedballs: big bundles of food and ammunition. So me and our wingman were on three different frequencies trying to coordinate between the helos, MEDEVAC, JTACs on the ground, and the guys back in the FOB. The guys on the ground were taking sniper fire, walking through trails, and at one point they got lost.

It was three or four hours of nonstop talking and tension. Every few minutes we were putting bombs on the ground trying to suppress fire. If you ask me I would say it was about a two-hour mission but in fact it was four or five hours. When you come back and land you're just exhausted. We were able to get the guys out. It's not one I'll forget.

Another tough mission for Major Ruona was in October flying support for teams looking for the British aid worker Linda Norgrove. She had been abducted by insurgents as she travelled in a convoy of two vehicles in Kunar province to attend a ceremony to inaugurate an irrigation project and was being held in the village of Dineshgal, Kunar province.

There were small [SF] teams set up along the ridgelines in the northeast in very isolated locations and apparently one of these teams got compromised.

Maybe three to six guys were on this very small peak. They said there were between 6 to 12 Taliban coming up the ridge and the team was taking fire.

We had to isolate their location to a peak where we couldn't actually see them, but they wanted us to engage only a couple of hundred yards down the ridge from them. It was a situation that I wasn't really comfortable with. There was a little saddle and I wasn't sure if he was talking about the close part or the near part but it was still Danger Close. I told him "I'm not going to drop here, but I'll drop back here and start walking closer."

I put the first bomb down just further out from where the team was and then adjusted fire. I felt really good [as the] first one went. Okay it wasn't near them and then more a little bit close. Three or four seconds prior impact where the ground commander said the attackers were they opened up with RPG right before the bomb hit. I was satisfied but nervous because it was so close. That's when you tell them on the radio "Bombs gone, thirty seconds, take cover."

It's a gut wrenching feeling.

Although the team was safe, Linda Norgrove was killed by her kidnappers during the rescue attempt by US SOF teams.

To keep the pressure on insurgents moving through Kunar province in RC-East, 1st Battalion, 327th Infantry Regiment, 101st Airborne Division and 1st Battalion, 75th Ranger Regiment, along with an ANA Kandak, air assaulted into the mountains surrounding the Watahar Valley, part of the eastern region of the Pech River Valley, on November 12.

Codenamed Operation *Bulldog Bite*, the multiple nighttime air assaults hit small villages to dig out insurgents. "There's a myth, I think, amongst us coalition forces and International Security Assistance Forces that there are some places we can't go," said US Army Lieutenant Colonel Joseph A. Ryan, TF Bulldog commander. "That is absolutely and unequivocally untrue. We can go anywhere we want to go. We have the technology to support it, but most importantly … our infantrymen are tougher, stronger, more capable, and better trained than the enemy is."

After conducting an air assault onto the high ground the troops moved out. "Picture the rockiest, crappiest terrain you can think of at 7,500ft with 75lb on your back taking you down the mountain," said Kammerer, a squad leader assigned to Company B.

The first US soldier was killed during combat on November 12. Two days later, US troops encountered heavy resistance, and five soldiers from Alpha Company were killed. A significant number were wounded during the six-hour-long firefight.

HH-60 Pave Hawk rescue flights Pedro 83 and 84 from USAF 33rd Rescue Squadron were first on scene at the firefight. The 33rd had been tasked to provide medical and casualty evacuation (CASEVAC) support for ground operations while deployed to Afghanistan. Captain Brown said he can recall the unsettling feeling he had the day his team was called to assist the Alpha Company of the Army's 1st Battalion, 327th Infantry Regiment, 1st Brigade Combat Team, 101st Airborne Division. "I had a gut feeling it was going to come to us," he said.

"It was a fairly routine call," pararescueman Master Sergeant Roger Sparks from Alaska's 212th Rescue Squadron said. "I thought: 'No big deal.'"

Within minutes of receiving the call to evacuate two wounded soldiers, Captain Marcus Maris (the flight lead and pilot for Pedro 83) and his team launched both helicopters, establishing on-scene overwatch of the battlefield. But on the five-minute flight into the zone, Sparks began to feel that something was wrong. The number of reported casualties jumped to six. "The guy on the radio was super emotional," Sparks said, "Cursing, freaking out."

The PJs (pararescue jumpers) were told that the area had been calm for 15 minutes, however, Sparks and Bailey prepared to be lowered by cable from the hovering chopper. Despite their rapid response, intensified RPG and machine-gun fire, interlocking enemy fields, and steep rocky terrain had forced Alpha Company into a defensive position, leading to a total of 11 casualties. A split second after Captain Koa Bailey, a combat rescue officer, and Sparks touched ground, the ear-shattering explosions of RPGs rang out overhead. "I don't know how we didn't get killed," Sparks said, "or why the helicopter didn't get hit and come crashing down on us."

Heavy machine-gun fire raked the area. The helicopter crew shot back, showering the two prostrate PJs with empty shell casings. "I cannot imagine a more comforting sound than the .50-cal firing and casings raining down on us," Sparks said. "You could feel the concussion from the RPGs while we sat in the hover," said Staff Sergeant Brandon Hill, a flight engineer with Kadena's 33rd Rescue Squadron. "The whole time we were being shot at."

Unrelenting enemy fire coupled with Alpha Company's depleting ammunition and increasing casualties made establishing a clear landing zone and protective cover for CASEVAC nearly impossible. The rescue mission quickly became a dangerous race against the clock.

"We knew based on the situation and the severity of the injuries, if we waited any longer, the risk of more US casualties expiring would increase exponentially," explained Captain Maris. "We devised a game plan and committed."

The two aircrews held a risky but offensive position that allowed them to suppress enemy aggression while hoisting down Captain Bailey and Sergeant Sparks to assess the situation on the ground and set up a small triage area. Technical Sergeant Mike Welles, the chalk two aerial gunner for Pedro 84, remembers the moment enemy forces focused their attention on the rescue teams: "I remember looking at them (Pedro 83) in the hover and looking at their gunner engaging. I could see a 3ft flame of discontent coming out of his gun. I followed where the rounds were going and could tell they were under our aircraft. As soon as you can hear your .50-cal on the other side of the aircraft go off, it's a good feeling."

Staff Sergeant James "Jimmy" Settle recalls an enemy round coming up through the deck of the helicopter he was riding in. The round struck him in the forehead between his skull and his combat helmet. With a now-wounded PJ onboard, the helicopter diverted to an emergency aid station where Settle was treated for 24 hours, as per protocol. "I wanted to get back into the fight," he says of this period on the ground. "I saw my guys bringing wounded in and going back out… I just knew I had to be there, too."

For the next two hours, Pedro 83 rotated through to a forward refuel and armament point, dropping "speedball" water and ammunition pouches to the remaining Alpha Company soldiers. By the end of the fight, both teams had resupplied the remaining soldiers and completed multiple pararescue insertions and patient extractions, saving the lives of seven wounded soldiers and bringing back the remains of four soldiers who had died.

"The people we're going to pick up, fellow Americans, are what it's all about," said Captain Thomas Stengl, the co-pilot for Pedro 84. "At the end of the day, we will do whatever it takes to bring them home," he added.[25, 26]

When the firefight ended there were only eight unwounded soldiers left in Alpha Company. The six-hour fight was one of the deadliest incidents of Operation *Bulldog Bite*.

Captain Joseph Andresky, an HH-60 pilot, says it was his worst mission. "It was madhouse. Five or six days of sustained operations. Pulling people out like cordwood. You compartmentalize, wait to the end, then bottle it up in a jar someplace, lock it in a safe, throw away the combination, and try not to go back there."[27]

After being wounded, Staff Sergeant Settle tended to the wounded and injured under constant fire. He was credited with saving 35 lives by the end of the operation and a high number of assists in supporting his fellow PJs. "I joined the PJs to help people, to save lives," he says.

By the time Operation *Bulldog Bite* ended on November 25 six members of the 101st, one Army Ranger, and three ANA soldiers had been killed. An estimated 52 insurgents were casualties, the majority occurring during the attack on Alpha Company. Major General John Campbell, 101st Airborne Division commanding general said: "This is a huge blow to the enemy. The operation also caught the fighters by surprise."

It turned out to be the last operation of the year by either side in RC-East.[28]

Down in RC-Southwest 3rd Battalion, 7th Marine Regiment (3/7) took over the infamous Sangin District, Helmand province. In four years the British had lost 106 men, including 36 in 2010 alone. In September, 3rd Battalion, 5th Marine Regiment (3/5) relieved 3rd Battalion, 7th Marine Regiment.

After taking over the Marines closed more the half of the 22 British bases around the town of Sangin. One British officer said: "It's a hard pill to swallow that the Rifles put so much sweat and blood into establishing these patrol bases only for them to be dismantled by the Americans. They are trying a new approach, but it was one tried by us in the past and gave the Taliban the chance to plant IEDs wherever they wanted."[29]

This proved to be the case. Between October 6 and 13 nine Marines were killed by IEDs. The rise in IED casualties was caused in part by the increased numbers of directional fragmentation-charge IEDs contained in a coffee can or another small, metal device and packed with nuts, bolts, or spark plugs, attached to 10–20lb of homemade explosives.

The area was on the road to the strategic Kajaki hydroelectric dam, which turned the deserts of the province into Afghanistan's breadbasket. The Marines found Sangin to be a major transit point for Taliban fighters and drug runners. Major General Richard P. Mills called Sangin, "the last piece of prime real estate that the insurgents are contesting [in Helmand province]. Once he loses that, having already lost the entire lower valley and the lower river basins, he will have a difficult time re-establishing himself in the province. He will be resigned to living in the desert, living in the fringes of the province." Lieutenant Colonel Jason Morris, commander of the 3/5, said, "Sangin has been an area where drug lords, Taliban, and people who don't want the government to come in and legitimize things have holed up."

The casualties kept rising even as the Marines tried to work with the local population. In November, a Marine was shot in the head and killed in an alley just off Sangin's bazaar shortly before a Marine civil affairs team arrived. The team was forced to lob green smoke grenades into the alley and sprint past to avoid being shot at themselves. Working with the people meant working with Afghans affiliated with the Taliban.

"There are checks and balances, but there is an inevitability that some money is going into people's pockets," said Phil Weatherill, a British government advisor. "Whether it's small-t Taliban or corrupt contractors, I don't know. But this is Afghanistan." Lieutenant Karl Kadon said it could be difficult to accept that Marines were coordinating with, and possibly even helping, the enemy, but saw no choice. "This is a tough job because I have friends who have gotten hurt or killed, and I know I'm conversing with Taliban on a daily basis," he says. "But it's one of those things where you have to give a little to get a little."

The Taliban was not always willing to cooperate. One case in point was a woman running an orphanage. "The woman said the Taliban told her that if they ever saw her taking any assistance from international forces, they would kill her or one of the children," Kadon said. Shortly after the message was delivered, a suicide bomber blew himself up nearby, but luckily he didn't harm the woman or the children.[30]

The Marines continued to take casualties. In November alone they lost 12 men in Helmand province, seven of them in Sangin. By early December they had lost 16 men and over 50 wounded in more than a hundred firefights.

When RC-Southwest was established, TF Wolfpack (3rd Squadron, 2nd Stryker Cavalry Regiment, or 3-2 Stryker), commanded by Lieutenant Colonel Bryan Denny, was assigned responsibility for the Maiwand District on the border between Kandahar and Helmand provinces. Task Force Wolfpack noted insurgents had previously been able to move with little difficulty along cultivated farmland south of Highway 1, which permitted them to bury IEDs along main routes across the district.

In late 2010, 3-2 Stryker constructed an 8km wall of barriers through a dry riverbed from Highway 1 directly southward to the Arghandab River, approximately 10km west of the Zhari border. The "Wolfpack Wall," named for 3-2 Stryker's Task Force call sign, had two primary crossing points along east–west routes of travel into Zhari district. Task Force Wolfpack established watchtowers, set up traffic control, and conducted inspections to limit the amount of illicit material traveling along those routes. Channeling civilian traffic through the monitored access areas forced insurgents away from cultivated land and into open exposed lines of travel. Although insurgents targeted the Wolfpack Wall with IEDs, 3-2 Stryker employed mine-clearing line charges (MiCLCs), a rocket with a long line of explosives attached to it, in an effort to detonate the buried explosives, the idea being that the explosive force from the MiCLC would set off any IEDs buried in the road. Once the wall was completed, 3-2 Stryker established overwatch through the winter months.[31]

The Marines also undertook to clear the main route into Sangin of IEDs. Starting on November 29, Operation *Outlaw Wrath* focused on clearing Route 611, an important route used to keep Sangin's patrol base supplied with food and water, and one known to be strewn with IEDs. "We've traveled that road plenty of times and every time we do, we get hit," said Lance Corporal Matt Dahlman, a heavy equipment operator attached to 3/5. "If eight days being stuck in a bulldozer is what it takes to stop that from happening then it was well worth it!"

The Taliban had set up checkpoints along portions of Route 611 where locals were taxed for money and items they had bought at the nearby bazaar. The taxation became so serious that the local economy was affected, causing prices to inflate.

"Our engineers were not only able to open up the route for mobility purposes, but also to better the economic problems that the citizens of

Sangin were facing," said Lieutenant Colonel Andrew Niebel, the battalion commander for 1st Combat Engineering Brigade (CEB).

MiCLCs were the main tool used to begin the clearing. After shooting an MiCLC, bulldozers would push away the rubble and uncover any unexploded IEDs, a dangerous job for those involved in the process.

"I never stopped getting chills while I was out there working, but the training the Marine Corps gives you helps a lot when trying to manage your fear," Dahlman explained. "It was easy to clear my mind and be unafraid. It is just one of those things that you have to deal with."

While the road was being cleared by the CEB, 3/5 along with ANA soldiers provided security and overwatch to the left and right of Route 611. Both groups worked together, ensuring that neither got too far ahead or behind.

Local Afghans were friendly toward many of the coalition forces, and appreciated their work to remove IEDs and push the Taliban out of the area. "It is important that we show them we are here to help them by keeping the roads free of IEDs," said 1st Lieutenant Chris Thrasher, a platoon commander.

After eight days of route clearing in Sangin, the Marines of 1st CEB and 3/5, along with ANA soldiers, had made Route 611 safe to travel along for the first time in three years, according to Bock. With more than 50 IEDs found and destroyed, coalition forces had helped bring security and stability to one of Helmand province's vital roadways.[32]

As casualties rose and COIN efforts continued, Major General Mills stated: "We are making steady progress. Overall we're all pointing in the right direction." According to the general, most of the Taliban's top commanders in Helmand had now been killed or captured: "Militarily we are hammering them. We're going to pressure this guy every step of the way. He won't get his two weeks in Florida this year, he won't get his vacation during winter time. We're going to push, because I want this battlefield to be completely different come spring."[33]

In November, NATO leaders endorsed a plan to wind down its combat mission by 2014. However, the announcement came with a warning that there would be "inevitable setbacks" in the work to complete the transition by the end of 2014.

Geoff Morrell, the Pentagon spokesman, added another caveat: "It does not necessarily mean that everywhere in the country [Afghan forces] will necessarily be in the lead and it does not mean that all US or coalition forces would necessarily be gone by that date. There may very well be the need for forces to remain in-country, albeit, hopefully, at smaller numbers, to assist the Afghans as they assume lead responsibility for the security of their country." US commitment remained open ended for at least another three years.

The year of 2010 was the deadliest yet for US forces, with 499 men and women killed and 5,246 wounded. One positive note was that poppy production had halved from 2009, largely due to a plant infection, which had drastically reduced yields. As for the war, US, ANA, and coalition forces had some successes in the field. However, in several instances operations had failed to complete their objective. There was also no measureable decrease in the enemy's fighting capability, and in fact it seemed to have increased in most of the country. Even though he was no longer in charge, General McChrystal's enhanced COIN strategy remained in place, but without measurable results.

Chapter 11
DRAWDOWN, 2011

At the beginning of January there were 97,000 US troops in Afghanistan, mostly stationed in RC-East and RC-Southwest. Of these, 18,500 were Marines in Helmand and Kandahar provinces. In anticipation of another Taliban spring offensive 1,400 Marines of 3rd Battalion, 8th Marine Regiment and helicopters stationed on board the USS *Kearsarge* (LHD-3, an amphibious assault ship) were deployed to Helmand to bolster security operations.

Keeping with Marine Major General Mills' statement about not giving the Taliban fighters a winter vacation, 400 Marines of 2nd Battalion, 1st Marine Regiment ran Operation *Godfather*, a three-day clearing mission in Durzay, Garmsir district, Helmand province, on January 14. Intelligence reported there were 30 insurgents in Durzay, one of the last Taliban-controlled villages in Helmand.

"If we were here alone, we'd be shot at," said Lieutenant Brett De Maria, while leading a morning patrol through farming villages. "But we've got air support and tons of vehicles."

"During the clear, we had numerous IED cache finds and opium cache seizures," said 1st Lieutenant Shannon Ashley, a platoon commander with Echo Company. Ultimately the Marines recovered about two dozen weapons caches. The operation in Durzay, considered the last real village in central Helmand province before the Pakistan border, left the Taliban with few places to go in south-central Helmand.

As part of ongoing counterinsurgency efforts in the province, engineers and heavy equipment operators with Combat Logistics Battalion 3, 1st Marine Logistics Group (Forward) constructed two bridges and improved several stretches of road leading into Durzay. Working continuously, approximately 25 Marines with CLB-3's Engineer Company completed these engineering projects in less than three days.

According to Lieutenant Elizabeth Stroud, platoon commander, Engineer Company, CLB-3, 1st MLG (FWD), in the nearly ten years that coalition forces have spent operating in Afghanistan, January marked the first time Durzay residents had seen examples of a US presence.

"I've spoken with many of the residents in Durzay, and they are very thankful for our work here," said Stroud. "In talking with them, I found that they realize [our] ultimate goal is to provide them with freedom, and that the Taliban has been driven out. We're also thankful that [the clearing operation] has provided us this opportunity to be some of the first individuals to interact with [Durzay's] residents."[1]

The ANA-led Operation *Omid Shash* ("Hope 6"), in mid-February, kept the heat on insurgents in the Nahr-e Saraj district, Helmand province. Afghan forces organized all phases of the operation, including a complex air assault involving approximately 750 ANA troops along with roughly 250 Marines from TF Helmand and elements of the British 2nd Battalion Parachute Regiment and 1st Battalion Irish Guards. It was the first operation in which ANA forces outnumbered coalition troops.

According to Marine Lieutenant Colonel David Eastman: "Operation *Omid Shash* is an incredible achievement. The [ANA] brigade's ability to plan and conduct successful operations combined with their martial spirit and determination to succeed is making them a force to be reckoned with in Helmand. We have been especially impressed with the development of their specialist capabilities, particularly in the vital area of countering the IED threat."[2]

The operation and its five predecessors were designed to assist the ANA in learning how to plan, coordinate, and execute complex operations. The series also allowed ANA and coalition forces to interact with the local population. This helped build rapport and assure them of the ANA's ability to protect them.

Map 4: ISAF Regional Commands, 2011

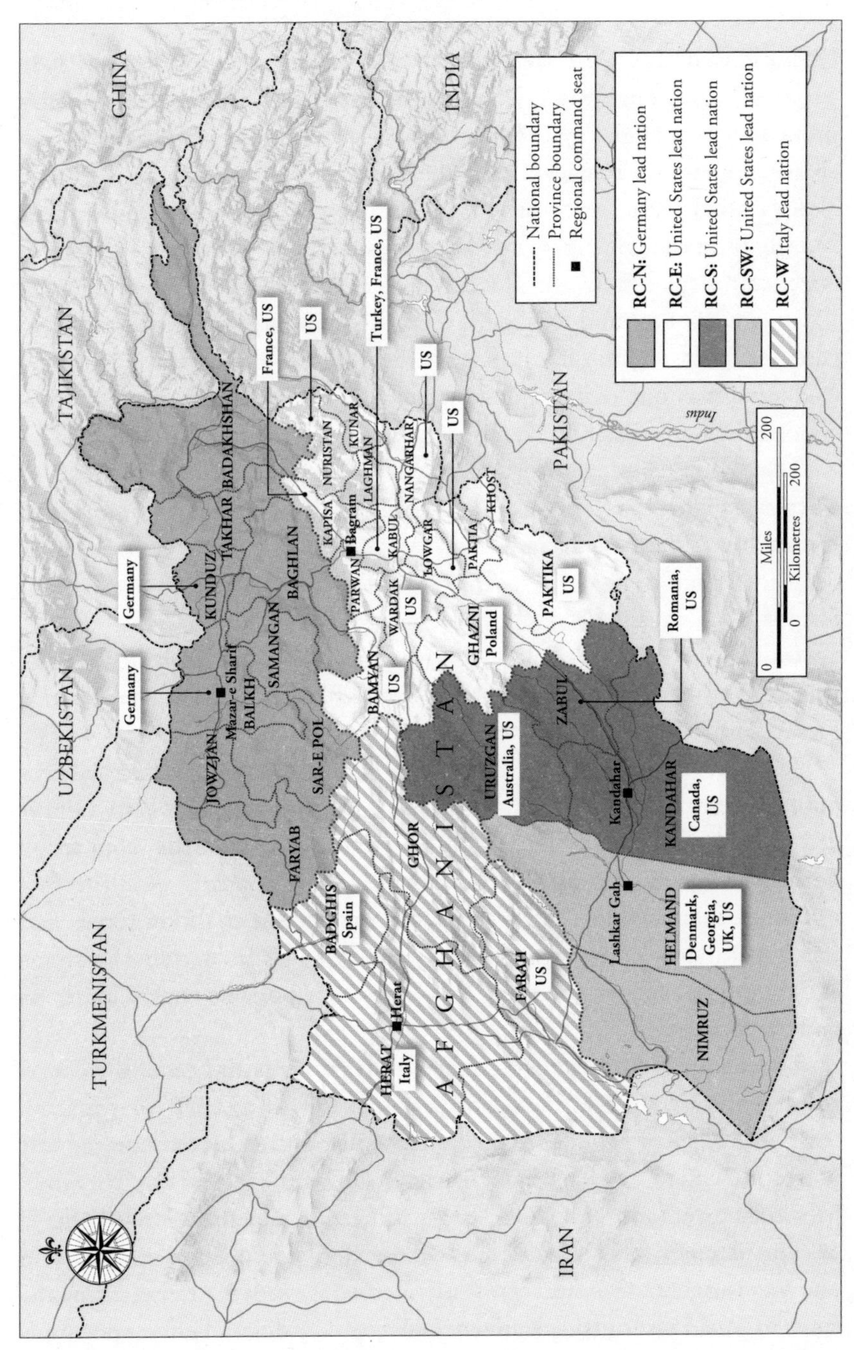

Operations in RC-West were mostly joint patrols by ISAF and ANSF personnel along Highway 1, which runs through Herat, Farah, and Badghis provinces, and Highway 8 from Herat City to the key northern border crossing point into Turkmenistan. The highways were clear, but the Taliban and its allies were active in villages and towns across the region. Bala Murghab in Badghis province was a sanctuary in which insurgents effectively displaced nearly all local farmers and villagers in the valley.

Unlike RC-East and RC-South there were no large-scale operations to root out the insurgents, but rather a series of small-unit actions. Operation *Red Sand* was one of these, held in northern Bala Murghab on April 2. Among the units was Red Platoon, Bulldog Troop's scouts.

The scout team members were Major Jonathan Lauer – the 7-10 Cavalry squadron operations officer, who was visiting from Camp Stone, Herat, for a battlefield circulation – Lieutenant Joseph C. Law, Staff Sergeant Mundo, Staff Sergeant Fletcher, Sergeant Amenta, Sergeant Sheppard, Sergeant Nalesnick, Sergeant Evenson, Specialist Evans, Specialist Newland, Specialist Aguirre, Specialist West, Private Budetti, Private Grubham, Private Kukosky, Private Bradley, Private Sims-Sparks, Private Hill, Sergeant Benavides, and Private Arnold.

Air Force journalist Technical Sergeant Kevin Wallace, Navy photographer Petty Officer 1st Class Pearl, Navy dog handler Petty Officer 3rd Class Ryan Lee, and his dog Valdo were also part of the scout troop during the operation. ANA forces accompanied the patrol.

The scouts patrolled farther into the valley than coalition forces had ever gone, and spent the night reconnoitering villages and plotting locations and fighting positions, for themselves as well as possible enemy locations and contact points.

The next night, all but one of the scouts, along with Lee, dog Valdo, a handful of ANA soldiers, Pearl, and Wallace returned to COP Metro. Army Staff Sergeant Ray Mundo, Red Platoon scout, injured his back on the first patrol and had to stay back at COP Metro during the second day. However, he waited on standby, in case a QRF was needed. The team moved out.

They secured an area of ruins where they could operate patrols in known insurgent areas, and egress by riverbed if needed. After securing the ruins in a field just outside Kamusari village, they dug in fighting positions and fortified the eroded walls and doorways with sandbags, all under the cover of darkness. They also patrolled the nearby Kamusari and Joy Gange villages, looking for evidence of mines, IEDs, or booby traps.

At daybreak, Bulldog scouts launched a patrol into a known insurgent hotbed and tried to convince locals to not support the insurgency and instead start supporting their government, with promises that a better life and development were being made possible.

"What we're doing here is vital to the security in this area," said US Army Lieutenant Joseph Law, Red Platoon leader. "This activity will hamper the [insurgents'] will to fight and may make them think twice before continuing to terrorize local villagers."

Not accepting Law's offers, the village elders became argumentative and accused the team of wrongdoing and trespassing. Tension grew in the air, and the villagers became visually upset, spitting and behaving in a way you rarely see in people who typically put a lot of stock into saving face and showing respect.

Petty Officer Pearl recounts what happened after the meeting:

> After a key leader engagement patrol through Kamusari village, we began our exfil south towards ruins just south of a two-story compound. I noticed the ANA company sergeant was pulled to the side by one of the local nationals, they whispered to one another and he immediately told our interpreter there was an IED in the ruins and we should not go through there. At around 0900 we noticed groups of women and children leaving Kamusari. Some headed across the western canal and some remained in the tree line on the canal, As we headed out of the village, around a dozen fighting-age men began to line rooftops, and we knew a battle would soon ensue.

Detouring through a canal east of the ruins to disrupt the enemy's tracking, the scouts arrived at the ruins, established Observation Post Reaper, and waited for the anticipated contact to begin.

"We headed back to our fortified ruins and dug our heels in for the inevitable battle that would find us," recalled Technical Sergeant Wallace. "[In] the ruins we established OP Reaper in an eroded and roofless dilapidated, old, three-room mud hut. I was in the western-most part of the ruins with scouts Sergeant Jeff Sheppard and Private Ben Bradley. Pearl, Lee, and Valdo were also in that room."

The central room housed an ANA soldier, his platoon sergeant, the interpreter, Lieutenant Law, scout Sergeant Peter Nalesnick, and Major Lauer. Three ANA soldiers, West, scout Specialist William Newland, and forward observer Specialist Dwayne Sims-Sparks were all in the eastern room.

The team soon began taking small-arms fire. They located its source and returned fire. Most of the incoming fire was originating from a compound several hundred meters to the north of OP Reaper. Insurgents were also using canals to the east and west, flanking the ruins.

Pearl was documenting the fight using video, while Wallace took still photos. Wallace picks up the story:

> They were able to maneuver up and down the canals, spraying rounds at us at will from a wide array of cover locations. Almost immediately the fighting reached a level of intensity that forced me to lay down my camera and volley rounds back at the insurgents. I could hear several whizzing bullets passing very near to my face and body, and their sound is unforgettable. At a distance, they sounded like pops; near my position, they sounded more like loud cracks; and when they passed within inches of my ears, they sounded like a high-speed bullet train roaring by. The Taliban were bombarding us with AK-47 and a barrage of heavy machine gun [PKM] fire. As we fought, I could literally see the mud walls of our ruins being cut down by the incoming PKM fire. We needed a mortar mission or CAS desperately as we were severely outgunned, had minimal cover in the ruins and field, and the insurgent force attacking us was growing very quickly.

Dropping their cameras and grabbing their weapons Wallace and POl Pearl immediately returned fire with a 240B machine gun and an M4 on the compound and other positions in that area as we continued to receive small arms right on top of the team's position and in the vicinity of bend in the creek bed.

"I called to troop requesting a fire mission and asking for CAS immediately," said First Lieutenant Law. "I told the ANA company sergeant to walk his RPG gunners on targets in the south side of Kamusari village, the firefight continued as Taliban dismounts fired the first RPG which landed just short of the patrol base impacting 150m in front of our position."

Italian Army soldiers from FOB Todd began laying mortar fire into the field west of where most the insurgents were attacking. The first mortar hit about 25 meters from OP Reaper's position. Wallace remembers each falling mortar shook the ground like an enormous bass drum, rattling his bones and soul. "The first mortar stunned me for a moment, then coming out of the haze I joined Sheppard and Bradley, calling out mortar positions to Law. Under Sims-Spark's directions, mortars moved closer and closer to the target. The enemy assault grew in intensity and I recall wondering if we'd make it out alive. Our 15-man team seemed doomed."

The firefight continued for more than an hour and insurgents began hitting the ruins with RPG fire from the northern compound. They initially hit the ground in front of the center room. Next they hit the front wall between the center and western room, and then directly hit the wall on the western room. At that time, Lt. Law was calling for close-air support because it seemed apparent the ruins could not handle more direct RPG hits. Before CAS arrived, the insurgents landed an RPG directly into the western room.

Wallace recalls:

> Law was calling on someone to verify no insurgents were approaching from our south. I remember thinking that in order to see over the southern wall, I would have to run, fully exposed, through a hail of enemy AK and PKM fire, jump up to grapple the top of the wall and peer over. Shaking and petrified, I garnered the courage and ran through the barrage of bullets and verified, indeed, we didn't have any surprises coming to attack us from the rear. When I raced back to the front of the room and returned scanning the western canal, Sheppard shouted at me to stay down. I knew any dumb move would burden my team and they'd have to carry my mangled body off that field. Still, keeping insurgents off our rear was worth the risk.

The fighting continued to intensify. Three RPGs hit back to back, nearly destroying the team's northern defenses. Sheppard knew it was time to move, and planned to lay down SAW fire to cover movement to the next room.

Before he had the chance to do so, the insurgents shot an RPG straight through the makeshift doorway in front of the ruins, and Wallace watched, as if in slow motion, as the grenade went straight over Bradley's head, skimmed within inches of his face and impacted the ground a few feet behind him.

"When the grenade exploded I was thrown into the front wall and saw nothing but sharp white light," Wallace says. "I couldn't smell, feel, see, and couldn't comprehend what was going on for moments. Then I heard, clear as day, Sheppard screaming, 'God damn it! Medic! Medic! Medic!' I stumbled and regained my footing and found that I had all extremities. Knowing Lee was dead, I shuddered to look back. When I did, I learned he was alive, but Valdo was in really bad shape."

The RPG struck right behind Valdo, and the dog took most of the blast. Lee seemed extremely concerned for Valdo, who was badly wounded in the stomach. Sheppard had taken shrapnel in the front of his arm, Bradley had shrapnel in his leg, and Wallace caught some in his upper back and had a concussion. But they were all alive, and while Lee and West tended to Valdo, the rest continued to fight.

As the dust cleared and there was a short break in insurgent machine-gun fire, Specialist West (the medic) made his way to the western room to assess and treat the casualties. Lieutenant Law continued requesting CAS, and planned an exfil under CAS cover. The team continued to fight, and relocated members from the western room into the central and eastern rooms, because Lieutenant Law feared the insurgents could easily target the western room again as the defenses there were in shambles. As an Italian fighter jet and a UAV arrived to provide CAS, the team, still under heavy fire, began to exfil.

Pearl said: "Lee was conscious but not reactive and appeared to be in shock. I tried to comfort him, then picked Valdo up and carried him on my shoulders as we exfilled toward the eastern canal. As I carried him, I became soaked in blood, vomit and feces. Major Lauer and Sergeant Nalesnick were already in the canal and under contact. We all worked our way about 2km south in the canal and remained under contact."

Wallace learned later that at one point, the ANA NCO, Company Sergeant Ali Ghouse, bravely protected Newland from a barrage of PKM rounds. "I had massive amounts of small-arms fire coming at me," recalled Newland. "He grabbed my shoulders and threw me to the ground and then he covered me with his own body. He stayed there until there was a break in incoming fire."

Meanwhile, the remaining team members battled their way into the canal through sporadic small-arms fire. The insurgents were seemingly coming from everywhere and descending on the canal.

Wallace says: "Though I didn't know it at the time, Law, a prior enlisted intelligence specialist with extensive tactics training, had a plan, and part of that plan was leading the insurgents into the open fields. Meanwhile, we had to get out of there, and with five of us wounded, this was no easy task.

"Once we made it to a clearing, I saw two M-ATVs [MRAP (Mine Resistant Ambush Protected) All Terrain Vehicle] waiting for us, which Law had already coordinated. Even coming out of the canal was intense, as we had to climb up about 9ft, while the roots we grabbed would break away. I had about 200 of the 550 rounds I was left with still on me, plus an AT-4 [antitank weapon], 9mm handgun, four grenades, camera gear, back-up camera gear, food, water and supplies – it was hard as hell to climb out of that canal."

The two M-ATVs were under attack in the field, and their crews answered with automatic weapons, firing at distant insurgents. Wallace says: "We could only get a handful of wounded into the back seats and in the rear of the M-ATVs so many of the team had to, once again, run across the open field dodging bullets as they made their way to COP Metro for medical air evacuation."

The COP was under attack, and the forces that stayed behind during the mission were up on the walls engaging the enemy. Law wrote about what occurred after he reached the COP: "Following the MEDEVAC, myself along with 1st Sergeant Dempsey and Major Lauer planned an immediate counteroffensive into Joy Gange village. Technical Sergeant Wallace volunteered to go with the counteroffensive dismount team, but due to limited space in the M-ATVs, had to remain at COP Metro. Unwilling to let his comrades go forward without him, Wallace quickly jumped into an ANA Ranger preparing to move north and assist. The ANA cancelled their mission, as they lacked armor and we were under heavy PKM and RPG fire. Without means to get north to assist, Wallace assumed an overwatch position on the COP Metro tower manning a sniper rifle."

Pearl was not done fighting either. "I assumed a firing position on top of COP Metro and provided overwatch for a QRF that had launched a mounted assault north of our location. Once Wallace's wounds were tended to, he joined me on a crew-serve weapon. A large-scale battle ensued, until a USAF B-l bomber dropped three bombs, one on an insurgent compound and two on an IED-making facility. The combat engagement continued until roughly 1300 hours."

Wallace concluded: "I was pleasantly surprised to find Pearl already up there on a machine gun. He and I had been through much together on that deployment and for all my life, I'll truly consider him my brother."

In the end the wounded all survived, and eventually all returned to full duty except the bomb dog Valdo. He was sent to a role-2 hospital at Camp Arena, Herat, where he was stabilized by a team of doctors. Once stable, he was transferred to Kandahar Airfield, where a veterinarian could treat him. Major Kristina Mcelroy, an Army veterinarian, was the deputy commander at Kandahar Airfield's veterinary clinic and, along with veterinary surgeon Major Ray Rudd, treated the K9. After his wounds healed, Valdo returned to full duty at Naval Station Rota, Spain, with Lee.

Operation *Red Sand*'s impact on the BMG Valley was impressive. The two-day operation destroyed insurgent compounds and IED-making facilities. Coalition forces composed primarily of the 7th Squadron, 10th Cavalry Regiment, killed an unknown number of insurgents and crippled anti-Afghan Government activities in Bala Murghab.[3]

The military working dog Valdo and his partner Petty Officer Lee had counterparts in the Air Force, Army, and Marines. Staff Sergeant Ben Seekell, Military Working Dog Handler, and his eight-year-old German shepherd Charlie were part of the USAF 4th Security Forces Squadron at Bagram Airfield.

Staff Sergeant Seekell talked about their job. "The only thing we had to worry about as dog handlers was let's go out and find some bombs and save some lives today. It's all about the job over there."

On May 8, Seekell and Charlie went out a routine patrol that turned out to be anything but routine. Seekell relates:

> It was a normal day, we were going out to look for some stuff, see what we could find. Get our hands dirty and whatnot. Mission brief early in the morning and this time went out a different gate than we normally do. No problem at all, just a change in the details.
>
> We went out just as the sun was just coming up. We were trying to get to this road – the ground we were on we weren't familiar with. We couldn't see the road, it was on the map but it wasn't in front of us. We walked a little ways and we're talking with our navigator and squad leader.

As dog team we're out front; usually me, the navigator, and my spotter led the patrol. There was a farmer's field in front of us with very deep furrows. It was also very muddy; it was hard going.

We're looking at the GPS trying to figure where we are. "Okay, we think we need to be over here, but there's no good way of getting there." So alright we're just going.

We went about a klick [kilometer] across this field and we could see the road but we weren't quite there yet. Just then out of nowhere there was a huge explosion behind us and off to the side. Me, my dog, and the navigator are about 50m out front and we hit the deck instinctively.

I tossed my dog into one of the depressions in the ground to keep him from getting hit by shrapnel. I didn't know if people were going to start coming out of the bushes or whatnot. We had rifles up, looking around. There were people screaming. We knew somebody was hurt but we couldn't see with all the vegetation. It felt like we sat there for an eternity, fingers on the triggers, waiting for somebody to pop out.

I had my spotter call back on the radio to find out what happened. It turned out Staff Sergeant Russell Logan from Memphis Air National Guard stepped on a mine. He was hurt pretty bad but luckily he was right next to our CLS [Combat Life Saver] who had the stretcher and all the med gear. He went to work on Logan as we sat in place trying to make a game plan. Our original plan was if we had contact or an incident we'd beat feet to the rally point and go back to the installation. At the time we didn't know if it was a mine or IED. The way the patrol sat, they decided to go back the way they came.

Where we were sitting was a little ahead of them and there was a small path leading back to the installation that we were pretty sure was solid ground. We let the rest of the patrol know we'd be traveling parallel to them and would meet at the rally point. Everybody circled up. Me and two other guys started down the path as the other got Sergeant Logan out.

We were moving pretty quick, checking side to side and behind us to make sure no one was following us or setting up an ambush. Finally we saw the gates, walls, and C wire. We relax and started to slow down a little. We could see our guys coming out of the brush off to the side into the clear zone. I thought, "Alright, cool, we're alright now, we got back. Maybe it was just a mine."

There was a gully right where the vegetation ended just before getting to the hard gravel surrounding the base. Me and Charlie stopped and took a look around. I told the other two go and I'd cover to make sure no one was following us. They went down one at a time and got to the other side and said, "Alright Sergeant Seekell, come on over, we got you."

I gathered up Charlie's leash and took maybe two or three steps before the ground exploded. The thing in the movies where everything is ringing, that's all I heard, just this ringing. I felt like I was thrown up not very far. Landed pretty hard. I didn't black out. I didn't feel pain; I felt a lot of pressure. Definitely knew something hadn't gone right. I smelled burning metal and what I'm guessing is burnt me.

I remember rolling over and pressure on my left foot but not wanting to look at it. I felt like it was bad. I looked at it and it just was bloody. Almost at the same instant I thought, "Where's my dog? Where's the dog?" I started calling: "Charlie! Charlie!" I found the leather leash cut in half. I remember my buddy yelling out to me, "I got him, I got him!"

Then I got fixated on finding my rifle. I saw it a couple of feet away and I was trying to get it. A couple guys came down close, but not too close, and told me not to worry about the rifle, that they'd get for me, and that I had bigger problems than the rifle. They eventually came down and dragged me out. Sergeant Estes, also from Memphis Air National Guard, pulled my tourniquet out of my gear patches and put it on my leg. I asked how bad was the bleeding. I knew I'd survived the blast but I didn't want to bleed out.

I was in a daze, the pain was coming on. I was lying on my back sort of taking it all in. Then the phone in my pouch started ringing. We have a phone for the "On Call" bomb dog handler. I was close enough to the installation that I got reception. I pulled it out and answered it. It was a natural reaction.

It was the operations center asking: "Hey, do know what's going on out there?" I said a few choice words and requested MEDEVAC. I can't remember what was said next but I remember throwing the phone away. That's the last I remember about the phone call.

The sad news for me was that we were too close for a MEDEVAC and we'd used the only litter for Logan. So they said: "Sergeant Seekell, you're going to have to hump it out to the gate." I was game.

They got one man each side and I started out on my one good leg. It was probably only 150 yards to the gate, but it felt like a long time. They got to the gate, put me on a litter, and then in the ambulance. Sergeant Logan was there already. He saw me and said something to the effect of "What took you so long?" The roads are terrible and I felt every single bump.

I wound up losing my left leg about half way down.

The first question I asked when I woke up is, "Where's the dog?" and they brought him right in. Charlie lucked out. He was on my left side when the mine went off and got some shrapnel in his left side and his ear drums were busted up. I have good memories of him coming to see me in the hospital.

He took care of me and in turn I took care of him. We had a really good relationship.[4]

On April 25, the top US commander in Kabul, Marine General Joseph Dunford, said that the security situation has improved across the country, with Afghan forces now leading 80 percent of all conventional operations. "As the traditional fighting season begins, the insurgency will confront a combined Afghan force of 350,000 soldiers and police," he said.

Two days later the Taliban announced it would launch its spring offensive named "Khalid ibn al-Walid" (the "Drawn Sword of God"), named after a legendary Muslim military commander and companion of Islam's Prophet Muhammad.

Even before the offensive started, April had been the worst yet month for combat deaths. According to an Associated Press tally, 257 people – including civilians, Afghan security forces, and foreign troops – had been killed in violence around the nation, against 217 insurgents deaths. The previous year during the month of April, 179 civilians, foreign troops, and Afghan security forces were killed, contrasted with 268 insurgents.

Afghanistan's defense ministry responded by saying its security forces were prepared for the Taliban's new campaign. "The Afghan National Army is ready to neutralize the offensive," the ministry said. However, the first attack was against the ANP, not the ANA, in Kandahar on May 7. In the early morning, 60–100 militants struck with RPGs, small arms, and suicide bombings.

It took three days for Afghan and NATO forces to defeat the attack. A reported 25 insurgents were killed along with seven captured. Government losses were 12 ANP and two ANSF killed and four ANP wounded in two different assaults. Despite the victory, the attack brought into question how effective nine years of war had been in securing the region.

On May 1, Operation *Neptune Spear*, an intelligence-driven operation in Pakistan, killed al Qaeda leader Osama bin Laden. A team comprised of members from SEAL Team 6, the CIA, and others air assaulted into bin Laden's compound from helicopters flown by the Army 160th Special Operations Regiment (SOAR). There were no US casualties. President Obama made the following statement at a press conference: "The death of bin Laden marks the most significant achievement to date in our nation's effort to defeat al-Qaida, yet his death does not mark the end of our effort. There is no doubt that al-Qaida will continue to pursue attacks against us. We must, and we will, remain vigilant at home and abroad."

It had taken eight years of gathering information and almost ten months of planning before the operation was launched.

As shown in Operation *Neptune Spear*, good intelligence both for long-term planning and for what's going on a few hundred meters from where you're patrolling is crucial. In Afghanistan, gathering information fell under Task Force ODIN (Observe, Detect, Identify, and Neutralize). Its function was intelligence, surveillance, and reconnaissance (ISR), with manned and unmanned aircraft. Army Aviation Major Eric McKinney, the operations officer commander (S3), tells about his part in ODIN:

> As the S3, you wake up pretty early. I would go to physical training, come back, and open up the e-mail. Usually that was about a hundred deep, and you'd sort through that looking for what was critical. By the time I could get my first sip of coffee and click on the first e-mail, the commander was usually calling me about some issues or problems that I had to solve, immediate fires that I had to put out. It was basically to oversee all the operations, but we ranged between 60–80 missions a day and, with that, problems would occur all the time. So, you were just constantly managing problems.
>
> I had a pretty big staff in the tactical operations center [TOC], and what they couldn't solve, I would usually get involved with. I also projected out and planned certain missions that were coming up, making sure that we had all the assets in the right place at the right time. It was just nonstop,

every day. I was probably in the office from around 0800hrs until about 2000hrs at night.

Major McKinney said his biggest problem when planning missions was the weather.

We were located in seven different FOBs in Afghanistan spread out in every regional command, and so if the weather was good in Balad, it might be bad in Kandahar, so you have supported units and when they can't get their collection, sometimes missions are contingent on the collection that they get.

We would be working with them to reschedule or find a different means to get the information they needed. It was mostly dealing with other S3s, collection managers, and intelligence officers [S2s] in different units to make sure we met their needs and priorities.

He says his greatest success came in the amount of information collected that translated to lives being saved.

You know, we would cover a lot of operations and give them early warning of any potential ambushes or other dangers. I can probably say I saved a lot of American lives, and coalition lives.

There were some instances where, because we were armed, there were dangers and threats that we eliminated, that were actively engaged, so I guess that stood out.

One important thing that I will never forget is to never confuse emotion with reality. Sometimes you can get caught up, but it doesn't affect reality. I thought that was huge. It's the little things sometimes. You need to hear them to mature quickly.[5]

As Major McKinney mentioned, weather played an important part in planning surveillance and reconnaissance missions. Because weather conditions were so changeable, particularly in the mountains, accurate on-scene forecasts were provided by the Air Force 10th Combat Weather Squadron (CWS). The CWS provided information on risk mitigation for commanders, based on weather and environmental factors. These included rivers, avalanche, and anything that dealt with the environment in relation to the battle space.

Captain Gary Charney, the Special Operations Team Weather Officer assigned to the 10th CWS Bagram, tells of what happened during his first mission and how dangerous it could be.

I was deployed pretty much all over Afghanistan except the west from August to December 2011. I was there leading an environmental recon team, the only one in CENTCOM. The toughest part was the transition seasons, spring and autumn, that's where we earn our money. Summer and winter pretty much everyone is a weatherman. In summer it's going to be hot and dusty and in the winter it's going to snow.

The first operation I went on was the first operation I got into a gun fight. Until that time everything was fairly benign with a lot of training of Afghan Local Police, assisting other special ops units with their missions based on the weather and environment. I was requested to go on this mission because the conventional army was clearing a valley in northeastern Afghanistan that was suspected of having a large bomb-making facility. At the time it was transitioning between September and October. In October, based on climatology, you have the largest variability of thunderstorms and the largest increase in visibility potential. With aircraft overhead, ISR, and close air support, it was supposed to be a ten-day operation with resupply.

So they said "We need your expertise for forward observation and Now Forecasting." Pretty much a 12-hour forecast based on what I was seeing and what I know sent back to a brigade level to determine tactical operations.

I went out to a forward deployed [National] Guard sniper team that would provide overwatch in a fixed location for the operation. This was ideal for me to set up shop with my communications and tactical equipment to observe the entire valley and over the mountain tops.

I asked the team what I needed to bring along with my equipment, and they said take five days of food and water. Which meant five MREs and ten liters of water. I filled my pack with food, water, and ammo. They showed me they were going 800–1,000m up a steep mountain. I'm looking at my pack and didn't have any room for extra clothes or anything to sleep on, just enough room for food, water, bullets, my radio, and weather equipment.

I didn't bring a sleeping bag. It's a three or four day op, not a ten-day op, which it turned out to be. I can go without for three of four days, not ten. I could have brought an extra pair of pants but I always carry a flag, so the flag came along and the pants didn't. I didn't know I was going to be sleeping on rock. I wore a hole in the seat of my favorite multicams sitting on a rock for three days.

The rumors and intel during our mission planning was that the governor informed higher ups we were coming in and when. We also learned there was a Russian PKM heavy machine gun in the area. I could only hope they left.

We infilled at night with Chinooks with an ANA platoon into a valley and started up the mountain with our 100lb packs. The weather was good so at that point I'm just another rifleman. At the peak we established a position where we could reach out and touch someone if they came close to any of our teams.

On the fourth day we started receiving sniper fire from about 400m out, which wasn't too bad for them. Our team leader almost got shot in the head. It missed by inches, splashing rock splinters in his face. At that time we had no idea where the fire was coming from. Then we saw two areas of movement. One about 400m away and at the top of the mountain.

We started firing at the closest sniper and he squirted down behind the ridge. The other was a group of six to ten guys much higher up than us. They had machine guns and RPGs. We started engaging them and directed in close air support. It was danger close. I remember hearing over the radio: "You guys may want to take a little more shelter because we're going to drop a 500lb bomb and a 2,000lb air burst."

It was definitely very close. Obviously gravity was going to pull some of the debris down but as it's coming down we're saying, "Hey, this is a little bit more than dust. Maybe we should put on our helmets." At the time we were helmets off and body armor off to conserve heat and water.

The bombs vaporized the top of the mountain, but the sniper was still loose and on the move. We did a presence patrol and found cigarette butts and shell casings. So we moved our position and kept our overwatch.

Down below the operation had cleared the valley, finding only one cache and detaining two people, clear indications that the enemy knew we were coming. Now the point was we have to get out of here. When we planned the mission it included how we were going to infil and exfil. But I'm talking with the team and they've said: "Yeah, that's always the plan, but we have walked kilometers out of a valley all the way back especially along the road searching for IEDs. We know you SOF get the luxury of having plenty of assets available to you, but be prepared to walk out."

I'm all right, I guess this is how conventional [forces] do things. It was a good experience for me on my first real operation.

The night before we were supposed to head out we get word that command could get a couple of Chinooks in the valley. Not all the way into the valley; we'd still have to walk out. I'm looking at my tactical visibility chart and we have to walk 10km, including through a village that was just cleared. Thank God my pack was no longer 100lb because we had to do this in one day after we got off the mountain. We were already smoked from going up the mountain.

Right before sunset I push out my last observation, still no crazy weather at this point, just some thunderstorms here and there. I get a call over the radio that some people were concerned about the thunderstorms. I say, "No, no, we're all good. They're not going to impact our operation." The storms didn't, but I was only half right, which I guess we're allowed to be.

I lay down and wake up to three or four thunderstorms all around us. All the guys on the team had heard me on the radio so now they're saying, "I thought this wasn't going to impact our exfil window."

We didn't get thunder but we got pelted with heavy rain and high winds. I'm definitely eating my forecast. Literally eating my forecast. I didn't even bring my poncho. The team is in half caves while I'm out in the rain sending in weather reports.

It rained so hard there were two inches of water in boots; the guys are drenched. This is the day we're walking out of the valley and if we lose air we have to walk another 15km.

I walked out with no socks, my feet were so wet. The Army guys didn't have as good multicams as we did. Their uniforms split from the crotch to the knees. You could see their boxer shorts.

As we're walking out I'm talking to the base on a cell phone trying to identify a window. Based on my forecast we got out a couple of hours early. As we're touching down at the main base the storms started again. At least I nailed that forecast right.

Overall it was a great experience.[6]

Although there was no apparent diminution in the Taliban's ability and willingness to fight, on June 22 President Barak Obama announced that starting in July the US would remove 10,000 of its troops from Afghanistan by the end of the year, and a total of 33,000 troops by the summer of 2012. He set 2014 as the end date for completing the process of transitioning responsibility for Afghan security to the Afghans. At that point the US mission would change from combat to support.

First to leave were 1,000 National Guardsmen from Parwan province in eastern Afghanistan, and from Kabul. Other troops to be redeployed to the States included more than 1,000 3rd Battalion, 4th Marines soldiers assigned to Regimental Combat Team 8, which was overseeing operations in Sangin, Musa Qala, and other districts in the northern part of Helmand province.

Speaking about the Marines' withdrawal, Major General Richard Mills said: "Their presence there in that area took a lot of pressure off those road builders and, again, disrupted the enemy in an area where he had not expected to see coalition troops. It was one of his few remaining hideouts, if you will, within the province. Because of the fact that you only have them for a short period of time, we're not in a hold phase with those troops, but we're doing some clearance and some disruptions."[7]

This statement was echoed in Operation *Dagger Fury*'s mission, which was to kill, capture, and clear insurgents out of villages in the Araban Valley, Wardak province, on July 25. Since the war began no major operations had been conducted in the valley. It was so bad there that ANA and ANP avoided the area.

The military decided to do something about the area after a massive suicide-bomb attack on COP Dash-e-Towp near the town of Sayed Abad blew a 30ft hole in one of the COP's barrier walls and wounded 22 troops in mid-July.

Since the US began turning control of the area over to ANSF in April security in the region had deteriorated and the number of attacks had increased, including ones against Highway 1, the arterial route connecting Kabul and Kandahar.

"It's of special concern because of the types of attacks we've seen coming out of here," said Major Heather Levy, an operations officer-in-charge with Task Force Dagger, 4th BCT, 10th Mountain Division. "The number of attacks has only risen."

Normally, operations were planned and executed primarily by combat units. This time it was a Brigade Special Troops Battalion (BSTB) that planned the operation, led by Lieutenant Colonel Blace Albert. BSTBs usually handle base organization and infrastructure, housing, and security. The BSTB troops were reinforced by three maneuver companies, including cavalry and infantry troops, and Task Force Knighthawk, 10th Combat Aviation Brigade, 10th Mountain Division, plus Air Force units in support.

"Knighthawk ensured that we, as the ground force, were able to rapidly mass our combat power," said US Army Lieutenant Colonel Blace C. Albert, TF Dagger, 4th BCT commander. "Before the sun came up, we owned the Araban Valley."

With CH-47 Chinook, AH-64 Apache, and UH-60 Blackhawk helicopters, the 10th CAB inserted personnel from TF Dagger and the ANA at night into several landing zones on July 25–26.

"We infilled nearly 450 personnel the first night plus we sling-loaded a 20ft container, which was used as a forward command post during the operation," said US Army Major Rich Tucker, TF Knighthawk, 10th CAB operations officer-in-charge. "81mm mortars, water, ammo, and an all-terrain tactical vehicle were internally loaded on one of the Chinooks."

On the fourth night of the operation, Apaches provided security and illumination in support of a complex MEDEVAC extraction.

"The [injured] soldier was located on a pinnacle observation post with 150–500ft cliffs on each side," said Chief Warrant Officer 4 Steve Donahue Jr., an AH-64 Apache helicopter pilot and master gunner with TF Knighthawk, 10th CAB. "[Our MEDEVAC crew executed] a hoist extraction with the aircraft at a hover, during extremely low illumination and with a light wind gust."

Over the course of the operation, the Apaches were called upon several times to provide CAS. "Knighthawk's air weapons team responded on multiple occasions to engage the Taliban with Hellfires," said Levy. "After a few days, the insurgents wouldn't attack when the AWT was in the air – that was pretty important for us since no other platform had the same deterrent effect."

The exfil began just before midnight on July 30 and continued for several hours into the early morning of the next day. The 10th CAB picked up and returned all personnel safely to their bases.

A US Air Force F-15E Strike Eagle aircraft flies over Afghanistan in support of Operation *Mountain Lion* on April 12, 2006. US Air Force F-15, A-10 Thunderbolt II, and B-52 Stratofortress aircraft provided CAS to troops on the ground engaged in rooting out insurgent sanctuaries and support networks. (DOD, photo by Master Sergeant Lance Cheung)

Above: A US Army M-ATV leads a resupply convoy during Operation *Helmand Spider* in Helmand province. The device attached to the grille of the vehicle is a counter-led device, designed to jam the signal sent to any remotely controlled electronic IED. (US Army)

Below: The High Mobility Multipurpose Wheeled Vehicle (HMMWV) is a lightweight, highly mobile, diesel-powered, four-wheel-drive tactical vehicle that uses a common chassis to carry a wide variety of military hardware ranging from machine guns to tube-launched, optically tracked, wire command-guided (TOW) antitank missile launchers. (Military.com)

Above: Snipers of the French 2nd Foreign Infantry Regiment using a PGM Hécate and a FR-F2 in Afghanistan in 2005. French troops were part of the ISAF contingent that expanded considerably after 2006. (Davric)

Below: A US Army staff sergeant looks over a cliff as he provides security while his fellow soldiers, Afghan National Army soldiers, and US Air Force airmen of the 755th Explosive Ordnance Disposal Unit move to an enemy weapons cache point on the side of a mountain on December 23, 2006. (DOD, photo by Staff Sergeant Marcus J. Quarterman)

Above: A British Army convoy makes a temporary halt in opium poppy fields outside the town of Gereshk in Helmand, 2006. The opium poppy is traditionally the main cash crop of Afghanistan. Until the late 1990s, Afghanistan was the world's leading supplier of opium. Whilst in government, the Taliban outlawed opium cultivation, nearly eliminating it from the country entirely by 2001. However, production revived quickly after American forces overthrew the Taliban government. (IWM, 12BDE-2007-010-343)

Below: Paratroopers from the 782nd Brigade Support Battalion, 4th Brigade Combat Team, 82nd Airborne Division watch as combat delivery system bundles carrying food and water come floating to the ground in the Paktika province of Afghanistan on October 11, 2007. (DOD, photo by Specialist Micah E. Clare)

A 120mm mortar is fired in support of combat operations in the Da'udzay Valley in the Zabul province of Afghanistan on October 23, 2007. This operation was a joint Afghan National Army and ISAF mission to clear anti-government elements from the Dawzi area. (DOD, photo by Sergeant 1st Class Jim Downen)

Above: Paratroopers from B Company, 1st Battalion, 508th Parachute Infantry Regiment, 82nd Airborne Division patrol the Ghorak Valley in Helmand during Operation *Achilles*, March 6, 2007. (Public Domain)

Below: A Marine Special Operations Company's leatherneck examines a poppy plant handed to him by an Afghan National Army soldier (right) during a patrol on February 25, 2008 through a village in Helmand where they were looking for Taliban fighters. (DOD, photo by Staff Sergeant Luis P. Valdespino Jr.)

Above: An F/A-18C Hornet aircraft from Strike Fighter Squadron 113 refuels from a US Air Force KC-10 Stratotanker aircraft over southeast Afghanistan during a mission supporting international security forces in Helmand on October 6, 2008. The squadron was embarked aboard the aircraft carrier USS *Ronald Reagan* to provide support to ground forces in Afghanistan. (DOD, photo by Commander Erik Etz)

Below: A Fairchild Republic A-10A Thunderbolt II, known as the Warthog from its less than pleasing aesthetics, sits on the strip at Bagram Air Base. The Warthog was introduced late into the battle and flew top cover for the extraction helicopters. (DOD)

Above: Members of ODA 3336, 3rd Special Forces Group (Airborne) recon the remote Shok Valley of Afghanistan where they fought an almost seven-hour battle with insurgents in a remote mountainside village as part of Operation *Commando Wrath*. (US Army)

Below: A US Army sniper teams provides overwatch while an officer surveys a village during a foot patrol near FOB Mizan on February 23, 2009. (DOD, photo by Sergeant Christopher S. Barnhart)

Above: US Marines and Afghan National Police officers conduct a security patrol through the Nawa district of Helmand province, August 3, 2009. The severity of the insurgency in Helmand meant that the British troops who had been based there since 2006 were heavily reinforced by US Marines and other troops in 2009. (DOD, photo by Corporal Artur Shvartsberg)

Below: A US Navy Petty Officer treats a Marine who was wounded during a firefight in the Nawa district of Helmand, August 14, 2009. Navy corpsmen are first responders to wounded Marines on the battlefield. (DOD, photo by Corporal Artur Shvartsberg)

A US Marine with 2nd Battalion, 8th Marine Regiment reaches for more rounds during an attack at Patrol Base Bracha in the Garmsir district of Helmand, on October 9, 2009. The Marines are deployed with RCT 3, whose mission is to conduct counterinsurgency operations in partnership with Afghan security forces in southern Afghanistan. (DOD, photo by Sergeant Pete Thibodeau)

Above: US Air Force F-15E Strike Eagle aircraft from the 335th Fighter Squadron drop 2,000lb joint direct attack munitions on a cave in eastern Afghanistan on November 26, 2009. (DOD, photo by Staff Sergeant Michael B. Keller)

Below: US Marines board a V-22 Osprey aircraft at Control Base Karma in Helmand on June 9, 2010. (DOD, photo by Corporal Lindsay L. Sayres)

Above: A group of houses surrounded by mountains sit over a rocky foundation across the river in the Dara District of Panjshir. (US Army, photo by Sergeant Teddy Wade)

Below: US soldiers patrol in Baghlan province in January 2011. The district saw a surge of Taliban attacks in the months around this image. (Corbis)

Above: US Marines with Lima Company, 3rd Battalion, 4th Marine Regiment patrol through Bar Now Zad, January 13, 2010. The Marines are moving into the area to deny the Taliban freedom of movement. (USMC, photo by Corporal Daniel M. Moman)

Above: US Air Force Captain Nick Morgans, a pararescueman with 46th Expeditionary Rescue Squadron, scans his sector on the way to a landing zone during a mission near Kandahar on December 24, 2010. A pararescueman's primary function is as a personnel recovery specialist with emergency medical capabilities. (DOD, photo by Staff Sergeant Eric Harris)

Below: Members of the US Army's 502nd Regiment fire a mortar during 2010's Operation *Hamkari* in Kandahar. This image is part of a winning portfolio for the army photographic competition in 2011 (© MOD, Crown Copyright, photograph by Sergeant Rupert Frere)

Above: US Army Private 1st Class Ben Bradley, left, a Bulldog Troop, Red Platoon scout from 7th Squadron, 10th Cavalry Regiment, ducks away from small-arms fire as fellow scout, Sergeant Jeff Sheppard, launches a grenade at the enemy's position during a combat engagement in northern Bala Murghab Valley, part of Operation *Red Sand*, April 4, 2011. (Strategypage.com, photo by Technical Sergeant Kevin Wallace)

Below: US Defense Secretary Panetta visits troops at FOB Shukvani, March 14, 2012. Following the massacre of 16 Afghan civilians by an American soldier, Panetta told troops that it should not deter them from their mission to secure the country ahead of their withdrawal. (Corbis)

Above: This Buffalo MRV, equipped with the anti-RPG "slat" armor, survived an IED attack that took the two front wheels off its axle. The crew survived. (US Army)

Below: As the US prepares to withdraw forces from Afghanistan, combat operations turn to training of Afghan troops. Here Afghan National Army soldiers train on a Humvee in Nuristan. (Corbis)

Above: President Obama and Afghan President Karzai hold a meeting at the White House, January 11, 2013, discussing the continued transition from US-led operations and the partnership between the two nations. (Corbis)

Below: As part of the effort towards withdrawal, US forces, as part of the Coalition, train Afghan security. Here a police officer graduates in Herat, December 2013. (Corbis)

In addition to 16 enemy killed, TF Dagger found four caches, which included weapons and bomb-making material in addition to extensive numbers of documents and amounts of equipment.[8]

As combat operations went on, so did efforts by the Afghan Government and coalition members to stabilize society. Among the men working to accomplish this was Air Force Major Matthew Brown assigned to the Afghanistan–Pakistan (AFPAK) Hands mission. There he faced the challenges of countering poppy cultivation and trying to reintegrate insurgents into a nonmilitant society.

> We are trained to be sort of counterinsurgency experts and we also get a little bit of the language training. The idea was that we would be out working very closely with the Afghan Government officials trying to build their capacity. I was assigned a specialty of working with the Afghan Peace and Reintegration Program, trying to reintegrate the Taliban into productive society.
>
> They wanted me to work at the main operating base in Lashkar Gah, which was essentially a Provincial Reconstruction Team [PRT]. The PRT in Lashkar Gah was civilian-run, which was unusual. It was also British civilian. The top guys there were from the Foreign and Commonwealth Office [FCO].
>
> [Lashkar Gah] is dirty, filthy, and hot, and it produces in the order of 85–90 percent of the heroin in all of Afghanistan, which in turn produces 85–90 percent of the heroin in the world. Afghanistan is amazing. When someone says Afghanistan doesn't have the capacity to do something I usually respond with, "Well, they've got the capacity to provide the entire world's worth of opium." It's not a matter of could they do it, it's a matter of directing them to do something different.
>
> The goal was to incentivize and create a legal framework where Taliban can renounce the past and say, "I'm on the winning team. I'm with the government of Afghanistan." They could basically get an ID card, so based on this date if we found something that would link them to the insurgency, they could say, "No, I've renounced all that activity."
>
> The British ... come at this with a very sober attitude and a very realistic attitude in terms of time frames. They're like, "You can make all the noise

you want but it's not going to change the reality in the next year and a half, the next three years, or the next five years."

Insurgencies, if you look at them through history, are long, grinding conflicts. They're more on the scale of 20–40 years, they're not five years. It doesn't matter how smart you are, it doesn't matter how much money you spend, it doesn't matter how little you sleep every night, you're not going to substantively change the environment you're operating in in the short term. It's like society will push back against you the harder you push.

It's not a matter of how much force I can apply in concentration, it's about relentless pressure in the long term. That's what they learned in Northern Ireland and that's what they've seen in Africa. The other thing they've seen is that once there's a political settlement between two warring parties there needs to be a way for those guys on the side that lost to come back into society so they're not outcasts forever.

There's a program called Disarmament of Illegally Armed Groups, which is a precursor to reintegration. We had a lot of interpretation questions about whether these guys were going to need to turn in their weapons and, if not, how do you prove you're Taliban or militia or a fighter. If you don't have a weapon, or you're not willing to show us your weapon, how do you prove you're a guerilla and not just a guy with no job wanting to get paid? How do we keep track of you after the fact? These are all questions and they need to work in different ways in different parts of Afghanistan because Afghanistan is very, very local, and very, very non-homogenous.

The government of Kabul wants to have the monopoly of power both armed and unarmed or armed and economic. There's the idea that there are places in Afghanistan as we draw it on the map that are not going to be governed in the short term and probably not in the medium term, so what happens there and who controls it? In a vacuum of power if it's not the government then it's going to be the guys who have the economic desire to do so. It's going to be smugglers or drug dealers, whoever has the most skin in the game. These guys have a history of smuggling and growing drugs that's second to none. They're really, really good at it.

We got some guys to come into the program. It's debatable how much of an impact that had in terms of whether or not these guys were the real deal or if they were sort of sent in just to test the system or if it was a negotiation. There's so many power brokers in Afghanistan that it could be as simple as the governor saying, "Hey, I'm getting a lot of heat from the coalition. I need you to cough up six bodies." Some guy's like, "Alright. If I do that will you do this for me?" The guy's like, "Yes. Please just get these guys off my back for a month." Miraculously six bodies get coughed up and it's a huge win for reintegration in Helmand.

When things are top-down driven you see a lot of hedging type of behavior. "I'll send six of my young men this way in case this side wins and I'll send another six that way in case that side wins." We congratulate the six that came our way thinking they had a moment of inspiration and did some soul searching and found we were the right ones. We never get the other side of the story. We think those bad guys are just bad guys and we need to kill them, but it may be more complicated than that. Those were the guys that whatever authority they recognized sent them to hedge the position of the group that's going to stay there for another thousand years and they can't afford to make enemies with their neighbors. It makes the Hatfields and McCoys look like a picnic.

It's kind of a mountain hillbilly culture that doesn't want a lot of government and the government doesn't want to go down and deal with those people because they know what the story is. Unfortunately, when you have that culture nothing great is going to happen. Afghanistan isn't going to put anybody on the moon because they're too busy fighting over little things. They're not going to do great things. You just need to make it so they can function and not be a threat to anybody else.

If the entire world wanted to focus on nothing but Afghanistan for 30 or 40 years, sure, we could fix it. When every story you read is another Afghan who turns and shoots somebody who's supposed to be their friend and they rip off the Royal Bank for like 200 billion dollars or something and no one gets arrested. They're like, "What? 200 billion dollars. I lost it. Give me some more money." People get tired and say, "What are we doing?" There seems to be very little reciprocity in their relationship.[9]

Air Force Captain Andrew L. Chaulk was Kunar Provincial Reconstruction Team Public Affairs Officer. His experiences were different from what Major McKinney encountered in Helmand.

We were less than 10km from the Pakistan border, which was a pretty volatile area. It was an unusual situation. I was an Air Force Public Affairs officer with one photographer with me in a Navy PRT working for a Navy commander and we fell under the Army brigade out of Jalalabad. I and my photographer were the token Air Force.

Our job was to aid and assist the local government in the recovery process and building the Rule of Law. We would do site surveys, and we helped them with the contracting process getting government buildings and schools built. Our focus was to transition from international funds to funneling things through their central government for funding. The Rule of Law piece was something we helped them implement.

Our normal week was spending five to six days outside the wire. We visited the schools we had built, were building, or looking to be completed to see how well they were maintained, what was the progress of a school being built or if one was finishing up whether it was to the correct quality standards.

We spent a lot of time at the governor's compound. We also had an amazing Department of State guy called Tom West, who spoke Pashtun. We had Abe Sutherland, a lawyer who was our Rule of Law guy. He advised the judges setting up the legal processes.

Some of my favorite missions were the ones where we'd go out to do publicity for a trial. They had public trials, which were very rare in Afghanistan, where they let people come and watch. We had a trial about a kidnapping. A man had kidnapped a girl, and her brother ran to report him. They caught the man before he got away.

There was one terrorism trial, which was very interesting. Men were trying to cross a bridge and the police tried to stop them. Shots were fired, killing two of the men. One was convicted to a long sentence, and a taxi driver got sentenced to three months in jail for driving without a license.

We had one corruption trial where administors in the Education Department were convicted of taking food supplies from the schools and selling them. They were convicted.

You could see real progress in rule of law. It was really strong.[10]

Although the Kunar PRT was doing good work, RC-East continued to be a lethal area for US and Afghan forces. On August 6 insurgents shot down a Chinook carrying US and Afghan troops, including 20 Navy SEALs, 12 US Army personnel, an interpreter, and seven Afghan Special Operations soldiers. The helicopter was returning from an assault on a Taliban compound in the village of Jaw-e-Mekh Zareen in the Tangi Valley. It was the largest single loss in one day since the war began.

US troops in Helmand, Kandahar, Kunar, and Paktika provinces suffered the most casualties in August and throughout autumn. IEDs, snipers, and small-unit actions claimed the lives of an additional 131 US military personnel.[11]

Operation *Eagle Hunt* on December 27 finished the year for the Marines in Helmand province. The Afghan-led operation was to clear the Taghaz area for future counterinsurgency operations. The forces included more than 75 US troops, dog teams, ABP, and Afghan Uniformed Police. Most of the US personnel were Marines and Navy members from Border Advisory Team 1 along with Marine combat engineers from 3rd Combat Engineer Battalion. The engineers were trained to lead patrols as point men and sweep for IEDs.

"As combat engineers we were there to ensure that the Border Advisor Team was able to maneuver wherever they needed to in a safe manner," explained Sergeant Joshua Malok. "As a squad leader I was there to ensure my Marines did that properly."

"You get used to the feeling of always being in front and accept the fact that it's a part of the job," said Corporal Andrew Eisen. "But you always have to be on the lookout for stuff no matter what the situation is or where you're patrolling."

There were no firefights or overt enemy action during the operation. Afghan forces did detain more than 100 local residents on allegations involving the growing and harvesting of illicit crops, such as poppy and marijuana, according to ABP officials. They also eliminated roughly 90–100 acres of hasheesh and confiscated at least 13 tractors in support of the Afghan Government's efforts to prevent the cultivation of illicit crops.

Although the Marines did not lose anyone, IEDs and small-unit attacks during December claimed the lives of 11 Army troops in RC-East and two in RC-Southwest.

During 2011 the US and coalition forces shifted more responsibility for operations and security to the ANA and all branches of the Afghan police forces. The level of ability was not yet consistent in all ANSF units, as seen during combined operations in several provinces. Also in question was the ANSF's ability to maintain security in areas previously pacified by US or coalition forces as the foreign troops pulled out.

Another area of concern was that opium production had increased by over 60 percent since 2010, with a value of $1.4 billion dollars.[12] Drug trafficking was so large in the western provinces that there were truck parks filled with vehicles waiting to cross into Iran. This huge amount of money continued to fuel the almost pandemic level of corruption throughout Afghanistan, undermining the rule of law in large portions of the country. A lack of counter-narcotics police officers and the limited time available to confront the problem before international forces pulled out exacerbated the situation.

For the US, casualties for the year were 418 KIA and 5,199 wounded, a slight drop from 2010 (499 and 5,246). IEDs were the major cause of casualties, with most occurring in Kandahar and Helmand provinces.

Although the war's end point had been established, there was still a long way to go.

Chapter 12

END GAME, 2012–13

US forces were now acting in conjunction with and in support of Afghan operations instead of mounting major independent operations. Although no longer engaged in large-scale missions, casualties from IEDs and roadside bombs continued to take their toll, with eight US troops killed in the first week of January 2012.

Explosive Ordinance Detachments (EODs) were assigned to infantry units to clear out any that were found. Master Sergeant William Kennedy, North Dakota Air National Guard EOD, talks about his experiences:

> We were embedded with the 172nd Infantry and later the 2nd Battalion, 16th Infantry Regiment [TF Ranger], Kansas National Guard. Two three-man EOD teams supporting 500 infantry in RC-East.
>
> In RC-East you could find yourself in a pickle really fast. Everybody has the image of EOD from *The Hurt Locker*, which isn't reality. EOD teams do a lot of Level One intelligence work, recovering info from IEDs we collect. DNA, the tape, whatever we can recover. The better we are at recovering the IEDs the better the labs can turn it around building target packages for getting the bomb maker.
>
> Post-blast investigations are the most dangerous thing we do because there are almost always others in the area. You start a post-blast investigation and you find number two, number three, number four IED within minutes, within feet. "Wow I'm in an IED minefield."
>
> When you have an IED, it's yours; you have to clear it before anyone can do anything. When you work with SF teams in theater, they tend [to] use you as bait. They know that when you're working an IED someone is

going to be watching you. "Yeah we'll pull security for you." Then when you get out there they'll say, "We're going to go and knock on some doors. See you later."

The last time we went out with regular infantry they treat you like gold. Security wise, they're not leaving.

One of the funniest things I can remember is when we air assaulted into a village and got in a fight. We found a cache and blew it up. And we got hit again. As an IED guy I'm not there to shoot. I can shoot, but the grunts are all there to shoot. They love to shoot. It's going on for a while and some people are running out of ammo. You had from every extreme: one squad leader fell asleep, one guy was shooting at birds, and artillery's dropping rounds near us. The Army missed and started dropping 120s on top of us. When the resupply came, they gave us the wrong ammo. There are hours and hours of this, but in the end of this nobody was hurt. I remember that day because everything went wrong.

One of the last IEDs I worked was a post-blast investigation. I could see the area from cameras inside the COP. We go out there; the infantry didn't have the basic tools to check for landmines and trip wires and didn't know how to use it. They'd lost several trucks in the last few weeks. So we go out and find the IED and they're working all around it. The bad guys are watching. They blow one truck; we check and find two, three nearby. The trucks move a hundred meters and BAM, they lose another truck. And, we find another three or four nearby. This is not the way to locate IEDs.

EOD in this time and in this part of the world is such a unique thing. I'm in this EOD job that I love and it's such a unique time in our history you felt you're part of something. This is way bigger than me. You feel it's something you can't walk away from. I want to do that one hard mission, I want my chance at it.[1]

Medevac helicopters were still the primary means of getting casualties from the battle to a Mobile Army Surgical Hospital (MASH) unit. Even with the reduction in major combat operations, the need for rapid response hadn't changed. Staff Sergeant Antonio Delvecchio, Special Mission Aviator with the Air Force 64th Emergency Rescue Squadron (ERQS), had been in Afghanistan in 2003 as a C-130 crewmember; now he was back as flight engineer on an HH-60.

For Air Force MEDEVACs, from the time the alert drops and we get the 9 Line to the time we're wheels up is generally about five minutes give or take a couple of minutes. We don't have to wait for Chase Birds [armed helicopter escorts] or any of that. We are our own armament. The enemy doesn't like to shoot at us as much as they do the Army because we're armed with two .50-cal machine guns. With a .50-cal I can reach out and touch someone at 1,500m. The PJs are carrying SAWs and we have our M-4s for personal weapons.

My first real mission was picking up a Marine shot in the chest and side. We're about five minutes out and we ask the Marines to pop smoke to show their position. The Taliban hears the helicopters coming in and the enemy pops smoke to draw us in. We know where our guys are and now we know there's somebody over there that doesn't want us in. It gives you that reality check that there's somebody that does want us here.

About three minutes after that we land with the Marines on the right side of our helicopter. When our wheels touch down we start taking fire from our 11 o'clock. The Marines that are covering start shooting across our nose. Then the enemy opens up at our 9 o'clock and our 2 o'clock. Three different points of origin. It gets very busy very quick, and time slows down at that point. The PJs go out and get the Marine in the helicopter. It seems like five minutes on the ground but in reality looking back and going through the tapes it's 45 seconds. It was pretty impressive to see everything we'd trained for work the first time we got shot at. It was eye-opening.

That sound never leaves you mind. From that point on if you heard a pop or a crack you knew exactly what it was. It shuts down the helicopter noises and you don't hear anything else. You can smell the gunpowder. It's crazy.

It's always back picking up other services' casualties that are out doing their normal job and then end up not making it. Or, you're picking up a couple of heroes and bringing them back to Bagram to start making their way home. That's eye-opening. You may not know them but it doesn't matter; you're all fighting for the same cause.

You learn to compartmentalize everything. The pilots look straight ahead. We had a very young copilot on his first mission. He turns around to see what was going on in the back. It wasn't a very good mission, we'd picked up five guys. One was a triple amputee; one was a double amputee. It was messy in the back. Another was a hero on another bird. It was a lot of things going on at once, and he looked back at the wrong time. From that point in the deployment on he was like, "How do I get rid of this image? How do I just not remember it?"

You train your eyes on other things. You know the PJs are there doing what they're supposed to be doing. You can hear the wounded guys screaming. You learn to keep focused, scanning outside the helicopter, making sure the systems are where they're supposed to be at. You do things to keep your mind off what's going on in the back of the helicopter.[2]

IEDs, rocket attacks, and small-unit ambushes were part of the day-to-day life of US troops, and could be dealt with. What occurred on February 22 was different. That day US troops assigned to the Parwan Detention Facility at Bagram Airfield mistakenly burned 1,652 damaged books and Islamic texts that had been culled from the library for storage by Afghan-American interpreters. Among the books were 48 copies of the Quran, which had been defaced by detainees. Some Afghan interpreters noticed the remnants of the Qurans and notified an Afghan commander. When word of the Quran burnings spread, riots erupted across the country.[3]

At COP Whitehorse near Kunduz in RC-North, soldiers of 1st Squad, 3rd Platoon, C Company, 1/125 Infantry were performing security missions to protect Security Force Advisory Teams (SFATs) working with ANP units. COP Whitehorse was an ANP installation containing an Afghan compound and an American compound divided by a wall. On February 26 intelligence was received indicating Colonel Abdul Latif Ibrahimi had called for a Jihad against the Americans in the Imam Sahib District in the northern part of Kunduz province.

Sergeant Michael McNichol said, "We received intel that the Afghans in the nearby town of Imam Saheb were going to protest at 1:00pm on the 26th, so we planned and rehearsed how we would occupy defensive positions and defend COP Whitehorse in case things became violent."

The squad was working out at 12:00pm when they heard gunfire. McNichol said, "The ANP began firing in the air when protesters led by Colonel Ibrahimi tried to get through the entry point to our outpost. We moved to our assigned positions the way we did in our rehearsals. My position was security on the door dividing the installation. Three other soldiers were in a position near mine, Sergeant Michael Anderson took up a position with his M-249 Squad Automatic Weapon in the guard shack, and medic Specialist Tommie Owens organized the casualty collection point [CCP]. All of our positions were behind a Mine Resistant All Terrain Vehicle that blocked the entry to our part of the outpost and it blocked most of the rocks and bricks the rioters were throwing at us."

The rioters continued to throw rocks and bricks at the defending soldiers. McNichol said:

> We held our positions while dodging rocks and bricks; some soldiers began suffering minor injuries from being hit. One soldier, Specialist David Fuentes-Bueno, was hit in the face and moved to my position behind the M-ATV. The SFAT team fell behind the M-ATV as well. Non-lethal rounds and tear gas were used to try and disperse the crowd. After a few minutes, I heard and felt a loud explosion; flames, shrapnel, and rocks were thrown all over us. Later, it was determined that we had been hit by a grenade.
>
> I saw several soldiers fall to the ground and I dropped to my knees. I regained my footing, went to the soldier who was standing next to me, and realized he had life-threatening injuries. I grabbed him and dragged him until another soldier helped me get him to the casualty collection point. The medics took charge of the soldier once we got him to the CCP. I noticed another soldier unresponsive and not breathing, so I helped Owens treat the soldier. We gave him first aid and I gave Owens a nasopharyngeal airway to get him breathing again. Once he was stabilized, I went back to the CCP to get a protective mask.

Owens described the events and challenges he faced that day as a combat medic:

> We had nine soldiers injured during the attack; fortunately, none were fatalities. Our main entrance was blocked by the M-ATV to keep the rioters out so we had to use buddy carries to drag and move the injured soldiers in body armor once the decision was made for the MEDEVAC Blackhawks to land on our COP to pick up the wounded.
>
> I met up with Sergeant 1st Class Travis Garza, our platoon sergeant, and he saw I was wounded so he told me to return to the CCP for treatment. After being treated, I got the M-ATV ready to secure the landing zone when Owens came to the vehicle and told me the MEDEVAC helicopters were going to

> land on our COP instead of using the landing zone. Our Air Force Joint Terminal Attack Controller called in a show of force by F-15 fighter jets to drive off the rioters. The show of force run worked and the crowd dispersed. The two MEDEVACs landed one at a time; each bird retrieved four wounded and flew them to the German base at Kunduz. The first bird returned and picked me and another soldier up and flew us to Kunduz as well.
>
> The German medical personnel at FOB Kunduz were very helpful and provided excellent treatment for our wounds. Six of our wounded required additional higher-level treatment and were flown to Bagram, then Germany, and eventually the United States for recovery. My stay was overnight and I was back at the COP within 48 hours.[4]

When the riots ended three days later, four US soldiers had been killed by members of the ANSF. There were 37 other deaths, and hundreds of soldiers and civilians were wounded or injured.

On March 11, less than two weeks after the Quran-burning riots ended, Staff Sergeant Robert Bales, acting alone, killed 16 men, women, and children as well as wounding six others in the Panjwayi district near Kandahar.

Following the attack, President Karzai called the incident "intentional murder" and stated "this is an assassination, an intentional killing of innocent civilians and cannot be forgiven." Karzai repeated his demands that the United States pull back troops from village areas and allow Afghan security forces to take the lead in an effort to reduce civilian deaths.

"This is a fatal hammer blow on the US military mission in Afghanistan. Whatever sliver of trust and credibility we might have had following the burnings of the Quran is now gone," said David Cortright, the director of policy studies at Notre Dame's Kroc Institute for International Peace Studies.[5]

There were protests but no riots over the killings. Contrary to Karzai's demand to turn over security to Afghan forces and Cortright's statement that all trust and credibility was gone, village elders meeting with US military officials requested that the Americans stay.

"We now know what happened is not like most Americans. We need them to keep us safe from the Taliban," one said to a member of US military staff who visited the scene.[6]

Operations continued throughout the protests. One involved another Air Force military working dog handler on April 9 as Navy SEAL Team 2 was conducting a village-stability patrol along the edge of a mountain. During their mission, the team was engaged by PKM and AK-47 fire, resulting in one of their team members being shot in the leg.

"We were pretty much going out every day," said Technical Sergeant Clifford E. Hartley, 628th Security Forces Squadron military working dog handler, who was at the time a staff sergeant and deployed with the 3-2 Stryker Brigade Combat Team at Forward Operating Base Laghman. "While I was supporting Task Force Trident [US Navy SEAL Team 2], our mission was to find improvised explosive devices and to clear out Taliban members from villages," he says.

Hartley was about halfway through his deployment when he was approached to join the SEAL Team. In early April, SEAL Team 2's dog was killed after an IED detonated. "The Navy SEAL team requested someone to fill the vacant spot and I just happened to be the one who answered the door," Hartley said jokingly. "It really didn't affect me. I've been outside the wire many times before. We were clearing IEDs, so if my dog showed interest or response on a possible threat – the EOD tech was right there to take care of it with his equipment."

It was approximately 11:50am on April 9 when the event occurred in the vicinity of Ulgay. The platoon was moving northeast along a footpath connecting Ulgay and Khvajeh in the Arghandab district, Zabul province. Upon rounding a bend near a large rock outcropping, the lead elements of the SEAL patrol was immediately engaged by effective PKM fire by more than eight enemy fighters, according to one of SEAL team members.

The main element was engaged from their right flank. Hartley, the EOD technician, and another SEAL were pinned down hard on the front side of the mountain. The third member was shot in the leg directly behind Hartley. The EOD tech immediately ran to the third person's position on the ledge and dragged him to cover, while Hartley positioned himself between them and the enemy forces and laid down covering fire. "I've been around gunfire before and everyone reacts differently," said Hartley. "A lot of people would automatically take cover or freeze. The shots were bouncing off the rocks behind me."

While the EOD technician performed medical treatment on the wounded soldier, Hartley spotted two enemy fighters shooting at them from their immediate left flank. "I kept my head on a swivel and noticed the two Taliban fighters popping up," Hartley recalled. "I took a few shots with my M4 carbine and hit the rocks in front of them. The enemy stood up again and I shot him in the chest and he went down."

The EOD technician still had to transfer the wounded SEAL to better cover to complete first aid and to stop the bleeding. During this movement, Hartley laid down effective cover fire and shot more than 100 rounds toward enemy positions, ensuring the SEALs made it safely. "You go through so much training, but you really never know what you're going to do [when the situation arises]," said Hartley.

"Without a doubt, Staff Sergeant Hartley's heroics that day kept myself and the other SEAL from sustaining any more injuries. Without Sergeant Hartley's swift and selfless actions, I could not have worked on the SEAL's injury and stopped his bleeding – ultimately saving his life," the EOD technician recalls.[7]

The Taliban was still a force to be reckoned with in the southern provinces, as were their allies the Haqqani network and al Qaeda in the eastern provinces. At this time intelligence estimated Taliban strength at 25,000. The estimates did not include criminal or warlord organizations. ISAF believed 25,000 fighters wasn't enough for the Taliban to regain control of the country. As of the middle of April there were approximately 129,000 coalition troops (of which 90,000 were US) and over 344,000 ANSF to combat the threat.[8] This almost 20-to-1 disparity in numbers did not deter the insurgents.

On April 15, coordinated attacks struck Kabul, Nangarhar, Paktia, and Logar provinces. In Kabul insurgents attacked the US, British, German, Iranian, and Japanese embassy compounds. Taliban fighters had stormed the Kabul Star hotel complex near the presidential palace. There was also fighting near the Afghan Parliament building.

Camp Eggers (a major ISAF base in Kabul), ISAF headquarters, Camp Warehouse, and Camp Ghazni on Jalalabad road were also targeted. The attacks in Kabul were the largest since 2001. Outside the capital attackers also targeted government buildings in Logar province, the airport in Jalalabad, and a police facility in the town of Gardez in Paktia province.

Afghan police also arrested 15 would-be suicide bombers in northern Afghanistan who were trying to launch attacks in Kunduz province. There were also reports of the arrest of suicide bombers in other areas.

ANSF led the counterattacks, augmented by British Special Boat Service (SBS) and Norwegian Forsvarets Spesialkommando (FSK) forces with US Blackhawk helicopters providing CAS. The attacks lasted 18 hours and resulted in 36 insurgents and four civilians dead, with several more civilians injured.

The ANSF received high praise for their efforts from General John Allen, ISAF Commander: "I am enormously proud of how quickly Afghan security forces responded to today's attacks in Kabul. They were on scene immediately, well-led and well-coordinated. They integrated their efforts, helped protect their fellow citizens and largely kept the insurgents contained."

Zabihullah Mujahed, a Taliban spokesman, said that the attacks were a message to the Afghan Government and its Western military backers. "The Kabul administration and the invading forces had said some time ago that the Taliban will not be able to launch a spring offensive. Today's attacks were the start of our spring offensive." US Ambassador Ryan Crocker said the ability of Afghan security forces to respond to the attacks was a "clear sign of progress," while ISAF labeled the attacks "largely ineffective."

President Karzai blamed Afghan and NATO intelligence for failing to predict the attacks. The US Defense Department spokesman George Little said the Pentagon did not believe there had been an intelligence failure. "If we're held to the standard to have to know precisely when and where each insurgent attack is going to occur, I think that's an unfair standard. This is a war zone."

Intelligence failure or not, the attacks proved the Taliban could still strike anytime and anywhere it chose.[9]

The April attacks did not impact US and NATO drawdown plans. On May 2, President Obama and President Karzai signed the Enduring Strategic Partnership Agreement, providing a long-term framework for relations between the two countries.

NATO representatives met in Chicago on May 20–21 to, among other agenda items, finalize the exit strategy and declare its long-term commitment to Afghanistan. Included in the Chicago Summit Declaration on Afghanistan transcript was the statement that by mid-2013, all parts of Afghanistan will have begun transition and the Afghan forces will be in the lead for security nationwide. The alliance pledged $16 billion in financial support over the next four years.

It also gave a firm final withdrawal date by which ISAF forces were to complete their combat mission: December 31, 2014. However, there was this caveat: "We will, however, continue to provide strong and long-term political and practical support through our Enduring Partnership with Afghanistan. NATO is ready to work towards establishing, at the request of the Government of the Islamic Republic of Afghanistan, a new post-2014 mission of a different nature in Afghanistan, to train, advise, and assist the ANSF, including the Afghan Special Operations Forces. This will not be a combat mission." The Declaration ended with: "Our task is not yet complete. But in the light of our substantial achievements, and building on our firm and shared commitment, we are confident that our strong partnership will lead Afghanistan towards a better future."[10]

The end date was set, but the fighting for US and NATO forces was not yet over.

Staff Sergeant Christopher R. Miller was a squad leader with 4th Security Forces, Bagram Airfield. Air Force Security Forces do everything from resource protection to flight line security. Staff Sergeant Miller and his squad were tasked as the QRF for attacks outside the wire, perimeter security, and checking Point of Origin (POO) and Point of Impact (POI) site investigation for rocket or mortar attacks. "We didn't see too much activity – a random RPG here, small-arms fire somewhere else. I worked 95 days straight without a break. At one point we went 31 days without a rocket attack when we were pulling security."

One time an Army convoy got hit by RPGs less than a mile away from their FOB. An RPG came through the lead vehicle's driver's window, killing the driver.

> We heard the RPGs hitting the trucks and saw one glance off the top of a vehicle before exploding in the air. We mounted up and started out to rescue

> the convoy. As soon as we got into the trucks my radio was lighting up from the command post telling us to get up there.
>
> When we showed up there was chaos everywhere. As we pulled up we started suppressive fire and the attackers stopped shooting and backed off. We had to put out a fire in a vehicle before towing it to the FOB. The FOB didn't have the necessary medical facilities to handle the casualties, so we had to CASEVAC them back to Bagram. We loaded them up and drove back at high speed. The driver was the only one killed that day.[11]

Roadside bombs, IEDs, rockets, RPGs, and attacks by small units continued throughout southern and eastern Afghanistan. No one and no place was safe regardless of where they were or how careful they were. Between June 2 and August 27, US forces lost 85 men and one woman in these types of attacks. Another six died in a helicopter crash.

Starting in June, the ANSF and ISAF initiated a transition that resulted in the ANSF leading operations, with ISAF and US support. Although the numbers of ANA, ABP, Uniformed Police, National Civil Order Police, and Local Police forces were growing and assuming responsibility for more areas, they were not able to overcome Taliban operations or influence in many areas.

"It goes back to the question that everyone asks: When we pull out, can the Afghan forces do what needs to be done to secure Helmand province?" said Lieutenant Colonel David Bradney, 1st Battalion, 7th Marines commander, in northern Helmand. "I would tell you that, yes, the Afghan National Security Forces are absolutely capable enough to beat the Taliban. It's all a question of gumption and will. Do they have the leadership to force the discipline of action, and the commitment to get their forces into the field and risk, perhaps at times, being unsuccessful, to achieve success?"[12]

After two years of fighting to clear the insurgency from Sangin and Kajaki in northern Helmand province, the Taliban retook sections after the Marines were replaced by a National Civil Order Police (ANCOP) unit. ANCOP personnel had training and experience in counterinsurgency operations, but the Taliban enjoyed superior numbers and a strong infrastructure, including a shadow government in the area. Facing an overwhelming force, the ANCOP unit withdrew, ceding control of the area back to the enemy.

In RC-East the 1-12th Infantry Division and ANA troops moved briefly into Nuristan province, an area abandoned by US forces after the attack on COP Keating on October 3, 2009. "Nuristan remains for me a challenge, a black hole. My line in the sand stops at the Kunar and Nuristan borders," said Lieutenant Colonel Scott Green, whose area of responsibility included Nuristan.

US intelligence gathered information about a possible attack by approximately 1,800 Taliban fighters with another 700 spread throughout the province. Insurgents controlled the roads into Afghanistan through Kunar, Waygal, and Parun valleys leading to Kabul. "We'll get some eyes overhead to check it out. If it's Taliban, we'll get a plane up in the morning and drop a bomb on it," said Major Jared Bordwell. "There are a lot of Taliban around. If the US supports the Afghan Government it will be very good in future. If not, it will be worse," said Afghan militia member, Mohammad Ghazi.

Lieutenant Colonel Rocky Burrell believed securing Nuristan would probably take thousands of Afghan soldiers that the government did not have, even though it is one of the country's most mineral-rich provinces. "I think we can transition in Kunar," Green. "But if we were to try and expand without increased combat power there, then yes, I do think that we would be spread so thin that it would start to break."

The operation lasted five days and then the troops pulled out, once again ceding control to the Taliban.[13]

There were successful combined operations leading to greater confidence in the ANSF. In May the 1/2-205 Afghan National Army Corps, Shamulzai Detachment, and 5th Battalion, 20th Infantry, teamed up to locate and destroy several acres of opium poppy fields outside the village of Samogay, in Zabul province.

On June 5 units of 2nd Battalion, 504 PIR, 1st BCT, 82nd Airborne, and 6th Kandak, 3rd Brigade, 203rd Corps, air assaulted into villages in the mountains west of Qara Bagh, Ghazni province.

According to Lieutenant Colonel Praxitelis Vamvakias, the BCT's commander: "This is part of our plan to keep the insurgents off balance, allowing Afghan National Security Forces and the district governance space and time to gain traction in improving security, governance, and economics."

Locations cleared included the agricultural-based settlements of Barlah, Lar, and several smaller villages, all of which were located at nearly 8,000ft of elevation in a remote valley. One of the company commanders involved in the operation, Captain Robert Gacke III, said that such operations were intended to knock insurgents out of their comfort zones, causing them to make mistakes that US and Afghan forces may capitalize on. Gacke, whose company partnered with ANA soldiers to clear Barlah, said he believed the biggest benefit from the most recent mission was that it was "the spark that began the transition of responsibility and mission-leading from us to the Afghans."

The mission used a "combined-arms rehearsal" beforehand, a significant planning tool during which each commander described in detail on a floor map his role in the operation. Major Shamhoon Saf, operations officer for 6th Kandak, 3rd Brigade, 203rd Corps, said that he planned to use the planning method for their own missions in the future. "We want to become this professional."

One of Gacke's platoon leaders, Lieutenant Kirk Shoemaker, explained that Afghan soldiers entered every home first and were always in the lead of moving formations. "In fact, sometimes they outpaced us climbing mountains. They are hungry to make sure the people are protected and the Taliban is eliminated from this area," he said. Shoemaker said that the safe havens they cleared were not nearly as menacing as the reports suggested, and that they lacked the IEDs, anti-personnel mines, car bombs, and suicide vests that planners had warned against. "There weren't any direct engagements with the Taliban," he said. "There was Taliban rumored to be there and have influence, but it was not as belligerent as we expected."[14]

The drawdown continued. By the end of September the remaining 23,000 troops brought over for the surge had redeployed to the US. Among the hardest hit by the withdrawal were the Marines at Camp Leatherneck.

Their force there had shrunk from approximately 17,000 to 7,400 during the middle of the fighting season, while their area of responsibility spanned roughly 36,000 square miles and included 196 combat outposts and FOBs within 19 districts. The drastic reduction in forces soon hurt the Marines.

On September 14 the Taliban executed a well-planned attack on coalition forces in Kandahar. At approximately 10:00pm on September 14, 2012, 15 heavily armed Taliban insurgents dressed in US Army uniforms breached the eastern perimeter of Camp Bastion, Camp Leatherneck, and Camp Shorabak (collectively referred to as the BLS Complex) undetected, split into three teams of five men each, and commenced a coordinated attack on the Camp Bastion airfield. At the time the perimeter of the two guard towers in the British sector of the camp were manned by Tonga Defense Force troops. US and coalition personnel present on the airfield responded immediately, and the US and UK QRFs made contact with the enemy shortly thereafter, beginning an engagement lasting into the early hours of September 15, 2012.

The multi-pronged attacks killed two US Marines, wounded eight other US personnel, eight UK personnel, and one civilian contractor. Six AV-8B Harriers were destroyed, and two AV-8B Harriers, one C-12 aircraft, three MV-22B Ospreys, one C-130E, and one UK Sea King were damaged, along with the VMA-211 hangar/maintenance facility.

When one attack team struck the British section of the base the RAF security force began to react within just 12 minutes when they established an MQ-9 Reaper UAV orbit over the camp. This was followed by the launch of a British Apache helicopter that immediately engaged the insurgents, killing several. In addition, the British ground security force alongside members of 2nd Battalion, 10th Marines, backed by British armored vehicles, fought their way toward Camp Barber over the main runway, reportedly expending around 10,000 rounds of ammunition in the process.

After a five-hour battle, 14 of the Taliban attackers had been killed and the one remaining attacker had been captured.[15, 16]

The Marines killed were Lieutenant Colonel Christopher Raible, commanding officer of Marine Attack Squadron 211, 3rd Marine Aircraft Wing (Forward), and Sergeant Bradley Atwell, assigned to Marine Aviation Logistics Squadron 13 and working for MALS-16 while deployed.

When the attackers hit his squadron, Lieutenant Colonel Raible hopped in an unarmored sport utility vehicle with another pilot, Major Greer Chambliss, and sped toward the flight line. The Marines got out of the vehicle and ran under fire, weapons drawn, to meet other men from the squadron who were hunkered down near an aviation maintenance building.

Raible, carrying only his pistol, led a counterattack on the marauding insurgents on the flight line. Then he returned to the larger group of Marines. He grabbed a rifle and again headed toward the gunfire and his burning Harrier fleet, but was killed when an RPG exploded overhead.[17]

Hearing the firefight and explosions, Major Robb T. McDonald, Raible's executive officer, and two other officers, armed only with pistols, immediately left the security of the billeting area, and maneuvered on foot more than a mile through an area dangerously exposed to both enemy fire and possible friendly fire.

When he reached the squadron maintenance building and learned that Raible had been mortally wounded, McDonald assumed command and began directing the tactical situation. Realizing the aluminum-skinned building was indefensible, he fearlessly exposed himself to danger by leading multiple groups of his Marines across 75m of open ground to get them to the more protected squadron headquarters. Leading a small team out to reconnoiter the flight line, he killed one enemy with a rifle he had borrowed, and then expertly coordinated two helicopter strikes to destroy all remaining enemy.[18]

The US Central Command investigation of the attack determined that Major General Charles Gurganus, RC-Southwest commander, and Major General Gregg Sturdevant, 3rd Marine Aircraft Wing (FWD) commander, had failed to construct a unified security plan.

There were no other major attacks against US or coalition bases or major cities through the fall and into winter. This didn't prevent more losses to IEDs, roadside bombs, and small-arms fire. There is little information about US operations during the fall, just a list of the names, locations, and cause of death, with one exception. On December 8, Petty Officer 1st Class Nicolas D. Checque, a member of SEAL Team 6, died of combat-related wounds suffered during the successful rescue attempt of Dr. Dilip Joseph about 50 miles from the Pakistan border in eastern Afghanistan on December 8, 2012. Joseph, a medical adviser for the Colorado Springs-based Morning Star Development, was kidnapped on December 5 along with two Afghans near the village of Jegdalek in the Sarobi district of Kabul province as they were returning from a rural medical clinic. The two Afghans were later released unharmed, but the kidnappers were reportedly asking for a $100,000 ransom for Joseph.

The rescue operation was ordered after intelligence showed that the doctor was in imminent danger of injury or possible death, according to a statement by the US-led military coalition. At 3:00am local time, SEAL Team Six, along with a team of Afghan commandos, landed near a group of huts where Joseph was being held. Alerted by the noise of the incoming helicopter, the kidnappers opened fire, hitting Checque in the head. The rest of the team assaulted the huts, killing five Taliban fighters before freeing Joseph.

Throughout 2012, ISAF began transferring responsibility for combat operations to the ANA, although ISAF still provided many of the assets needed such as CAS and assault helicopters. As of November, the number of US troops in Afghanistan had dropped to approximately 68,000. Even with fewer troops in country and the ANA assumption of operation responsibility, the US lost 310 killed in 2012. Most of the casualties occurred during the heavy fighting in January, April, May, June, July, and August. Among the 310 deaths, IED fatalities amounted to 132.

With the ANSF taking the lead in operations and the continuing drawdown, 2013 was an unusual but still lethal year for US forces. Much effort was being expended preparing for the final withdrawal of troops and equipment in 2014. Combat operations focused on training and mentoring ANA and police units. However, as it had been for the previous 11 years, nowhere was safe.

Attacks occurred frequently in Nangarhar, Kandahar, Helmand, Maiwand, Wardak, Kabul, Paktia, and Ghazni Paktya provinces. Two Pennsylvania National Guard pilots died on April 9 when their AH-64 Apache attack helicopter crashed during a reconnaissance mission in the

Gera Khel area of Pachir Wa Agam district, Nangarhar province. On May 3, a three-man KC-135 tanker crew was lost when their aircraft crashed near Chon-Aryk, Kyrgyzstan. One IED claimed the lives of three soldiers from 3rd Battalion, 15th Infantry Regiment, 4th Infantry Brigade Combat Team, 3rd Infantry Division on July 23 in Soltan Khely. The 4th Battalion, 320th Field Artillery Regiment, 4th Brigade Combat Team, 101st Airborne Division lost three of its men to indirect fire in Paktia province on August 11.

Two particular attacks, occurring a month apart, one in Wardak province and the other in Kunar province, showed that the Taliban were not relenting in their efforts.

The first took place on March 11. Air Force Special Operations Command Technical Sergeant Delorean M. Sheridan was preparing for a mission with his Army Special Forces team when an ANP officer working with the team opened fire from a machine gun at 25ft. The teammates to Sheridan's immediate left and right were hit. Puffs of smoke blew up around him. As he turned to react, Sheridan saw his team leader shot in the head at close range.

Occurring simultaneouly with this attack, 15–20 insurgents located 150m south of his position also engaged the base with heavy AK-47 and PKM fire. To Sheridan the insider attack was like "having someone sneak into your house in the middle of the night."

It provoked an instantaneous reaction. He ran toward the shooter, jumped into the turret of an armored vehicle, and shot him twice with his pistol and nine times with an M4 rifle until the shooter was dead. With the immediate threat neutralized, Sheridan quickly exited the vehicle, returning to the kill zone in order to extract his wounded teammates.

He then maneuvered through the heavy volume of gunfire streaming into the base and grabbed his wounded team leader by the shoulder strap, pulling him some 20ft out of the field of fire to medical assistance. Still undaunted by the enemy fire, Sheridan charged into the kill zone a third time in order to retrieve the infantry squad NCO in charge, pulling him to the casualty collection point.

Within the next 30 minutes, Sergeant Sheridan methodically sequenced six medical evacuation aircraft, assisting with the litter transfer of wounded personnel while simultaneously directing CAS and surveillance aircraft. With the medical evacuation complete, Sheridan located and directed aircraft to engage insurgents maneuvering towards the friendly location, resulting in four additional enemy fighters killed. He helped save the lives of 23 critically wounded personnel.[19]

The second attack, on April 6, also involved Air Force and Army Special Forces operators. Technical Sergeant Christopher G. Baradat, Air Force 21st Special Tactics Squadron, was working as part of an Army Special Forces team tasked as a QRF to retrieve a group of pinned-down coalition forces. Upon notification, Baradat, his Special Forces team, and attached Afghan forces sprang into action, entering the treacherous Sono Valley, a known sanctuary for Taliban and al Qaeda militants.

As the team moved through the tight valley on foot, they came under heavy enemy attack as they closed to within 800m of the pinned-down element. His job was to control the air assets supporting the team on the mission. When they came under fire, Baradat directed the 30mm guns of the A-10s overhead onto the enemy, prior to taking cover with his teammates. When he realized he could not control the aircraft effectively from his covered position, he moved from safety to the center of the compound, where he was sprayed with dirt from constant machine-gun fire. Standing in the thick of the firefight did not phase Baradat, though his teammates were urging him to take cover. "That was where I needed to be standing to communicate with the aircraft and to get the mission done," he said.

For the next three hours Baradat calmly directed lethal engagements from A-10 and AC-130s onto 13 enemy fighting positions consisting of over 100 fighters, while ignoring enemy machine-gun rounds impacting all around him. When all friendly forces had consolidated and egressed from the valley, Baradat once again showed incredible bravery when he purposefully jumped onto the running board of a vehicle, where he was continuously exposed to enemy fire, so he could maintain communications. With rounds again impacting all around him, he continued to control AC-130 and A-10 strikes to destroy the enemy attempting to cut off the coalition forces.

As a result of his actions, 150 coalition members were saved and more than 50 enemies killed. "We lost two-thirds of our team [on the mission] and half of the guys who were there were wounded in the firefight," Sheridan said.[20]

The ANSF was increasing its capabilities as the year progressed. One weak point had been the Afghan Air Force's ability to provide CAS and logistic support. With about 60 Russian Mi-17 helicopters whose pilots and crews where trained by units from the Mongolian Air Force, the Afghan Air Force took over the resupply mission of Afghan bases in the spring of 2013.

Captain Derek Forst, commander of Company A, from the Missouri National Guard's 1st Attack/Reconnaissance Battalion, 135th Aviation Regiment, which was flying in support of Task Force Tigershark, 10th Combat Aviation Brigade, said that without the aerial resupply missions, many of the OPs would be dependent on supplies brought in by foot and pack mule.

"It would take weeks for a convoy to get to most of the OPs," Forst explained. "These missions are keeping the OPs open. It's their livelihood. If it weren't for these resupply missions, the Afghan forces would not have food and water; those outposts would not be open."

Afghan Air Force Mi-17 helicopter crews fly resupply missions nearly once a week to the remote Afghan OPs and bases. Although each Mi-17 was armed with two M-240H machine guns, AH-64 Apache helicopters provide security overwatch for them due to the higher level of threat in some areas of the resupply route. In addition to providing greater firepower against threats on the ground, the AH-64 Apaches could alert other aircraft, as well as troops on the ground, of enemy activity in the area.

"We provide security and deterrence," said Captain Steven Lancianese, an AH-64 Apache pilot who also serves as the 10th Combat Aviation Brigade assistant operations officer. "In the areas they are flying, the tactical threat is significant."

"They are not junior pilots," Forst said. "They are excellent pilots. They know what they are doing. They tell us that if we ever have to make an emergency landing, they will pick us up – and they will."[21]

As joint operations continued, so did the logistical challenge of bringing out $17 billion worth of equipment. On October 2, Lieutenant General

Raymond V. Mason, the Army's top logistician and Deputy Chief of Staff, told members of the House Armed Services Committee that he remained "cautiously optimistic" that the Army will complete its withdrawal from Afghanistan on schedule. "Right now we are on the glide slope we had planned, but that can change overnight. One incident at a border could cause us challenges."

Critical to the success of meeting the December 2014 deadline were the Pakistan ground lines of communication (PAKGLOC) and, to a lesser extent, the Northern Distribution Network (NDN), a series of commercially-based logistical arrangements connecting Baltic and Caspian ports with Afghanistan via Russia, Central Asia, and the Caucasus. Both of these land routes involved less expense than air transportation.

"Unfortunately, the PAKGLOC and the NDN are not always viable and open," Mason said. "Additionally, other variables, including increased enemy activity or potential delays in Afghan elections, would most certainly affect our retrograde and drawdown plans."[22]

The withdrawal was not going to happen without more casualties. Patrols still went out regularly and the Taliban was still attacking. By December 31, 2013, 127 US military personnel had lost their lives, 52 of them to IEDs.

By July 3, 2014, the US had lost 2,335 men and women and 19,728 wounded in Afghanistan as part of Operation *Enduring Freedom*.[23] These included 34 dead in 2014. At the time, 32,800 US troops remained in Afghanistan, along with 17,102 other NATO and coalition forces.[24]

With the drawdown of US and other forces and with ANSF now running operations, the Taliban, Haqqani Network, Hezb-e Islami Gulbuddin, their allies, and criminal networks gained territory. According to some informed sources, the Taliban maintains a shadow government that has more influence than the central government in Kabul in some provinces. These same sources told the author that the western provinces are under the influence or control of drug-trafficking organizations. These organizations are well funded and continue to be funded by the sale of opium poppies.

Although not a primary US military mission, opium poppy eradication was important to help stabilize Afghanistan and cut off funding to anti-government forces. This, too, has failed. The Afghan Government has conducted a sustained campaign against poppy production with mixed results, and in 2013 suffered a setback when farmers in two previously poppy-free provinces once again began cultivation.

In 2013 opium poppy cultivation reached a record level of 5,500 tons, most of the production coming from the southern and western provinces. Although increased production led to lower prices, the crop was still valued at $950 million. The central government appears to be incapable of stopping the trade, since it is prevalent in all but 15 of the country's 34 provinces.[25]

The Afghan Government's influence does not extend far beyond Kabul. There is a growing number of the population who are actively opposing the return of the Taliban in their villages and towns, but these are few in number. Several informed sources said they believe what has happened in Iraq will happen in Afghanistan, but more quickly.

In addition, al Qaeda has not been defeated. After losing Afghanistan as a base of operations and moving to Pakistan, it has continued to grow in numbers and influence throughout the world.

In a press conference on May 27, President Obama presented the final steps to end US involvement in Afghanistan. "At the beginning of 2015, we will have approximately 9,800 US service members in different parts of the country, together with our NATO allies and other partners. By the end of 2015, we will have reduced that presence by roughly half, and we will have consolidated our troops in Kabul and on Bagram Airfield. One year later, by the end of 2016, our military will draw down to a normal embassy presence in Kabul, with a security assistance component, just as we've done in Iraq." The President included one caveat: "we will only sustain this military presence after 2014 if the Afghan Government signs the Bilateral Security Agreement that our two governments have already negotiated."

As of the end of June 2014 there was no clear winner in the presidential elections, which were held in April with a runoff election held in June. According to President Obama, both of the final two candidates indicated they would sign the agreement upon taking office.[26]

After 13 years of war there will not be a quick, clean, successful exit for the US, as was originally envisioned. Afghanistan will continue to be a place of war, as it has been for 35 years. For a generation of America's military women and men, the risk of being killed or wounded in Afghanistan will likely continue for two more years. Regardless of how long the fighting continues, the scars from the war will take a long time to heal.

EPILOGUE

While conducting research for this book I spoke with shopkeepers in Kabul and Kunduz, former Mujahadeen fighters, military personnel from several countries, civilian contractors, and consultants. They all raised the same three points regarding how long it will take for stability to come to Afghanistan. One pertains to the Afghans' perception of time and history and is presented thusly. In the US, people seem to think in terms of two- or four-year electoral cycles when setting policy, Russians think in terms of decades, while the Chinese think in terms of centuries. The Afghans have no sense of time. What happened when the British invaded in the mid-19th century, or if a family member was insulted 200 years ago is contemporary to them. This is a generalization, but one that's not too far off the mark.

The second is that the level of corruption has to be brought down to acceptable levels. It will take 20–25 years before Afghanistan will become a stable nation governed by an Afghan version of democracy. This timeframe is set by the maturing of men and women now in their 20s and 30s who have been exposed to western culture most of their lives. They have access to the Internet and social media almost everywhere in the country, strange as it sounds for a country without good roads, a nation-wide power grid, or other infrastructure, which developed nations take for granted.

I fell in love with the country and the people I had the chance to meet and share meals with (by the way, the food is fantastic). Each person has the same hopes for peace as everyone else, and the same wish for a better life for their children. For many, their hopes were raised with the defeat of the Taliban. Now, 13 years later, they realize that these hopes will be delayed, possibly beyond their children's lifetimes.

What the men and women who fought in Afghanistan feel about the situation, I don't know, and it's a question I won't ask. They fought, and many of their friends were killed or wounded to secure enduring freedom for the Afghans. Whatever they feel, their voices leave an enduring record of their accomplishments and sacrifices. May they forever be remembered, and may we all keep the faith with them.

LIST OF ABBREVIATIONS

AA	antiaircraft
ABP	Afghan Border Police
ACM	Anti-Coalition Militia
AFB	Air Force Base
AFSOC	Air Force Special Operations Command
AIA	Afghan Interim Authority
AMF	Afghan Militia Forces
ANA	Afghan National Army
ANG	Air National Guard
ANP	Afghan National Police
ANSF	Afghan National Security Forces
AO	area of operation
AOR	area of responsibility
ARNG	Army National Guard
ARSOF	Army Special Operations Forces
ASF	Afghan Security Force
ASOC	Air Support Operations Center
ASOS	Air Support Operations Squadron
AWACS	Airborne Warning and Control System
AWT	air-weapons team
BN	battalion
BP	blocking position
C3	command, control, and communications
CA	civil affairs
CAGC	Combined Air Operations Center
CAS	close air support
CASEVAC	casualty evacuation
CAT	Crisis Action Team
CAT-A	Civil Affairs Team-Alpha
CAV	cavalry

CENTCOMUS	Central Command
CERP	Commander's Emergency Response Program
CFACC	Combined Forces Air Component Commander
CFC-A	Combined Forces Command-Afghanistan
CFLCC	Combined Forces Land Component Command
CG	commanding general
CHLC	Coalition Humanitarian Liaison Cell (Chicklet)
CIA	Central Intelligence Agency
CJCMOTF	Combined Joint Civil Military Operations Task Force
CJSOTF	Combined Joint Special Operations Task Force
CJSOTF-A	Combined Joint Special Operations Task Force-Afghanistan
CJSOTF-S	Combined Joint Special Operations Task Force-South
CJTF	Combined Joint Task Force
CMIC	Civil–Military Cooperation
CMO	Civil–Military Operations
CMOC	Civil–Military Operations Center
COIN	counterinsurgency
CP	command post
CS	combat support
CSAR	Combat Search and Rescue
CSS	combat service support
CSTC-A	Combined Security Transition Command-Afghanistan
CTC	Counterterrorism Center
CTF	Combined Task Force
DDR	Disarmament, Demobilization, and Reintegration
DEVGRU	Naval Special Warfare Development Group
DOD	Department of Defense
DOS	Department of State
DRA	Democratic Republic of Afghanistan
DS	direct support
EOD	explosive ordnance disposal
ETT	embedded training team
FA	field artillery
FARP	forward arming and refueling point
FM	field manual
FOB	forward operating base
FORSCOM	Forces Command
FSB	forward support base
G2	Intelligence Section at Corps and Division Staff

G3	Operations Section at Corps and Division Staff
GDI	ground-directed interdiction
GPS	Global Positioning System
GWOT	Global War on Terrorism
HAST	Humanitarian Assistance Survey Team
HDR	humanitarian daily rations
HHC	headquarters and headquarters company
HIG	Hezb-e Islami Gulbuddin
HLZ	helicopter landing zone
HMMWV	high-mobility multipurpose wheeled vehicle (Humvee)
HQ	headquarters
HSC	headquarters and service company
HUMIN	Thuman intelligence
HVT	high-value target
ID	Infantry Division
ISR	Intelligence Surveillance Reconnaissance
IED	improvised explosive device
IMIN	Timagery intelligence
INL	International Narcotics and Law Enforcement
IO	international organization
ISAF	International Security Assistance Force
ISI	Pakistan Inter-Services Intelligence
ISOFA	Cisolation facilities
ISR	intelligence, surveillance, and reconnaissance
ITGA	Islamic Transitional Government of Afghanistan
JAG	Judge Advocate General
JCS	Joint Chiefs of Staff
JDAM	Joint Direct Attack Munition
JFACC	Joint Forces Air Component Command
JFSOCC	Joint Force Special Operations Component Command
JPOTF	Joint Psychological Operations Task Force
JRT	joint regional team
JRTC	Joint Readiness Training Center
JSOTF	Joint Special Operations Task Force
JSOTF-N	Joint Special Operations Task Force-North
JTAC	Joint Terminal Attack Controller
JTF	joint task force
K2	Karshi-Khanabad (air base)
KIA	killed in action

KMTC	Kabul Military Training Center
LAV	light armored vehicle
LOC	line(s) of communications
LOO	line of operation
LTF	Logistics Task Force
LZ	landing zone
MASH	Mobile Army Surgical Hospital
MEDCAP	Medical Civic Action Program
MEDEVA	Cmedical evacuation
MEU	Marine Expeditionary Unit
MI	Military Intelligence
MiCLC	mine-clearing line charge
MIT	mobile interrogation team
MOD	Ministry of Defense
MOI	Ministry of Interior
MP	Military Police
MRE	meal, ready to eat
MTT	mobile training team
NA	Northern Alliance
NATO	North Atlantic Treaty Organization
NCO	noncommissioned officer
NGO	nongovernment organization
NSA	National Security Agency
NVG	night-vision goggles
ODA	Operational Detachment Alpha
ODC	Operational Detachment Charlie
OEF	Operation *Enduring Freedom*
OIF	Operation *Iraqi Freedom*
OMC-A	Office of Military Cooperation-Afghanistan
OP	observation point
OPCON	operational control
OPORD	operation order
OSC-A	Office of Security Cooperation-Afghanistan
PIR	Parachute Infantry Regiment
PJ	pararescue jumper
PL	phase line
POG	Psychological Operations Group
POL-MIL	Political-Military
PPCLI	Princess Patricia's Canadian Light Infantry

PRT	Provincial Reconstruction Team
PSYO	Ppsychological operations
PUC	persons under control
PZ	pickup zone
QRF	quick reaction force
RC-East	Regional Command-East
RC-South	Regional Command-South
RC-West	Regional Command-West
ROC	Rear Operations Center
ROE	rules of engagement
RPG	rocket-propelled grenade
RTO	radio-telephone operator
SAR	search and rescue
SASR	Special Air Service Regiment
SATCOM	satellite communications
SAW	Squad Automatic Weapon
SEAL	Sea, Air, and Land
SF	Special Forces
SFAT	Security Force Advisory Team
SFG	Special Forces Group
SIGINT	signals intelligence
SO	Special Operations
SOAR	Special Operations Aviation Regiment
SOCCENT	Special Operations Command Central
SOCOM	Special Operations Command
SOF	Special Operations Forces
SOP	standing operating procedure
SOSB	Special Operations Support Battalion
SOSCOM	Special Operations Support Command
SR	Special Reconnaissance
SSE	sensitive site exploitation
TAC	tactical command post
TACON	tactical control
TACP	Tactical Air Control Party Specialist
TALC	Theater Airlift Control Element
TF	Task Force
TIC	troops in contact
TLAM	Tomahawk Land Attack Missile
TOC	tactical operations center

TOE	table of organization and equipment
TOW	Tube-Launched Optically-Tracked Wire-Guided Missile
TRANSCOMUS	Transportation Command
TSC	Theater Support Command
UAV	unmanned aerial vehicle
UK	United Kingdom
UN	United Nations
UNAMA	United Nations Assistance Mission in Afghanistan
USAF	United States Air Force
USAID	United States Agency for International Development
USASOC	United States Army Special Operations Command
USMC	United States Marine Corps
USSOCOM	United States Special Operations Command
UW	unconventional warfare
WSO	Weapons Systems Officer
WIA	wounded in action
XO	executive officer

NOTES

Chapter 1

1. 9/11 Commission Report, formally titled *Final Report of the National Commission on Terrorist Attacks Upon the United States*, August 2004, Chapter 1: 'We Have Some Planes.'"
2. There hadn't been a hijacking in the US since December 7, 1987 when a recently fired US Air employee used his invalidated credentials to a board Pacific Southwest Airline (USAir had recently purchased PSA) with a pistol and apparently killed his former manager and both pilots. The remaining five crew members and 37 other passengers were killed when the aircraft crashed. Source: AirSafe.com Foundation, http://www.airsafe.com/events/hijack.htm.
3. *Cape Cod Times*, Kevin Dennehy, Staff Writer, August 21, 2002.
4. Author interview with Colonel David A. Wood, August 2013.
5. Franks, General Tommy, with McConnell, Malcolm, *American Soldier*, HarperCollins, New York, 2004, p.240. Reprinted with permission.
6. Source: Author interview.
7. United Nations Security Council Resolution 1368 (2001).
8. Source: The Heritage Foundation, http://www.heritage.org/research/projects/enemy-detention/response-to-911.
9. Address to a Joint Session of Congress and the American People, Source: The White House, Office of the Press Secretary, September 20, 2001, http://georgewbush-whitehouse.archives.gov/news/releases/2001/09/20010920-8.html.

Chapter 2

1. 9/11 Commission Report, formally titled *Final Report of the National Commission on Terrorist Attacks Upon the United States*, p.208.

Chapter 3

1. Franks, *American Soldier*.
2. The Northern Alliance, officially known as the United Islamic Front for the Salvation of Afghanistan, was formed from the military wing of the government

ousted by the Taliban in 1996. Many of the alliance followers were part of the Mujahedeen guerillas who fought the Soviets in 1979–89. The Alliance's strongest member and US asset, Ahmad Shah Massoud, was assassinated on September 9, 2001. Two individuals disguised as reporters exploded a bomb hidden in a camera.

3. US Army Peacekeeping and Stability Operations Institute's Study of Civil Military Operations in Afghanistan, September 2001 to December 2002.
4. Ryhne, Major Richard G., *Special Forces Command and Control in Afghanistan*, Command and General Staff College, Fort Leavenworth, Kansas, 2004, pp.39–40.
5. Global Security, http://www.globalsecurity.org/military/agency/dod/tf-11.htm. TF 11 eventually established a base of operations in Khost, Afghanistan.
6. The full composition of TF K-Bar was Navy SEALS, Marines, Navy Seabees, Army Special Forces, Air Force Special Operations Command (AFSOC) troops, Army helicopter support, and Army 4th Psychological Operations Group personnel. Task Force K-Bar included Special Operations personnel from Joint Task Force 2 (Canada), the Australian Special Air Service Regiment, New Zealand Special Air Service, Kommando Spezialkräfte (Germany), Jægerkorpset og Frømandskorpset (Denmark), Jegerkommando og Marinejegerkommandoen (Norway), and Turkish Special Forces.
7. Zimmerman, Dwight Jon, *Task Force K-Bar – Special Operations Forces and Operation Enduring Freedom: Operation Enduring Freedom: The First 49 Days – Part 6*, Defense Media Network, September 19, 2011. Reprinted with permission.
8. Source: Price, Johann, "Operation Enduring Freedom: Commands and HQs" June 1, 2002, v.1.1 June 23, 2002, http://www.orbat.com/site/agtwopen/oef.html.
9. Source: American Special Ops, United States Military and Law Enforcement, http://www.americanspecialops.com/cia-special-operations/jawbreaker/.
10. Naval Historical Center, Department of the Navy, *US Naval Aviation 1910–2010*, Appendix 38 (unedited draft), Operation *Enduring Freedom* Phase I, October 7 to November 20, 2001, Washington, DC.
11. Afghan Media Dossier: 4, US Military Psychological Warfare, October 2001–2002.
12. Special Forces groups are organized in small teams of 12 men known as an Operational Detachment Alpha (ODA). A typical Green Berets team structure usually consists of two each of the following: weapons sergeants, communications sergeants, medical sergeants, and engineering sergeants. A commander, assistant commander (warrant officer), operations/intelligence sergeant and non-commissioned officer in charge (NCOIC) complete the team. The composition of these teams can change according to the type of mission. Source: US Army Special Forces website, http://www.goarmy.com/special-forces/team-members.html.
13. Combined Force Research Library Interview, Operation *Enduring Freedom*, Afghanistan 09/11/2001 through 04/01/2002, 92Y5S2S, Task Force Dagger, Master Sergeant Dale G. Aaknes, J-4 NCOIC, September 29, 2006. Reprinted with permission.
14. *United States Special Operations Command History 20*, 1987– 2007, USSOCOM/SOCS-HO, MacDill Air Force Base, Florida.

15. Information gathered from American Special Ops website, http://www.americanspecialops.com/operations/sof-afghanistan/task-force-dagger.php.
16. Sources: Author phone interview and material from http://projects.militarytimes.com/citations-medals-awards/recipient.php?recipientid=3774; http://www.sgtmacsbar.com/CCTPhotos/Gallery24/Silver%20Stars/Markham.html. Master Sergeant Markham was awarded a Silver Star for his actions.
17. The primary difference between a Spooky and Spectre is the armament: AC-130H Spectre: 1) 40mm (1.58in) L/60 Bofors cannon; 2) 105mm (4.13in) M102 howitzer. AC-130U Spooky II: 1) General Dynamics 25mm (0.984in) GAU-12/U Equalizer 5-barreled Gatling cannon; 2) 40mm (1.58in) L/60 Bofors cannon; 3) 105mm (4.13in) M102 howitzer.
18. Author interview with Captain Allison Black, the first female Air Force Combat Action Medal recipient.
19. Dictionary of American Fighting Ships, USS *Kitty Hawk* (CV(A)-63), Naval History and Heritage Command, Washington, DC.
20. American Special Operations, United States Military & Law Enforcement Special Operations website, http://www.americanspecialops.com/operations/rangers-delta-afghanistan-2001/.
21. *United States Special Operations Command History 20*, 1987–2007, USSOCOM/SOCS-HO, MacDill Air Force Base, Florida, p.90.
22. US Marine Corps 15th MEU website: http://www.15thmeu.marine.mil.
23. Interview with Major Lou Albano, Combat Studies Institute, the Operational Leadership Experiences, Fort Leavenworth, Kansas, January 21, 2009.
24. USSOCOM History, pp.93–94.
25. Major Richard Obert, US Air Force, Combat Studies Institute, the Operational Leadership Experiences interview collection, Fort Leavenworth, Kansas, reprinted with permission.
26. Wright, Donald P., Ph.D. (et al), *A Different Kind of War, The United States Army on Operation Enduring Freedom (OEF) October 2001 – September 2005*, Combat Studies Institute Press, US Combined Arms Center, Fort Leavenworth, KS, 2009.
27. United Nations Security Council Document 1154, http://www.un.org/news/dh/latest/afghan/afghan-agree.htm.
28. US Army in Afghanistan, p.30.

Chapter 4

1. Zimmerman, *Task Force K-Bar – Special Operations Forces and Operation Enduring Freedom: Operation Enduring Freedom: The First 49 Days – Part 6.*
2. *Army Guardsman Completes Special Duty in Afghanistan*, Sergeant 1st Class Eric Wedeking, US Army Public Affairs, Washington, DC, February 10, 2003.
3. Author interview with Staff Sergeant Scott Kaufman and Master Sergeant Ernest Svenkerud, July 26, 2013.
4. David King, Personal recorded interview, October 6, 2005, Operational Leadership Experiences Project, Combat Studies Institute, Fort Leavenworth, Kansas.

5. Ibid.
6. Major Jeremy Turner Operational Leadership Experiences interview, Combat Studies Institute, Fort Leavenworth, Kansas, May 11, 2006.
7. *Operation Anaconda, An Air Power Perspective*, Headquarters United States Air Force, AF/XOL, February 7, 2005.
8. Major David King, Operational Leadership Experiences interview, Combat Studies Institute, Fort Leavenworth, Kansas, October 6, 2005.
9. MAJ Mark Quander, Operational Leadership Experiences interview, Combat Studies Institute, Fort Leavenworth, Kansas, 7 March 2007.
10. Wright, *A Different Kind of War*, Chapter 6.
11. Operation Anaconda Case Study, ADA463075, College of Aerospace Doctrine, Research and Education, Maxwell AFB Alabama, November 13, 2003.
12. Wright, *A Different Kind of War*, p.151.
13. Kugler, Dr Richard L., *Operation Anaconda in Afghanistan: A Case Study of Adaptation in Battle*, National Defense University, Center for Technology and National Security Policy, Fort Lesley J. McNair BG 20, Washington, DC, 2007.
14. Wright, *A Different Kind of War*, p.152.
15. Major Jeremy Turner interview.
16. Lieutenant Colonel Scott "Soup" Campbell, Operational Leadership Experiences interview Part II, Combat Studies Institute, Fort Leavenworth, Kansas, May 15, 2009.
17. Sources: Executive Summary of the Battle of Takur Ghar, Released through the Department of Defense, May 24, 2002; Technical Sergeant Keary J. Miller interview, *Air National Guard at 60: A History*, pp.46–49; *Battle Attack at Takur Ghar: Roberts Ridge*, National Museum of the Air Force, August 4, 2009.
18. Author interview with Colonel Christopher Short, Mountain Home Air Base, Idaho, July 2013.
19. Executive Summary of the Battle of Takur Ghar.
20. Wright, *A Different Kind of War*.
21. Annan, Kofi, "The situation in Afghanistan and its implications for international peace and security," *Report to the Secretary-General, General Assembly Fifty-Sixth Session*, United Nations, NY, March 18, 2002.
22. Wright, *A Different Kind of War*, p.202.
23. *US Troops Finish 'Operation Mountain Lion*, CNN, Aired April 7, 2002. Reprinted with permission.
24. Wright, *A Different Kind of War*, p.338.
25. Brigadier General Robert L. Caslen, Jr., Operational Leadership Experience interview, Combat Studies Institute, Fort Leavenworth, Kansas, April 4, 2008.
26. Master Sergeant Carl A. Richards, 18Z50/1st Battalion, 19th Special Forces Group (Airborne), Operation *Enduring Freedom*, Afghanistan, 11/30/2001-10/30/2002, Riverton, Utah 84065, June 1, 2008.
27. Author interview with Command Sergeant Major Richard Lopez, Fayetteville, August 2013.

28. Author interview with Staff Sergeant Antuan Ray, Hurlburt Air Field, Florida, August 2013.
29. Sources: Global Security "Operation Mountain Sweep"; Garamone, Jim, *Coalition Forces Complete Operation Mountain Sweep*, Armed Forces Press Service, US Department of Defense, August 26, 2002; Wright, *A Different Kind of War*, p.221.
30. Wright, *A Different Kind of War*, pp.223–24.
31. "Tactics In Counterinsurgency, FM-3-24.2 (FM 90-8, FM 7-98), Headquarters Department of the Army, Washington, DC, April 21, 2009.
32. Sources: Kennedy, Harold, *Back From Afghanistan, Civil Affairs Unit Deploys to Iraq*, National Defense Industrial Association, Arlington, Virginia, February 2004. Reprinted with permission; Company Sergeant Major James W. King interview, United States Combined Arms Center, Fort Leavenworth, Kansas, January 2008.
33. James W. King interview, United States Combined Arms Center, Fort Leavenworth, Kansas, January 2008.

Chapter 5

1. Major Del Monroy, Operational Leadership Experiences interview, Combat Studies Institute, Fort Leavenworth, Kansas, January 9, 2009.
2. Ibid.
3. Author interview, Fargo, Idaho, July 2013.
4. Author interview, Hurlburt Field, Florida, July 2013.
5. Desert Devil Dispatch, *TF Devil Newsletter* I, Issue 7, February 28, 2003, p.3.
6. Excerpts from *Operation Valiant Strike* by Specialist Marie Schult, Army, May 2003.
7. "Operation Iraqi Freedom — By the Numbers," US Central Air Forces, Assessment and Analysis Division, April 30, 2003, p.3.
8. Franks, *American soldier*.
9. Global Security "Operation Desert Lion."
10. Rorke, Private Terri, 11th Public Affairs Detachment, "Carpathian Lightning strikes largest cache," *Freedom Watch Newspaper* published under the supervision of Combined Joint Task Force 180, April 22, 2003.
11. Rorke, Private Terri, 11th Public Affairs Detachment, "Devils craft Vigilant Guardian in Kandahar," *Freedom Watch Newspaper* published under the supervision of Combined Joint Task Force 180, May 10, 2003.
12. Rorke, Private Terri, 11th Public Affairs Detachment, "No findings, still success for 'White Devils,'" *Freedom Watch Newspaper* published under the supervision of Combined Joint Task Force 180, May 2, 2003.
13. Rorke, Private Terri, 11th Public Affairs Detachment, "The beauty behind the burqa," *Freedom Watch Newspaper* published under the supervision of Combined Joint Task Force 180, May 10, 2003.

14. Global Security, Fire Base Shkin, Fire Base Checo.
15. Angell, Lieutenant Cory, 10th Mobile Public Affairs Detachment, "Female MPs patrol 'just another Joe,'" *Freedom Watch Newspaper* published under the supervision of Combined Joint Task Force 180, June 21, 2003.
16. "Secretary Rumsfeld Joint Media Availability with President Karzai," Department of Defense news transcript, May 1, 2003, http://www.defense.gov/transcripts/transcript.aspx?transcriptid=2562.
17. Wright, *A Different Kind of War*, pp.256–57.
18. Author interview, Fort Indian Town Gap, August 2003.
19. Ibid.
20. Ibid.
21. Captain Bakhtiyorjon U. Hammidov, Uzbekistan Armed Forces, *The fall of the Taliban Regime and its Recovery as an Insurgent Movement in Afghanistan*, Tashkent Higher Military Academy of Combined Arms, Tashkent, Uzbekistan. Master of Military Art and Science General Studies Thesis presented to the US Army Command and General Staff College, Fort Leavenworth, Kansas, 2004.
22. Ibid.
23. *Defend America*, US Department of Defense news about the War on Terrorism, September 2003.
24. Global Security.
25. Sullivan interview.
26. Sources: Wright, *A Different Kind of War*, pp. 258–59; US Department of Defense, *Heroes*, *Ryan Worthan*, http://ourmilitaryheroes.defense.gov/profiles/worthanR.html; Mcgirk, Tim, "Battle in the Evilest Place," *Time*, October 27, 2003.
27. Wright, *A Different Kind of War*.
28. Thiel, Joshua, *COIN Manpower Ratios: Debunking the 10 to 1 Ratio and Surges*, *Small Wars Journal*, January 15, 2011.
29 "Tora Bora Revisited: How We Failed To Get Bin Laden And Why It Matters Today," A Report to the Members of the Committee On Foreign Relations United States Senate, 111th Congress, First Session, US Government Printing Office, November 30, 2009.
30. Sly, Liz, *Offensive Targets Taliban, Al-qaida*, *Chicago Tribune*, December 9, 2003. [Author's Note: This air strike and the casualties have been attributed to both Operation *Mountain Resolve* and Operation *Avalanche* by different sources.]
31. Sources: NJ Run For the Fallen and Arlington National Cemetery website.
32. Heath, Sergeant Greg, 4th Public Affairs Detachment, "2-87 Catamounts keep rolling in Afghanistan," *The Mountaineer Online*, January 8, 2004.
33. Summary of Afghan National Army (ANA), Program for Culture & Conflict Studies.
34. Wright, *A Different Kind of War*, p.319

Chapter 6

1. American Forces Press Service, *Coalition in Afghanistan Wraps Up Mountain Blizzard*, March 13, 2004.
2. Some information obtained from Synovitz, Ron, *Afghanistan: US-led Commando Teams Fight Taliban With Unconventional Warfare*, Radio Free Europe Radio Liberty, March 15, 2004, http://www.rferl.org/content/article/1051894.html.
3. Forward-looking infrared imaging systems.
4. Garrett Hopkins interview, *Saving the Legacy: An Oral History of Utah Veterans*, J. Willard Marriott Library, Special Collections Department, American West Center, University of Utah, Salt Lake City, Utah, January 22, 2010.
5. Wright, *A Different Kind of War*, pp.288–89.
6. Ibid, p.290.
7. Colonel Walter M. Herd, interview by Contemporary Operations Study Team, Combat Studies Institute, Fort Leavenworth, KS, June 22, 2007.
8. Bogart, Adrian T. III, *One Valley at a Time*, Hurlburt Field, FL: Joint Special Operations University Press, 2006, pp.59–62.
9. Personal Experience Paper of Dwight C. Utley, "Operation *Enduring Freedom*, Kunar Valley, Afghanistan, May 15 – December 1, 2004," Fort Bragg, North Carolina, August 20, 2006.
10. Lieutenant General David W. Barno, interview by Center for Military History, May 3, 2006.
11. US Institute for Peace Afghanistan USIP – ADST Experience Project interview #5, reprinted with permission.
12. Ibid.
13. US Institute for Peace USIP – ADST Afghanistan Experience Project interview #45, reprinted with permission.
14. US Institute for Peace USIP – ADST Afghanistan Experience Project interview #51, reprinted with permission.
15. Personal Experiences Paper of Dwight C. Utley.
16. Sources: Milks, Gunnery Sergeant Keith A., *22nd MEU Afghanistan Recap: Operation ASBURY PARK*, 22nd Marine Expeditionary Unit, II Marine Expeditionary Force, United States Marine Corps website, September 1, 2004; Sellers, LTC Terry L., *MEMORANDUM FOR BOBCAT FAMILIES, Update from Afghanistan*, department of the army, headquarters, 2nd battalion, 5th infantry regiment, 2nd brigade, 25th infantry division (light), July 13, 2004.
17. Clawson, Sergeant Jeremy A., 105th Mobile Public Affairs Detachment, "Operation Dragon Tree takes root," *Hawaii Army Weekly*, July 16, 2004.
18. Sources: Dietl, Gulshan, *War, Peace and the Warlords: The Case of Ismail Khan of Herat in Afghanistan*, Alternatives: Turkish Journal of International Relations, Vol. 3, No. 2&3, Summer & Fall 2004; Wright, *A Different Kind of War*, p.297.
19. Sources: The Cater Center Country Profile: Afghanistan; CRS Report for Congress, Afghanistan: Elections, Constitution, and Government, updated May 25, 2006.

20. Operation *Enduring Freedom* Deployment Photos, http://www.25idl.army.mil/deployment/oef%20afghanistan/deployment/13dec04pictures.htm.
21. "US Begins New Offensive Vs. Afghan Militants," *Wall Street Journal*, December 11, 2004.
22. CTF Thunder covered the central and eastern region of the country. It included: 2nd Battalion, 27th Infantry Regiment of the 25th Infantry Division (Light); 3rd Battalion, 6th Marine Regiment, 2nd Marine Division; 3rd Battalion, 116th Infantry Regiment of the Virginia Army National Guard; 1st Battalion, 505th PIR 82nd Airborne Division, along with many smaller attachments. CTF Thunder was also responsible for Provincial Reconstruction Teams supporting security and reconstruction efforts in the Parwan, Bamyan, Ghazni, Gardez, Khost, Sharona, Asadabad, and Jalalabad areas. Source: US Department of Defense, http://osd.dtic.mil/home/features/1082004d.html. Colonel Gary H. Cheek commands Combined Task Force Thunder.
23. Rhen, Staff Sergeant Bradley, *Coalition begins winter offensive in Afghanistan*, Army News Service, December 20, 2004.
24. Mattingly, Corporal Rich, *3/3 Marines, Sailors Repel Christmas Eve Ambush*, Task Force Trinity, 3rd Battalion, 3rd Marines in the Global War on Terror, http://www.taskforcetrinity.com/archives/146#more-146.
25. According to a Congressional Research Service report in December 2004, Afghanistan was the source of 87 percent of the world's opium and heroin. CRS Report for Congress, Afghanistan: Narcotics and US Policy, December 7, 2004.
26. CRS Report to Congress, US Military Operations in the Global War on Terrorism: Afghanistan, Africa, the Philippines, and Colombia, August 26, 2005.
27. Wright, *A Different Kind of War*.
28. Major General Jason Kamiya, interview by Contemporary Operations Study Team, Combat Studies Institute, Fort Leavenworth, Kansas, September 11, 2007.
29. The ANP is the primary police force of Afghanistan, serving as a single law enforcement agency all across the country. The Afghan Border Police (ABP) provides law enforcement capabilities at borders and entry points, including Afghanistan's airports, in order to deter criminal activity and the movement of insurgents into Afghanistan.
30. GAO Report, "Afghanistan Security: Efforts to Establish Army and Police Have Made Progress, but Future Plans Need to Be Better Defined," June 2005.
31. Rhen, Staff Sergeant Bradley, "Team trains, assists Afghan police," *Sentinel*, February 15, 2005.
32. Command Chronology for 3rd Battalion, 3rd Marines, January–June 2005.
33. Mattingly, Corporal Rich, 3rd Battalion, 3rd Marines, *Operation Mavericks Captures Suspected Terrorist*, April 5, 2005.
34. Command Chronology for 3rd Battalion, 3rd Marines, January–June 2005.
35. Looker's Personal Experience Paper, Operation *Enduring Freedom*-Afghanistan, AO East, Afghanistan, 11/07/2004–06/04/2005, Center for Army Lessons Learned, September 4, 2006.

36. Sources: Leo, Roger, "*No letup for Marines*," *Worcester Telegram & Gazette*, July 5, 2005; Dickerson, Corporal Michelle M., *Marine recalls Silver Star actions*, Marine Corps Base, Hawaii, February 10, 2006.
37. Scavetta, Sergeant 1st Class Rick, *Marines Return to Tora Bora for Operation Celtics*, Special to American Forces Press Service, Department of Defense, May 31, 2005.
38. Sources: Caldwell, Staff Sergeant Jacob, Combined Task Force Bayonet, "Operation *Diablo Reach Back* Targets Militia," *Defend America*, June 28, 2005; CRS Report to Congress, August 26, 2005.
39. For details see "Operation Red Wings Summary of Action," http://www.navy.mil/moh/mpmurphy/soa.html.
40. Pryor, Private Mike, 1/352 Public Affairs Detachment, "Operation Neptune strikes Taliban in Afghan desert," *ARNEWS*, August 22, 2005.
41. Mraz, Steve, "Operation *Pil* targets Taliban in Kunar province," *Stars and Stripes*, October 24, 2005
42. Fusco, Private Vincent, 20th Public Affairs Detachment, "US Paratroopers Complete Operation Pizmah," *Defend America News*, January 5, 2006.
43. CRS Afghanistan Casualties: Military Forces and Civilians, December 6, 2012.

Chapter 7

1. Cole, Beth Ellen and Hsu, Emily, *Afghan Insurgency Still A Potent Force*, US Institute for Peace briefing, February 2006.
2. CRS Report to Congress, *US and Coalition Military Operations in Afghanistan: Issues for Congress*, June 9, 2006.
3. Ibid.
4. US Field Manual (FM) 3-24 Para 5-51 – 5-78.
5. Master Sergeant Michael Threatt, Combined Studies Institute interview, Fort Leavenworth, Kansas, September 20, 2006.
6. Perito, Robert M., *The US Experience with Provincial Reconstruction Teams in Afghanistan: Lessons Identified*, United States Institute for Peace Special Report 152, USIP, 1220, 17th Street NW, Washington, DC, October 2005.
7. Commander John Wade and Commander Mike Vaney interviews, Operational Leadership Experiences, Combat Studies Institute, Fort Leavenworth, Kansas.
8. Commander Wade interview.
9. Commander Vaney interview.
10. 1st Sergeant Arthur L. Fredericks, Operation *Enduring Freedom* 01/04/2006 to 05/22/2007, United States Army Sergeants Major Academy, SMNRC Class 35 Phase II, 02/27/2010.
11. CJTF-76 composition: 10th Mountain's 3rd Brigade Combat Team; USMC 1st Battalion, 3rd Marine Regiment; brigades from the ANA 201st and 203rd Corps; 10th Combat Aviation Brigade (TF Falcon); multicomponent Special Operations Forces (SOF); 710th Brigade Support Battalion, various support elements; joint

PRTs to coordinate R&D activities, engineers to provide mobility and support R and US military embedded training teams (ETTs) to train and mentor the ANSF.

12. Sources: CRS Report to Congress, June 9, 2006; Coss, Colonel Michael A, "Operation Mountain Lion: CJTF-76 in Afghanistan, Spring 2006," *Military Review*, January–February 2008; Lindsay, Sergeant Joe, USMC, "Operation Mountain Lion Roars Into Korengal Valley," Special to American Forces Press Service, US Department of Defence, May 8, 2006; Zenk, Major Eric, "'Lion's Pride' Brings Medical Care to Afghans," *Defend America News*, May 5, 2006.
13. Connors interview by Douglas Cubbison, the Command Historian for the 10th Mountain Division.
14. Jorgensen interview by Douglas Cubbison, the Command Historian for the 10th Mountain Division.
15. Nilon interview by Douglas Cubbison, the Command Historian for the 10th Mountain Division.
16. Sax interview by Douglas Cubbison, the Command Historian for the 10th Mountain Division.
17. CRS Report for Congress, *US Forces in Afghanistan*, March 27, 2007.
18. Institute for War & Peace Reporting, *Helmand Residents Question NATO Success Claims*, ARR Issue 257, June 29, 2007
19. Ibid.
20. Sources: (Dutch) Uruzgan Weblog: Uruzgan: Het gevecht om Chora; (Dutch) Infanteristen, commando's: iedereen vecht tegen Taliban – Binnenland – de Volkskrant; *Battle for Chora*, War and Tactics, http://www.warandtactics.com/smf/afghanistan-476/battle-for-chora-june-2007/, March 12, 2010; Honor the Fallen, *Military Times*.
21. Author interview.
22. The US Air Force Combat Search and Rescue (CSAR) helicopters handled the problem by not displaying a Red Cross and mounting crew-served weapons on both sides (more on this in Chapter 7).
23. Major Gary Means interview, Operational Leadership Experiences, Combat Studies Institute, Fort Leavenworth, Kansas, February 1, 2010.
24. Regional Command East, Institute for the Study of War, Washington, DC.
25. Caldwell, Jacob, USA, "Company Works to Flush Out Taliban During 'Rock Avalanche,'" Armed Forces Press Service, October 31, 2007.
26. Rubin, Elizabeth, "Battle Company Is Out There," *New York Times Magazine*, February 24, 2008.
27. Sources: Staff Sergeant Salvatore A. Giunta Medal of Honor Official Narrative; Tilghman, Andrew, "Medal of Honor bittersweet, Giunta says," *Army Times*, September 15, 2010.
28. Author interview with Captain Angelina Stephens, Mountain Home Air Base.
29. "Afghan flag flies over Musa Qaleh once again," *Defence News*, British Ministry of Defence. December 12, 2007.

Chapter 8

1. The French Government reduced its caveats and agreed to allow its forces in Kabul and elsewhere come to the assistance of other NATO forces in an emergency. Germany also allowed its forces to respond in an emergency, but German troops reportedly patrol only in armored personnel carriers, and do not leave their bases at night. Turkey refused to change its proscription against its forces' use in combat. The Italian and Spanish governments allowed that their force commanders in the field could make the decision to send forces to assist in an urgent situation. CRS Report for Congress, *NATO in Afghanistan: A Test of the Transatlantic Alliance*, Updated January 7, 2008.
2. RC-North – Germany, RC-East – US, RC-South – Britain, RC-West – Italy, RC-Capital – Turkey.
3. Sources: Associated Press, 1/15/2008; *The Guardian*, 14 January 2008; BBC News, January 15, 2008.
4. www.army.mil: the Official Homepage of the United States Army, December 15, 2008.
5. Captain Kyle Walton, Master Sergeant Scott Ford, Staff Sergeant Dillon Behr, Staff Sergeant Seth Howard, Staff Sergeant Luis Morales, Staff Sergeant Ronald Shurer, Staff Sergeant John Walding, Sergeant David Sanders, Sergeant Matthew Williams, and Specialist Michael Carter were awarded Silver Stars for their actions. SrA Zachary Rhyner became the third and only living Air Force Cross Combat Controller in the Global War on Terrorism to be awarded the Air Force Cross.
6. Dupee, Matt, "Kapisa province: The Taliban's gateway to Kabul and ANA Commandos and US Special Forces capture and kill insurgents in Kapisa province," *The Long War Journal*, Foundation for the Defense of Democracies, April 29, 2008, updated on April 30, 2008.
7. Sources: 24th Marine Expeditionary Unit, *Operation Azada Wosa: Recounting the 24th MEU's progress in Garmsir*, July 19, 2008; 24th Marine Expeditionary Unit, *24th MEU flips to COIN*, July 7, 2008.
8. Author interview with General David D. McKiernan.
9. Sources: Cavallaro, Gina and Fuentes, Gidget, "Valor awards mount up for little-known battle," *Marine Corps Times*, Gannett Company, July 17, 2011; Lamothe, Dan, "'We drove them from the battlefield': Marines overcome 8-to-1 odds during an 8-hour battle," Marine Corps News Room, December 22, 2008; Lowe, Christian, "Marines Prevailed in a Day of Battle," Military.com, December 3, 2008.
10. Congressional Research Service, *Afghanistan Casualties: Military Forces and Civilian*, December 8, 2010.
11. Source: Defense Manpower Data Center, Report DRS 11280, Modified Location Country Report, December 2008.

Chapter 9

1. Fair, Christine C., Jones, Seth G., *Securing Afghanistan Getting on Track*, United States Institute for Peace Working Paper, January 23, 2009.
2. Combating Terrorism Center, CTC Sentinel, West Point, February 15, 2009.
3. "Dozens killed in Afghan fighting," BBC News, January 7, 2009, http://news.bbc.co.uk/2/hi/south_asia/7814995.stm.
4. Sources: ISAF Press Releases, "Joint ANSF, ISAF operation disrupts IED networks in Kandahar," January 13, 2009 (PR# 2009-043) and "ANSF and ISAF disrupt terrorist bomb-making network," February 6, 2009 (PR# 2009-117).
5. Ibid.
6. Major Casey Crowley interview, Operational Leadership Experiences Project, Combat Studies Institute, Fort Leavenworth, Kansas, September 2011.
7. Ibid.
8. Blanchard, Christopher M., *Afghanistan: Narcotics and US Policy*, Congressional Research Service, April 21, 2009.
9. Ibid.
10. Major Kurt C. Merseal, Team Chief, CNIK ETT, ARSIC-K, Memorandum Subject: Serious Incident Report (SIR) for Troops in Contact (TIC), department of the army, counter narcotics infantry kandak embedded training team (CNIK ETT) camp Dubbs, Darulaman, Afghanistan, AFGHANISTAN APO AE 09320.
11. Report on Progress toward Security and Stability in Afghanistan Report to Congress in accordance with the 2008 National Defense Authorization Act (Section 1230, Public Law 110-181), June 2009.
12. Among the sources are: DoD News Briefing with Brigadier General Nicholson from Afghanistan, Presenters: Commander, Marine Expeditionary Brigade-Afghanistan Brigadier General Lawrence Nicholson, July 8, 2009; Sheppard, Ben, "US Marines battle on in Afghanistan," *The Sydney Morning Herald*, July 3, 2009; Strazious, Jason, "Marines suffer first casualties in Afghanistan offensive," Associated Press, July 1, 2009; Shanker, Thom and Oppel, Jr., Richard A., "In Tactical Shift, Troops Will Stay and Hold Ground in Afghanistan," *New York Times*, July 2, 2009; Youssef, Nancy, "Taliban scatters in Afghanistan, but the threat survives," *McClatchy Newspapers*, July 8, 2009; Chandrasekaran, Rajiv, "Taliban Insurgents Step Up Attacks on Marines in Southern Afghanistan," *Washington Post*, July 4, 2009.
13. Youssef, Nancy A., "Afghans: Taliban have escaped Helmand and Marines," *McClatchy Newspapers*.
14. Among the sources were: de Montesquiou, Alfred, "Marines Assault Dahaneh, Afghan Town Held By Taliban, For First Time," *The World Post*, August 13, 2009; Nelson, Soraya Sarahaddi, "Marines Find Afghan Mission Is A Matter Of Trust," NPR, August 24, 2009.
15. Regimental Combat Team 3 Public Affairs, *Regimental Combat Team 3, First Marine RCT in Afghanistan concludes historic deployment*, October 26, 2009.
16. Major Louis Gianoulakis interview, Operational Leadership Experiences Project, Combat Studies Institute, Fort Leavenworth, Kansas, October 12, 2010.

17. "Commander's Initial Assessment," Headquarters, ISAF, Kabul, Afghanistan, August 30, 2009.
18. Sources include: Leipold, J.D., *Battle of Ganjgal: Army's first officer to receive Medal of Honor from OIF/OEF recounts ambush*, www.army.mil, October 15, 2013; Lamothe, Dan, "Heroism in ambush may yield top valor awards," *Marine Corps Times*, August 2, 2010.
19. Westbrook was evacuated to Walter Reed Army Medical Center in Washington, DC, and seemed on the verge of recovery, then complications developed as the result of a blood transfusion in Afghanistan, which initially saved his life. He passed away October 7, a month after the battle.
20. Captain William D. Swenson and Corporal Dakota Meyer received the Medal of Honor for their actions during the battle. Corporal Meyer is the first living Marine to receive the Medal of Honor since the Vietnam War, and Captain Swenson is the fifth living soldier to receive the Medal of Honor since the Vietnam War. Staff Sergeant Juan Rodriguez-Chavez and Captain Ademola Fabayo received the Navy Cross.
21. US soldiers killed in the battle were: Justin T. Gallegos, Christopher Griffin, Kevin C. Thomson, Michael P. Scusa, Vernon W. Martin, Stephan L. Mace, Joshua J. Kirk, and Joshua M. Hardt.
22. Sources include: Defense Department interview posted online; US Army Executive Summary – AR 15-6 Investigation re: Complex Attack on COP Keating – 3 October 2009.
23. Official Narrative: Staff Sergeant Clinton L. Romesha, Medal of Honor, http://www.army.mil/medalofhonor/romesha/narrative.html.
24. Hitesman, Lance Corporal John, *Marines clear Taliban from Buji Bhast Pass*, Defense Video & Imagery Distribution Center (DVIDS), October 16, 2009.
25. Nola, Corporal Zachary, "Marines face two-front engagement during Operation North Star," Marine Official website, December 2, 2009.
26. Sources: Marino II, Lance Corporal Walter D., *Cobra's Anger: Marines assault into Now Zad*, Regimental Combat Team-7, 1st Marine Division Public Affairs, December 13, 2009; Adkins, Sergeant Lia, *Lima Company comes full circle in Now Zad: Marines reflect on progress, sacrifices*, ISAF Regional Command South, August 18, 2013.

Chapter 10

1. Congressional Research Service (CRS) – War in Afghanistan: Strategy, Military Operations, and Issues for Congress June 8, 2010.
2. Ibid.
3. Afghanistan: The London Conference, January 28, 2010 communiqué.
4. Ibid.
5. Afghan National Security Forces (ANSF), NATO OTAN Media Backgrounder, October 26, 2010.
6. February 14, 2010, 6:57pm. "Opium city captured," http://www.heraldsun.com.au/archive/news/opium-city-captured/story-e6frf7lf-1225830238012.

7. NATO-ISAF Briefing, Major General Nick Carter, February 18, 2010. IJC Public Affairs Office, http://www.nato.int/isaf.
8. ISAF Joint Command – Afghanistan News Release 2010-02-CA-59 Operation Moshtarak, February 13, 2010.
9. CRS – War in Afghanistan: Strategy, Military Operations, and Issues for Congress June 8, 2010.
10. The information and quotes regarding the operation were taken from two press releases filed by Marine Sergeant Brian Tuthill, Regimental Combat Team-7, 1st Marine Division Public Affairs. Links: http://www.dvidshub.net/news/45179/marines-fight-insurgents-secure-key-intersection-road-marjeh#.UkWKZD8jaSq; http://www.dvidshub.net/news/46619/marines-name-new-outpost-near-marjah-fallen-brother#.UkWHwT8jaSq.
11. Major Robert Lee interview, Operational Leadership Experiences, Combat Studies Institute, Fort Leavenworth, Kansas, March 2011.
12. Norton-Taylor, Richard, "Nato offensive aims to tackle bribery and corruption in Kandahar," *Guardian*, April 18, 2010 6:22pm EDT.
13. McKenzie, Jean, "Dread surrounds Operation Hope," *Global Post*, April 19, 2010.
14. Operation *New Dawn* was also referred to as Operation *Cobra* in news releases.
15. Fayloga, Sergeant Mark, *America's Battalion, Afghan Army complete first task in Operation New Dawn*, Regimental Combat Team-7, 1st Marine Division Public Affairs, June 20, 2010.
16. Staff Sergeant Matthew Loheide was awarded the Silver Star for his part in the battle.
17. The information for this operation was excerpted from: "Operation Strong Eagle: The Brutal Battle of Sangam," by Dianna Cahn, *Stars and Stripes*, September 20, 2010; "Fort Campbell soldier Sergeant 1st Class Matthew Loheide received Silver Star in Ceremony on Friday," *Clarksville Online*, April 8, 2013.
18. 300th Mobile Public Affairs Detachment Press Release, "No Slack" Continues Clearing the Ghaki Valley, July 24, 2010.
19. Sources: Padula, Sergeant Joe, "Operation Dragon Strike: Mission improves Kandahar security," 2nd Brigade Combat Team, October 7, 2010; Pendlebury, Richard and Wiseman, Jamie, "Dicing with death in the devil's playground: In a heart stopping dispatch, the Mail's Richard Pendlebury joins troops clearing roadside bombs in the Afghan valley where every step could be your last," *Mail Online*, October 25, 2010; Millham, Matthew, "Compensation in Kandahar," ISAF HQ Public Affairs; ISAF News, "Afghan Security Forces, ISAF Assist Residents In Returning Home," ISAF Joint Command –Afghanistan," 2011-01-D-328; Barikzai, Naweed, Operation *Dragon Strike* – Afghanistan, Center for Conflict and Peace Studies Afghanistan, October 2010.
20. Task Force Bastogne Public Affairs Office, "Security forces begin operations in the Pech River Valley, October 15, 2010.
21. Combined Joint Special Operations Task Force – Afghanistan, "CDO, USSF reduce caches, kill 13 insurgents in Kunar," October 23, 2010.

22. Security forces begin operations in the Pech River Valley.
23. The defense of COP Margah resulted in award or recommendation for one Silver Star, three Bronze Star Medals with Valor, 12 Army Commendation Medals with Valor, two Purple Hearts, ten Combat Infantryman Badges, and one battlefield promotion.
24. Sources: Boothe Jr., Specialist Luther L., "The Defense of COP Margah: a story of valor," Task Force Currahee Public Affairs, December 11, 2010; Axe, David, "US Kills 70 Taliban, Loses No One In Huge Outpost Battle," Danger Room, *Wired*, November 17, 2011.
25. For their heroism and valiant efforts, members of the 33rd RQS are being recognized with the Jolly Green Association Rescue Mission of the Year Award. The association is composed of military service members and veterans who have flown in or otherwise supported "Jolly Green" rescue operations. The 33rd RQS, which has as its home base Kadena A.B. in Japan, was chosen from a competitive field that included US Air Force rescue units from across the globe.
26. Over the course of the five days of Operation *Bulldog Bite*, the three pararescuemen from the 212th Rescue Squadron conducted 25 CASEVAC and MEDEVAC missions, and retrieved 49 coalition personnel.
27. Author interview with Captain Andresky.
28. Sources: Burrell, Sergeant Mark, "'Bulldog Bite' clears Pech River Valley," Task Force Bastogne Public Affairs, November 30, 201; Hostullier, Senior Airman Shaunlee, "33rd RQS wins third straight 'Jolly Green Rescue Mission of the Year,'" 18th Wing Public Affairs, May 2, 2011; Lowery, Jake, "3-star: Operation Bulldog Bite disrupts Taliban," *The Leaf-Chronicle*, November 18, 2010; Dunham, Mike, "Alaska squadron rescues troops in fierce battle," *Anchorage Daily News*, August 20, 2011.
29. "American Marines pay a heavy price in fight for Sangin," factstoknow.co.uk, December 6, 2010.
30. Abbot, Sebastian, "In Afghan cauldron, realism can trump the rulebook," Associated Press 10:07am, December 2, 2010.
31. Shukla, Paraag, BATTLEFIELD UPDATE: TASK FORCE DREADNAUGHT IN MAIWAND DISTRICT, KANDAHAR, Institute for the Study of War Backgrounder, January 23, 2012.
32. McCall, Corporal John, "1st CEB, coalition forces complete Outlaw Wrath, destroy more than 50 IEDs," 1st Marine Division, December 12, 2010.
33. Truscott, Claire, "US commander inherits tough fight for Taliban state," AFP, December 6, 2010.

Chapter 11

1. Sources: Lim, Lieutenant Alex, "2/1 clears Durzay in Operation Godfather," Regimental Combat Team, January 14, 2011; Woodall, Corporal Daniel, "Engineer Marines begin civil development projects in Durzay," 1st Marine Logistics Group,

February 11, 2011.

2. Ross, Staff Sergeant Jeremy, "Afghan soldiers, coalition Advisors sweep villages during Operation Omid Shash," Regional Command Southwest, February 18, 2011.
3. Sources: Wallace, Technical Sergeant Kevin, "Operation Red Sand destroys insurgent compounds in Bala Murghab," ISAF Joint Command, April 6, 2011; Wallace, Master Sergeant Kevin, "Flashbacks of War, Remembering Red Sand," 100th Air Refueling Wing Public Affairs, July 26, 2012; Wallace, Master Sergeant Kevin, "To hell and back: The Bala Murghab saga," 336th Fighter Wing, April 4, 2013; Petty Officer 1st Class John A. Pearl, Sworn Statement on the events that occurred on April 4, 2011 in Bala Murghab, Badghis province, Afghanistan; Lieutenant Joseph Cecil Law, Sworn Statement COP Metro, Bala Murghab, Afghanistan, 2012/01/10; Author interview with Technical Sergeant Kevin Wallace.
4. Author interview with Staff Sergeant Ben Seekell, June 2013.
5. Major Eric McKinney interview, Operational Leadership Experiences, Combat Studies Institute, Leavenworth, Kansas, February 2013.
6. Author interview with Captain Gary Charney, USAF.
7. Sources: Radin, C.J., "US begins drawdown of forces from Afghanistan," *The Long War Journal*, July 15, 2011; Lamothe, Dan, "3/4 eyed as part of Afghanistan drawdown," *Marine Corps Times*, July 6, 2011.
8. Sources: Shea, Neil, "Unlikely unit of cooks, fuelers, and mechanic and clerks leads assault into a Taliban stronghold," *Stars and Stripes*, August 21, 2011; Pouliot, Staff Sergeant Todd, "TF Knighthawk supports Operation Dagger Fury," Task Force Falcon Public Affairs, August 10, 2011.
9. Major Matthew Brown interview, Operational Leadership Experiences, Combat Studies Institute, Leavenworth, Kansas, July 2012.
10. Author interview with Captain Andrew L. Chaulk.
11. US War Casualties – Afghanistan, http://citizenjournalistreview.wordpress.com/us-war-casualties-afghanistan-by-date/.
12. United Nations Office of Drugs and Crime, *Afghanistan opium Survey 2011 Summary findings*, October 2011.

Chapter 12

1. Author interview with Master Sergeant William Kennedy.
2. Author interview with Staff Sergeant Anthony Delvecchio.
3. Sources include the author's discussion with Afghan-American interpreters in Kabul, February 2013.
4. Downen, Sergeant 1st Class James, "Squad defends combat outpost against rioters," Joint Force Headquarters, Michigan National Guard, February 26, 2012.
5. Quote excerpted from "US Soldier Massacres 16 Afghan Civilians In Shooting Rampage – Dead Include 12 Women And Kids," by Heidi Vogt and Mirwais Khan, Associated Press, March 11, 2012.

6 Author interview with personal source.
7. Hyatt, Staff Sergeant Anthony, "Airman's actions in support of OEF result with AFCAM," Joint Base Charleston Public Affairs, August 8, 2013. Technical Sergeant Clifford Hartley was awarded the Air Force Combat Action Medal and Bronze Star for his actions.
8. Livingston, Ian S. and O'Hanlon, Michael, *Afghanistan Index*, Brookings, May 16, 2012.
9. Sources include: Smith, Bernard, "Taliban 'spring offensive' rocks Afghanistan," Al Jazeera, April 17, 2012; Mojaddidi, Mushta, "Taliban's 'spring offensive' rocks Afghanistan," AFP, April 15, 2012; Solheim, Simon, "Omfattande angrep i Kabul i Afghanistan (Comprehensive attacks in Kabul in Afghanistan)," *Norwegian Defense Media*, April 15, 2012; Stone, Mark, "UK Troops Crucial In Ending Kabul Attack," Sky News, April 19, 2012.
10. NATO Summit, *Chicago Summit Declaration on Afghanistan Issued by the Heads of State and Government of Afghanistan and Nations contributing to the NATO-led International Security Assistance Force (ISAF)*, Chicago, Illinois, May 21, 2012.
11. Author interview with Staff Sergeant Christopher R. Miller, USAF.
12. Excerpts from Lamothe, Dan, "Taliban make gains as Marines take back seat," *Marine Corps Times*, October 29, 2012.
13. Excerpts from Taylor, Rob, "US troops return to Afghanistan's 'lost province,'" Reuters, June 13, 2012.
14. MacLeod, Sergeant Michael J., "Bragg paratroopers, Afghan soldiers disrupt insurgent safe havens in Ghazni province," www.army.mil, June 11, 2012.
15. United States Central Command Camp Bastion Leatherneck Shorabak (BLS) Investigation Enclosure 3 Executive Summary.
16. Gresham, John D., "Attack on Camp Bastion: The Destruction of VMA-11," *Defense Media Network*, September 20, 2012.
17. Lamothe, Dan, "Fallen Marine commander up for Silver Star," *Marine Corps Times*, October 12, 2012.
18. Excerpted from Major Rodd T. McDonald's Silver Star citation.
19. Caldwell, Rachel and Savage, Major Craig, "Special Tactics Airmen awarded Silver Star, Bronze Star with Valor, and Purple Heart medals," 24th Special Operations Wing Public Affairs, January 13, 2014, and Master Sergeant Delorean M. Sheridan's Silver Star citation.
20. Ibid.
21. Sources: Pouliot, Staff Sergeant Todd, "Afghan aviators resupply remote bases with partnered close-air support"; 10th Combat Aviation Brigade, October 28, 2013; Author interview with Mongolian Air Force personnel.
22. Piper, Sergeant 1st Class Raymond, "Army's top logistician remains 'cautiously optimistic' on Afghanistan withdrawal," www.army.mil. October 4, 2013.
23. Sources: Defenselink Casualty Report, http://www.defense.gov/news/casualty.pdf; icasualties.org/oef/.

24. Source: International Security Assistance Force – Afghanistan, troop numbers and contributions,http://www.isaf.nato.int/troop-numbers-and-contributions/index.php.
25. United Nations Office of Drugs and Crime and Islamic Republic of Afghanistan Ministry of Counter Narcotics, "Afghanistan Opium Survey 2013 Summary Findings," http://www.unodc.org/documents/crop-monitoring/Afghanistan/Afghan_report_Summary_Findings_2013.pdf.
26. Source: ISAF Transcript: President Obama's May 27 speech on Afghanistan, http://www.isaf.nato.int/article/isaf-news/transcript-president-obamas-may-27-speech-on-afghanistan.html.

INDEX

References to illustrations are in **bold**.

ABOUT THE AUTHOR

Michael G. Walling is author of several books, including *Bloodstained Sea*, the recipient of the 2005 Samuel Eliot Morison Award for Naval Literature. An internationally recognized World War II expert, Walling is a contributing author to the US Naval Institute's *Naval History* Magazine and has appeared on The History Channel and PBS as an aviation and naval expert. After graduating from Montclair State College with a BA in Biology, Walling served in the US Coast Guard for six years as a commissioned officer and a senior petty officer. He has spent more than 45 years collecting stories from veterans from World War II, Korea, Vietnam, Iraq, and Afghanistan as well as those of pilots, merchant seaman, and civilian personnel. His research has included visits to London, Sarajevo, Baska Voda, Croatia, Halifax, Nova Scotia, St. John's, Newfoundland, New Orleans, and, more recently, Afghanistan.